ABOUT TEACHING MATHEMATICS

A K–8 Resource

Second Edition

ABOUT TEACHING MATHEMATICS

A K–8 Resource

BY MARILYN BURNS

Second Edition

MATH SOLUTIONS PUBLICATIONS
Sausalito, California

Math Solutions Publications
A division of
Marilyn Burns Education Associates
150 Gate 5 Road, Suite 101
Sausalito CA 94965
www.mathsolutions.com

Library of Congress Cataloging-in-Publication Data
Burns, Marilyn, 1941–
    About teaching mathematics : a K–8 resource / by Marilyn Burns.—2nd ed.
      p. cm.
    Includes bibliographical references and index.
    ISBN 0-941355-25-X (pbk.)
    1. Mathematics—Study and teaching (Elementary) I. Title.
  QA135.5.B83963 2000
  372.7—dc21   00-036177

ISBN-10: 0-941355-25-X
ISBN-13: 978-0-941355-25-4

Cover design: Leslie Bauman
Cover photo: Bob Adler
Book design: Aileen Friedman
Illustrations: Marilyn Burns

Printed in the United States of America
06   ML   11 12 13 14 15

A Message from Marilyn Burns

We at Math Solutions Professional Development believe that teaching math well calls for increasing our understanding of the math we teach, seeking deeper insights into how children learn mathematics, and refining our lessons to best promote students' learning.

Math Solutions Publications shares classroom-tested lessons and teaching expertise from our faculty of Math Solutions Inservice instructors as well as from other respected math educators. Our publications are part of the nationwide effort we've made since 1984 that now includes

- more than five hundred face-to-face inservice programs each year for teachers and administrators in districts across the country;
- annually publishing professional development books, now totaling more than fifty titles and spanning the teaching of all math topics in kindergarten through grade 8;
- four series of videotapes for teachers, plus a videotape for parents, that show math lessons taught in actual classrooms;
- on-site visits to schools to help refine teaching strategies and assess student learning; and
- free online support, including grade-level lessons, book reviews, inservice information, and district feedback, all in our quarterly *Math Solutions Online Newsletter*.

For information about all of the products and services we have available, please visit our Web site at *www.mathsolutions.com*. You can also contact us to discuss math professional development needs by calling (800) 868-9092 or by sending an e-mail to *info@mathsolutions.com*.

We're always eager for your feedback and interested in learning about your particular needs. We look forward to hearing from you.

Math Solutions®
PUBLICATIONS

Preface to the Second Edition

*T*his book has a lengthy history. I wrote a first version of it in 1981 for a class I was teaching to K–8 teachers. During the following years, as I revised, amplified, reorganized, and clarified my ideas, the book evolved into *About Teaching Mathematics*, first published in 1992. With the current changes, the book has been a work in progress for almost twenty years, just as my teaching of mathematics has been a work in progress for almost forty years.

I decided to publish this second edition for several reasons. The one wielding perhaps the greatest influence was the volume of letters I've received over the years from teachers and students asking for help with specific problems and activities in the book. These requests came from learners who were eager for confirmation, partially stuck, completely stuck, or even mathematically desperate. I responded to and saved these letters, and they are the inspiration for the biggest change in this edition — the entirely new *Part IV, Mathematical Discussions,* in which I discuss the mathematics involved in about forty activities. Since I believe that an answer to a specific problem is only as useful as its connection to other problems and its contribution to developing mathematical understanding and intuition, I not only provide the support of answers but, more important, describe how I thought about the mathematics and how the problems helped me think mathematically in new ways.

Another reason for revising the book is my recent thinking about teaching arithmetic, specifically as it has been informed by the teaching I've been doing in grades 4 and 5. As a result, in *Part III, Teaching Arithmetic,* I've added a new section. Titled "Extending Multiplication and Division," it addresses how to help students deal with multiplication and division of large whole numbers. I've also made changes to the section on fractions to offer teachers the benefit of what I've been learning from my recent work with students.

As I entertained the idea of making these additions and changes, I began to think about what else I thought would make the book a more effective resource. Although I had dipped into the book from time to time when I needed something specific, I now reread the book thoroughly and thoughtfully. I also reread my collection of other letters I've received from teachers, letters that didn't relate to the problems and activities but that offered feedback and asked other questions. (I save everything!) Then I began making changes — again revising, adding, deleting, reorganizing, and clarifying. These changes are sprinkled throughout the book — a paragraph here, a page there, word tweaks from time to time — all to make ideas as clear and accessible as possible. Most of the mathematics activities remain intact, but some have been removed or revised and others added to reflect what I've learned from students I've taught and from teachers who have shared their experiences with me.

This second edition of *About Teaching Mathematics* is a continuation of a work in progress. Being a teacher demands that we are learners ourselves, not only about our pedagogical craft, but also about the subject matter we teach. My hope is that this book will contribute to your ongoing learning both of mathematics and how to teach it.

Table of Contents

Table of Contents

Table of Contents

Table of Contents

PART I

Raising the Issues

Introduction

Teachers are the key to improving mathematics education.... Regardless of the curriculum or the assessment process in a school district, the person in charge of adapting materials for a particular classroom and student is the teacher. It is through teachers' efforts that students have opportunities to learn mathematics. If students are to have better programs in mathematics, teachers need access to high-quality materials, the support of parents, and on-going, focused professional development.

— Glenda Lappan, President's Message, *NCTM News Bulletin,* October 1998

Students who understand mathematics can think and reason mathematically and use what they've learned to solve problems, both in and out of school. Teachers who teach for understanding must find ways to engage students actively in their mathematics learning. The goal of this book is to provide teachers with the direction and assistance needed to implement instruction that develops students' mathematical confidence and competence. Specifically, the book is designed to help teachers:

- examine how children learn mathematics
- develop a positive attitude toward and an interest in mathematics
- teach mathematics with problem solving as the primary focus
- understand the elements of a comprehensive mathematics curriculum
- establish a classroom environment that supports children's learning of mathematics

The book is organized into four main parts. *Part I, Raising the Issues,* addresses topics basic to mathematics teaching — the content of the curriculum, problem solving as the focus of math teaching, how children learn, and the place of arithmetic in mathematics instruction. Also, sections on managing the classroom and organizing the instructional program contain information about structuring classes for cooperative and independent learning.

Part II, Problem-Solving Activities in the Strands, is a sampler of explorations for each area of the mathematics curriculum — measurement; probability and statistics; geometry; logical reasoning; patterns, functions, and algebra; and number. The activities are models for classroom problem-solving experiences.

Arithmetic instruction is of major concern to teachers, parents, and administrators and is the focus of *Part III, Teaching Arithmetic.* This section addresses the role of arithmetic in the mathematics curriculum and how to teach arithmetic in a way that develops both understanding and skills.

It's important that teachers understand the mathematics that underlies the activities with which students are engaged. *Part IV, Mathematical Discussions,* addresses the mathematical ideas and skills for about forty of the activities included in the book. Many of the discussions provide solutions to problems, always with guidelines for thinking about the mathematics and explanations about why the solutions make sense.

Also included in the book are a bibliography of books, articles, videotapes, and audiotapes, as well as blackline masters needed for activities.

A Perspective on Arithmetic

*A*ttending to the development of problem-solving abilities does not imply a lack of concern for arithmetic. Standard 1 in *Principles and Standards for School Mathematics* (National Council Teachers of Mathematics, 2000) addresses the importance of giving attention to arithmetic: "Number, operation, and computation have a long and prominent history in the school mathematics curriculum. In addition, this area of mathematics, perhaps more than any other, is widely recognized and valued beyond the school setting."

Arithmetic instruction has traditionally focused on students' proficiency with paper-and-pencil calculations. However, a broader view of arithmetic instruction is required. Computation is still important, of course, and students must learn how to compute accurately and efficiently. In addition, instruction must help students learn to apply computational skills to problem-solving situations so that when they face problems that call for numerical calculations, students know how to choose the operations needed, decide on the numbers to use, do the necessary calculations, and then appropriately interpret the results. Arithmetic instruction must also give attention to developing students' number sense so that students are able to make reasonable estimates, think and reason flexibly with numbers, make sound numerical judgments, and see numbers as useful. Computation, problem solving, and number sense are the essential three legs on which arithmetic instruction rests.

In order to examine instructional decisions, it's useful to consider the place of arithmetic in real-life situations. When teachers are asked to list the occasions they use arithmetic outside of the classroom, most responses include the following types of situations: when I calculate my checkbook balance, when I'm in the supermarket figuring how much I'm spending or doing price comparisons, when I need to know how much wallpaper or floor covering I need, when I'm deciding on the tip in a restaurant, when I want to know the mileage I'm getting on my car, when I'm figuring how long a roast or turkey needs to cook, when I'm deciding on the time to leave to arrive at the movies on time. Using a calculator and doing arithmetic mentally are the two most frequently reported methods for doing arithmetic. Using paper and pencil is not the usual choice. When evaluating their lists to decide when being accurate was necessary and when an estimate would do, teachers generally find a 50-50 split between the two needs. Complete the questionnaire on the following page to analyze your own use of arithmetic.

At the same time, teachers admit to spending more than 75 percent of their math time (closer to 90 percent for many) on paper-and-pencil drill, with students practicing arithmetic skills in isolation from problem-solving situations. The arithmetic exercises are

1. List all the situations outside of school responsibilities for which you've used arithmetic during the past month.

   _____   _____

   _____   _____

   _____   _____

   _____   _____

   _____   _____

   _____   _____

   _____   _____

2. There are three methods people generally use when doing arithmetic:
   (1) calculator,
   (2) paper and pencil,
   (3) mental arithmetic.

   Number each item on your list to indicate the method you usually use to do each task. Which method do you use most often? _____
   Least often? _____

3. Review your list once more and mark each item with *estimate* or *accurate* to show which is usually required for each situation you listed. What percentage of your items did you mark *estimate*? _____ Accurate? _____

usually provided on worksheets or textbook pages, neatly arranged and ready for children to apply their computation skills to figure answers. Yet in all the real-life needs for arithmetic, problems do not present themselves ready for calculation. Deciding what to do is the important first step before doing any calculation.

Learning to do paper-and-pencil arithmetic on isolated examples does nothing to ensure that children will truly understand the algorithms or develop the ability to use them when needed. This fact is obvious to teachers when addition problems are assigned and a child asks, "Do I have to carry on this page?" It's obvious when word problems are assigned and a child asks, "Do I need to add or subtract?" It's clear when a child makes a division error, omitting a zero in the quotient so the answer is ten times too small, and the child doesn't even notice. All of these examples indicate students' lack of understanding and are substantiated by research findings.

This does not mean that children do not need to learn arithmetic. Doing arithmetic mentally demands mastery of basic facts along with the ability to estimate. Using a calculator successfully requires understanding of the arithmetic processes called for in a variety of situations. But there's no place in our schools for teaching arithmetic by focusing on computation in isolation from the problem situations that require those skills. And there's no place for requiring students to practice tedious calculations that are more efficiently and accurately done by using calculators.

Can students determine whether it's cheaper to buy things two for a nickel or three for a dime? Can they name a fraction that is larger than one-third yet smaller than one-half? Can they figure out what to do when halving a recipe that calls for three-fourths of a cup of sugar? (What would you do?) Merely learning to perform arithmetic algorithms with paper and pencil is not sufficient for success with problems that demand reasoning ability, not just computation ability. Arithmetic must be taught in the context of problem solving so it can assume its proper role of providing tools to use for solving problems.

Examining Children's Common Arithmetic Errors

*E*xamining the errors children make during arithmetic drill can provide additional insights into their thinking and our instructional problems. Do each of the arithmetic exercises below, making the kinds of errors that children commonly make. Purposely find incorrect answers, ones that come from common mistakes.

1. $3 + \boxed{} = 7$	2. $\begin{array}{r} 35 \\ +67 \\ \hline \end{array}$
3. $\begin{array}{r} 42 \\ -17 \\ \hline \end{array}$	4. $\begin{array}{r} 300 \\ -136 \\ \hline \end{array}$
5. $12\overline{)3840}$	6. $1/2 + 2/3 =$
7. $2.06 + 1.3 + .38 =$	8. $\begin{array}{r} \$5.40 \\ \times .15 \\ \hline \end{array}$

With the exception of errors that result from carelessness with basic facts, the errors children make are not random. They are remarkably consistent. Teachers see the same mistakes over and over, year after year. In most instances, children's errors are rule-bound, the result of applying an incorrect procedure in place of the correct algorithm. This incorrect procedure, however, has some logic for the child, even though that logic is incorrect. Often, the child has been taught the rule by a teacher but applies the rule in an inappropriate situation. When performing isolated arithmetic calculations, children have no way to check their logic against the real world. The following explanations describe the kind of incorrect thinking children typically apply.

1. $3 + \boxed{10} = 7$ A plus sign means to add.

2. $\begin{array}{r} 35 \\ +67 \\ \hline 912 \end{array}$ Add the numbers in each column and write the sums under the line.

3. $\begin{array}{r} 42 \\ -17 \\ \hline 35 \end{array}$ When you subtract, you take the smaller number from the larger.

4. $\begin{array}{r} \overset{299}{800} \\ -136 \\ \hline 163 \end{array}$ You can't subtract a number from zero, so you change the zeros into nines.

or   or

$\begin{array}{r} \overset{2}{800} \\ -136 \\ \hline 174 \end{array}$ You can't subtract from zero, so you borrow from the three and the zeros become tens.

5. $12\overline{)3840}$ with quotient 32 You can drop the zero at the end of the problem.

6. $1/2 + 2/3 = 3/5$ When you add fractions, you add across the top and across the bottom.

7. $\begin{array}{r} 2.06 \\ 1.3 \\ .38 \\ \hline 2.57 \end{array}$ Line up the numbers and add.

8. $\begin{array}{r} \$5.40 \\ \times .15 \\ \hline \$81.00 \end{array}$ After you figure the problem, bring down the decimal point.

It's important to examine erroneous reasoning in light of the instruction that occurred. When learning arithmetic processes, children focus on the symbols. Children tend to see arithmetic as doing something to those symbols to get the right answers. The same children who incorrectly put 10 in the box in the first example most likely know that 3 + 10 is not equal to 7. However, when tackling the missing addend problem, they're not focusing on the meaning of the problem but on the symbols in the example. They see a plus sign, they know a plus sign means add, and therefore they add. Children given a subtraction problem in a context, and asked to solve it with objects instead of symbolically, rarely do something as ridiculous as the common error children make when dealing with the same type of situation on a workbook page.

The implication in each example is that children rely on following recipes rather than reasoning what is sensible to do. Following recipes results from learning arithmetic as a collection of specific methods used to arrive at answers. Many teachers have experienced consternation when students come to class and want to know if they can do the division using the method someone at home showed them. (What would you do in that situation?) It's not uncommon for a teacher to respond that children must learn to do it the way the book says. The implication is that the specific algorithm is important, not that children should understand that different algorithms are possible and they should make sense of whatever method they use.

When making errors, children rarely notice or even seem to care when they arrive at an absurd answer. Though teachers urge children to estimate or check their answers, generally children are concerned primarily with finishing. Their goal seems to be to get the problem or page done, not to evaluate their answers. They figure a 15 percent tip on $5.40, produce a result of $81.00 (as shown on the previous page), and accept the answer without question. The problem springs from an educational issue larger than mathematics instruction. If children believe that getting quick, right answers is what is valued in school, then this response is an obvious result. Instruction should not aim toward an answer-oriented curriculum, but toward one that values reasoning processes and calls for evaluating answers as an essential part of any assignment.

Not only is the mastery of algorithms presented as the most important goal in elementary mathematics instruction, but the algorithms taught are often presented as if they are the only way to perform a calculation. In this light, the following exercise is revealing:

Mentally double 38. Then analyze the method you used in order to arrive at the answer.

When teachers are asked to double 38 mentally and then describe how they accomplished this, methods vary. Some visualize the problem symbolically and perform the algorithm mentally, seeing two 38s lined up on their mental chalkboards, adding the 8s, carrying the 1, and so on. Some use this approach, but mentally multiply 38 by 2 instead of adding. Some add the 30 and 30 first, and then add on 16. (And we know that children are discouraged from ever adding the numbers in the tens place before those in the ones place.) Some double 40 and subtract 4. Some double 35 and then add 6. Invariably, such a range of methods is offered. Why, in school, is the implication that there is one right way to do arithmetic? And why is the symbolic method used to produce arithmetic results so often separated from the meaning in the situation?

Using Word Problems to Develop Arithmetic Understanding

*I*f teaching computation skills by starting with numerical symbols is a backward approach, the traditional sequence of teaching computation first and then applying those skills to problem situations is just as backward. It doesn't make sense to teach arithmetic skills in isolation from situations for which those skills are needed. As supported by research findings, this pedagogical version of putting the cart before the horse doesn't work.

When research studies examined why children's ability to solve word problems falls far below their ability to compute, they found certain common myths to be untrue. For example, children's difficulties are not caused primarily by poor computation skills or insufficient reading ability. When given a word problem, children simply do not know how to choose the correct operation to apply to the problem. In order to solve word problems, children have to connect the suitable arithmetic processes to the situations presented in the stories. Although children can perform the computations adequately, they do not understand the arithmetic processes in ways that enable them to make those connections to the word problems.

Try the *Dealing in Horses* problem on the facing page. It will help you experience the kind of difficulty children encounter with story problems. (It's also an interesting problem to discuss with friends or present to a class, if the children are old enough to be comfortable with the numbers.)

Generally, people offer different solutions and reasoning for the *Dealing in Horses* problem. It's not typical of the word problems children face. Although it can be translated into an arithmetic sentence and solved by computation, it involves more than the usual word problem demands. However, the difficulty adults have deciding on the solution is similar to the difficulty many children have when applying their arithmetic knowledge to common word problem situations.

Understanding the situation is not the difficulty with *Dealing in Horses*; the scenario is clear. Adding and subtracting the numbers in the problem also is not difficult; the numbers are easy to handle mentally. Yet deciding precisely what to do isn't obvious to everyone. The difficulty is knowing the correct way to connect the arithmetic operations to the situation in order to arrive at a solution. The confusion that adults experience with this situation is similar to the confusion that children experience when presented with a page of mixed word problems that leads them to ask: "Do I need to add or subtract?"

Dealing in Horses

A man bought a horse for $50 and sold it for $60. He then bought the horse back for $70 and sold it again for $80. What do you think was the financial outcome of these transactions?

☐ Lost $20   ☐ Earned $10

☐ Lost $10   ☐ Earned $20

☐ Came out even   ☐ Earned $30

☐ Other (describe) _____

Explain your reasoning: _____

_____

_____

_____

Facility with computation does not ensure children's ability to know when to use those skills in problem situations. Problem situations should be the starting place for developing arithmetic understanding, thereby establishing the need and context for computation skills. Children need to see that learning to compute serves a purpose — for solving problems. Too often, the message is reversed, and children see word problems as a way of providing computation practice, and a mysterious way at that.

This suggestion does not mean that teachers should begin arithmetic instruction by assigning the word problems in the textbook. Assigning word problems accomplishes no more than testing students' abilities to solve those problems. It's teaching that is needed, not testing. Teachers should present word problems for children to discuss and find solutions, without the distraction of numerical symbols. This needs to be done frequently, several times a week throughout the entire year, at all grade levels. The goal is for the children to generalize for themselves — from many, many experiences — how the arithmetic operations are described in the language of the real world. Also, students should be encouraged to figure their own ways to arrive at solutions and make sense of situations numerically.

A caution: Teachers often resort to helping children solve textbook problems by providing word cues: When it says "altogether," you are supposed to add; "how many more" means to subtract. Teachers provide these cues to help children be more successful with word problems. However, instruction of this type does little more than give children tricks to find answers. Even worse, the implication is that getting the answer is most important and that relying on tricks is an effective strategy for finding those answers. This message often results in children's looking for tricks, rather than trying to make sense out of problems.

Beyond Word Problems

*T*he mathematical problem-solving situations that children encounter in the elementary grades should include problems that require broader thinking than traditional word problems demand. Word problems require children to focus on the meaning of the arithmetic operations. To solve a word problem, a child needs to translate the situation into an arithmetic sentence (or sometimes more than one sentence) and then do the computation called for in that sentence. There is usually one right way to get the answer; there is always one right answer.

Making traditional word problems the only or main emphasis of the problems children encounter is not sufficient for the elementary curriculum. Doing so gives an unrealistic message to children about the way mathematics will serve them as adults. Most daily problems adults face that require mathematics reasoning and skills are not solved by translating the available information into arithmetic sentences and then performing the needed calculations.

In real-life problems, you're rarely given all the information you need in one tidy package; you often have to collect the data and often from a variety of sources. There's rarely only one possible method or strategy that emerges from real-life problems; usually you choose one from several viable possibilities. You don't always know for sure if the solution you choose is the "right" or "best" one; you decide on one plausible solution and it may be only later that you can evaluate your choice. Sometimes you never find out for sure; life has no answer book.

When solving problems in real life, you call upon all the resources you've developed in other situations — knowledge, previous experience, intuition. You need to analyze, predict, make decisions, and evaluate. In order to function in our complex and changing society, people need to be able to solve a wide variety of problems. The elementary math curriculum must prepare children to become effective problem solvers.

Teaching children to be problem solvers does not minimize the importance of arithmetic. Arithmetic is necessary for solving many problems in life. Also not all the problems children deal with in school need be real-life problems. Although many situations that arise daily in classrooms afford opportunities for the application of math skills — collecting lunch money, deciding on how many cars are needed for a field trip, taking attendance, and so on — children also benefit from contrived problem situations that build their problem-solving abilities. After all, school is the place where children can safely develop and practice problem-solving skills. The challenge for curriculum choices is to provide motivating problems that spark children's natural curiosity and allow them to use, in a safe and supportive environment, the skills they'll need later. The following exercise provides a classroom application for these ideas:

---

1. If a = $.01, b = $.02, c = $.03, and so on, what is the value of your first name? _____

2. Using this alphabet system, one of the days of the week is worth exactly $1.00. Which one is it? _____

3. Find other words that are worth exactly $1.00.

How did you go about figuring the value of your name? Did you write the alphabet and list the value of each letter? Did you separately figure out the value of each letter in your name? (Did you use your fingers for this?) Did your method for figuring out the value of your name help you find the day of the week worth exactly $1.00? How did you go about finding which day of the week is the $1.00 word? These are the kinds of questions that are valuable to discuss with students. It gives them the opportunity to see that there are different ways to approach a problem. Also, not providing a list of the alphabet letters and their values gives students a chance to decide how they'll collect the data they need.

Finding $1.00 words opens up addition practice to a multitude of possibilities. Over 1000 $1.00 words have been found by students and teachers across the United States. Some teachers have organized class or school $1.00 word contests. Some have students write computer programs that make it possible to type in words to check their values. Some have simplified the problem for young children to one of finding the most expensive and least expensive three-letter or four-letter words. Students develop different strategies for searching for $1.00 words, and these are useful to discuss in class. This type of problem provides arithmetic practice while also providing a broader problem-solving experience.

WHAT IS AND IS NOT A PROBLEM?

What is the definition of a problem? A problem is a situation in which a person is seeking some goal and for which a suitable course of action is not immediately apparent. In the context of the mathematics curriculum, a problem is one requiring that mathematical skills, concepts, or processes be used to arrive at the goal.

Whether a situation is a problem is an individual matter, depending on an individual's reaction or relationship to that situation. The individual must understand the situation and be interested in resolving it, yet there must be some block preventing immediate resolution. If these conditions do not exist, then a situation is not a problem for that individual.

What may be a problem for one student may not be a problem for another. Analyzing the definition produces four criteria that define mathematical problems for students:

CRITERIA FOR MATHEMATICAL PROBLEMS

1. There is a perplexing situation that the student understands.

2. The student is interested in finding a solution.

3. The student is unable to proceed directly toward a solution.

4. The solution requires use of mathematical ideas.

Refer to these four criteria in answering these questions:

1. Was the *Dealing in Horses* problem a problem for you? Why or why not? Answer in terms of the four criteria.

_____

_____

_____

2. Was finding the value of your first name a problem for you? Why or why not?

_____

_____

_____

3. Was finding $1.00 words a problem for you? Why or why not?

_____

_____

_____

4. Would these be problems for your students?
   Solving *Dealing in Horses*: Yes ☐ No ☐
   Finding the value of your first name: Yes ☐ No ☐
   Finding $1.00 words: Yes ☐ No ☐

   Why? _____

   _____

Do not confuse arithmetic exercises with problems. If a student meets a situation that calls for two-place multiplication and has not been taught the algorithm for this process, then this might be a problem for that student. Generally though, arithmetic exercises are used to provide students practice with using standard mathematical procedures. Although a child may have difficulty arriving at a correct arithmetic answer, deciding on the method for getting the answer is not usually part of the child's task. Executing specific procedures — the algorithms — is the child's task.

Textbooks often present word problems so that all those on the same page are solved with the same operation. The first one on the page may be a problem for a student. But if the student realizes that the same procedure can be used for all the others (and students are quick to notice this), the rest are not problems. They are merely exercises that do not require thinking or reasoning but rather repetitive application of the same algorithms.

Problem-solving situations, on the other hand, each demand that the child develop a plan for solution as well as execute the plan. Problem-solving techniques do exist, but they are general approaches, not algorithms that can be routinely applied to specific problems. Although arithmetic is essential for solving many problems in life, it is not the only mathematical skill generally needed. Figuring how much floor covering is needed for a room requires applying both geometry and measurement skills. Deciding on the best place to put savings involves ideas in the areas of probability and statistics. Assembling a bicycle that arrives in a crate calls for the application of logical thinking skills.

At each of the grade levels, mathematics instruction should provide children problem-solving experiences in all of the areas of the elementary math curriculum. The areas are not strictly separate concepts; they overlap. Although arithmetic is part of the number area, for example, arithmetic skills are needed to understand ideas and to solve problems in each of the other areas as well.

AREAS OF THE ELEMENTARY MATH CURRICULUM

Measurement

Probability and Statistics

Geometry

Logical Reasoning

Patterns, Functions, and Algebra

Number

PROBLEM-SOLVING STRATEGIES

Students benefit from learning about problem-solving procedures that are useful for analyzing and solving problems. Problem-solving procedures are called strategies. Strategies are not specific to particular problems or to particular areas of the mathematics curriculum but can be applied alone or in combination with other strategies to solve a wide variety of problems. Students use many strategies intuitively when they solve problems. However, gaining familiarity with a collection of strategies by seeing them modeled, and then by trying to apply them, provides students with useful tools for tackling problems and broadens their problem-solving abilities. The following is a list of useful problem-solving strategies:

PROBLEM-SOLVING STRATEGIES

Look for a pattern

Construct a table

Make an organized list

Act it out

Draw a picture

Use objects

Guess and check

Work backward

Write an equation

Solve a simpler (or similar) problem

Make a model

It's important to discuss with students both the specific strategies they use to solve problems and whether those strategies were effective choices. Class discussions are useful because they provide opportunities for students to hear others' points of view. Having the list of problem-solving strategies posted in the room is also helpful. That way, when a problem is summarized in class, the list serves as a reference for helping students label their methods. As students become familiar with the various strategies, they can refer to the list as a source for approaches.

Usually, it's possible to solve a particular problem using different strategies or combinations of strategies. The following exercise focuses on this issue. For each of the three problems provided, decide which strategies are possible or reasonable to use. After making a list of these strategies, choose one or a combination of strategies to try first in solving each problem. Then solve the problem. Record for each of the problems as indicated.

Problem 1: Show all the ways that 15 objects can be put into four piles so that each pile has a different number of objects in it.

Possible or reasonable strategies:

_____ _____

_____ _____

_____ _____

Which strategy or combination of strategies will you try first to solve the problem?

_____

Solution: _____

_____

Did you change strategies or use others as well? Describe. _____

_____

Problem 2: Lisa and David are playing a game. At the end of each round, the loser gives the winner a penny. After a while, David has won three games, and Lisa has three more pennies than she did when she began. How many rounds did they play?

Possible or reasonable strategies:

_____ _____

_____ _____

_____ _____

Which strategy or combination of strategies will you try first to solve the problem?

_____

Solution: _____

_____

Did you change strategies or use others as well? Describe. _____

_____

Problem 3: **If you spend $1.85 and pay with a $10.00 bill, you get $8.15 in change. Notice that the digits in your change are the same as the digits in what you spent. There are four other amounts you could spend so that the change has the same digits. Find them.**

Possible or reasonable strategies:

_____   _____

_____   _____

_____   _____

Which strategy or combination of strategies will you try first to solve the problem?

_____

Solution: _____

_____

Did you change strategies or use others as well? Describe. _____

_____

THE PROS AND CONS OF PROBLEM SOLVING

Some teachers think that a problem-solving mathematics curriculum is too demanding or unrealistic. Several arguments have been raised: There isn't enough time; the tests we have to give mainly test arithmetic; parents expect us to teach arithmetic; problem solving is too hard for the slow students who need work in basic skills; I was never very good in math myself and I don't feel comfortable teaching what I don't understand. It's important to examine each of these issues.

Argument 1:

There isn't enough time. The reality of the classroom is that teaching the basic skills of arithmetic is a time-consuming and difficult task. There is just so much time in the school day, and over the years, more and more curriculum responsibilities have been added. Now it's problem solving. Focusing mainly on problem solving is too much to expect; it isn't realistic. Besides, the major complaint of secondary math teachers is that the students aren't well enough prepared with basic arithmetic skills.

There's no quarrel with the reality of how difficult and time-consuming the task of educating children is. It's never been easy. But that's no excuse for not taking a serious and critical look at how the math time, no matter how limited, is being spent. Research has shown that spending the bulk of mathematics instructional time to teach arithmetic skills does not prepare students to solve problems. Teachers are well aware of this, even when the most rudimentary of word problems are assigned and students are unable to solve them. Continuing to emphasize arithmetic in isolation rather than in the context of problem solving makes little sense. It's an irresponsible choice when considered in the perspective of children's needs to function in our complicated world.

Argument 2:

The tests we have to give mainly test arithmetic. Accountability is a big issue in education today. Teachers are under a great deal of pressure to prove they are teaching children the needed basics. Taking time away from teaching the basic skills for problem solving may result in lower test scores, and test scores are viewed as an important measure of the quality of the education being provided. Schools cannot risk increased negative public opinion about our educational system.

The evaluation of mathematics instruction should be based on the goals of that instruction. If a standardized test is the tool for evaluation, then the test items should match the goals of the instruction. However, it seems that the available tests dictate what should be taught, rather than the other way around. This doesn't make sense. Remember, the issue is not to avoid arithmetic instruction but to keep in mind that arithmetic skills reflect minimal competencies and cannot be the mainstay of elementary math programs.

Argument 3:

Parents expect the school to teach arithmetic. Parents are concerned about their children's arithmetic skills. They want their children to bring home papers that show the arithmetic work they are doing in school. They don't want another rerun of the "new math" fiasco. Parents argue that they learned arithmetic when they were in school without all this fuss about problem solving, and that should be good enough for their children.

Teachers need to explain program goals to parents, students, and the general public. These goals need to be stated in the context of what children require to function in our changing society. The world differs greatly today from when parents were in elementary school; the technological explosion has affected all areas of everyone's lives. To cling to what was suitable when parents were in school is clinging to nostalgia rather than examining what is currently essential. Professional educators have the job of reeducating parents, not just complying with demands that are obsolete.

Argument 4:

Problem solving is too hard for students who have difficulty with the basic skills. Some students require more time to learn. For many of them, mastering basic computation requires both more instructional time and more practice. Without this, they are not able to perform arithmetic calculations. It's better for slow students to concentrate on the skills rather than attempt to do even more complicated problem solving.

Instead of merely considering how to give the slower students more instructional time to learn to do arithmetic, why not examine what is really basic for those students? Skills are tools. The value of a tool is its usefulness. Being able to do paper-and-pencil computation will not serve students without the ability to interpret a problem, analyze what needs to be done, and evaluate the solution. If a problem calls for arithmetic, a calculator is as sensible a tool (even more so in many cases) as paper and pencil. Therefore, there must be a redefinition of what is really basic to mathematics instruction.

Argument 5:

Some teachers are not very good in math and do not feel comfortable teaching what they do not understand. Some teachers took only what was absolutely required in mathematics, and for some this means that their last math course was in high school. To be afraid of mathematics, to feel inadequate, or even to hate it are not uncommon reactions from people, professional educators included. All teachers can do arithmetic; not all have that same facility in the other strands of mathematics. It's not fair to expect teachers to teach what they don't understand themselves.

There are indeed professional educators who are not comfortable with mathematics. Too often, it is taken for granted that teachers have a firm grasp of the content of grade K–12 mathematics when they leave high school. This isn't always the case. Many teachers have taken only two years of high school mathematics, and many who have taken more courses still have not developed a full understanding of the ideas and relationships in the high school mathematics curriculum. It is a myth that some people do not have a mathematical mind and therefore cannot learn mathematics. All teachers responsible for teaching mathematics face the challenge of introducing children to important mathematics concepts and motivating them to enjoy and appreciate mathematics. Teachers who have never been at all interested in mathematics or who have a limited background in it can continue their learning of mathematics through mathematics courses, conferences, inservice workshops, and other professional development activities.

How Children Learn Mathematics

Not only is it important to consider the content of the elementary math curriculum, it's important to make use of what is known about how children learn mathematics. Children need to learn mathematical concepts and to see relationships among these concepts. Because mathematical concepts and relationships are constructed by people and exist only in their minds, to learn mathematics, children must construct these concepts and relationships in their own minds.

In much of math instruction, children are expected to accept an entirely organized intellectual discipline, usually presented symbolically. They may learn to deal with symbols well enough to perform arithmetic operations. However, having learned arithmetic procedures is not a sufficient indicator that children truly understand the concepts that symbolic manipulations represent. It does not guarantee that they will be able to use those concepts to solve problems.

Learning mathematics requires that children create and re-create mathematical relationships in their own minds. Therefore, when providing appropriate instruction, teachers cannot be seduced by the symbolism of mathematics. Children need direct and concrete interaction with mathematical ideas; ideas are not accessible solely from abstractions. Continuous interaction between a child's mind and concrete experiences with mathematics in the real world is necessary. The following exercises are designed to help you experience this process of interaction.

The Ratio of Your Height to Your Head

How many times do you think a piece of yarn or string equal to your height would wrap around your head as a headband? _____

Unless you've done this before, your initial response most likely was based purely on your perceptions. You have some mental picture of your body, and you rely on that perception to make a guess. Adults' answers to this question usually range between 2 and 10. (Ask at least five others this same question to verify this for yourself.) Few make an accurate estimate based on their perceptions.

Perceptions are not always based in reality. We see this with young children who are shown five objects and claim that there are more when the objects are spread out. This is what they perceive. Their response is not based on logical reasoning but on their perception. If you've never explored the ratio between your height and your head, there is no reason to assume you have learned that relationship. You need to do the measurement to find out the ratio. To learn concepts, experience in the real world is needed.

Height/Circumference

Imagine a soft drink can. Suppose you take a piece of yarn and wrap it around the can to measure its circumference. Do you think the circumference is *longer, shorter,* or about the *same* as the height of the can? Indicate on the drawing how high you think the circumference measure will reach.

As with the previous experience, many people guess incorrectly. The common misperception is that the yarn will be about the same length as the height of the can. There's an element of surprise when that perception is proved to be incorrect. More than surprise, there is often a feeling of consternation, of being puzzled about what has been shown, often of uncomfortableness. It's as if you thought you had more understanding about the relationship between the height and circumference of a soft drink can.

The realization of a misperception produces mental confusion. You now have a problem — you've been faced with a contradiction. This state of confusion is what Piaget calls *disequilibrium*. It is at this moment that you have the greatest potential to learn, to gain new understanding about a relationship. To develop the understanding that takes you beyond your misperception to what really is so requires that you reorganize your mental construction (about the relationship between the circumference and height of the can) that led you to the erroneous conclusion in the first place.

This reorganization can be done only by you, in your own mind. When you come to new understanding — based in reality rather than on how you perceive reality — you no longer are confused. You are in what Piaget terms the state of *equilibrium*. Your intellectual balance is restored, and you no longer experience uncomfortableness or confusion.

To follow up the experiment of measuring the soft drink can, you would benefit from additional experiences with cylinders that have different proportions. One experience is not generally sufficient to cement understanding of a relationship that is new to a learner.

Repeat the experiment with the soft drink can using at least six other cylindrical containers. Use glasses, jars, paper cups, waste paper baskets — whatever is available. For each, make a drawing of the object and predict before measuring. Record your prediction (longer, shorter, or same) and the actual result for each.

What conclusion can you now make about the relationship of the circumference and the height of a cylindrical container? If it's not possible for you to make a conclusion, what more might you do?

_____

_____

_____

The process of resolving disequilibrium is called *equilibration*. This process requires ample concrete experience by the learner. It's not enough to be taught a concept abstractly. Actually, when you studied geometry in high school, you were most likely "taught" this concept. You were taught that the circumference of a circle is equal to pi times the diameter ($c = \pi d$ or $c = 2 \pi r$). You may have learned the formula and also may have been successful applying it in textbook situations. But you did not learn the concept in a way that made it accessible for you to apply in a new situation; that is, that the circumference is about three times the diameter and that using this information enables you to make better estimates in measurement situations.

For many people, there is little relationship between the abstractions of math and the concepts those abstractions represent. It's helpful to relate this to the instructional practice of teaching children through abstractions. The danger is pointed out by the joke about the used car salesman who reported to his boss: I sold the car, but the customer didn't buy it. It's not enough to "teach" without careful attention to what is "learned."

Learning often begins with the recognition of a problem. The process of equilibration is one in which there is continuous interaction between your mental conceptual structures and your environment. It's a repeated cycle of going from confusion to new understanding. Confusion is essential to the process. Yet in school, confusion is often seen negatively, as a hindrance rather than an opportunity for learning. It's as if the goal for a child is to be right all the time, to complete papers correctly, to be successful continually. This makes no sense when the process of learning implies that some concepts have not yet been learned.

Try the following experiment with cylindrical containers. Take two 5-by-8-inch cards and roll each into a tube, rolling one the short way and the other the long way. Tape them. As in the previous experiments, predict whether the circumference is *longer, shorter,* or about the *same* as the height. Also predict *how much* longer or shorter the height is. Then measure.

Prediction: _____   Prediction: _____

How much: _____   How much: _____

Result: _____   Result: _____

Suppose you filled each tube with rice or beans to compare how much each holds. Do you think each holds the same? If not, which one do you think holds more than the other? Why?

_____

_____

Follow the procedure shown and record the results.

_____

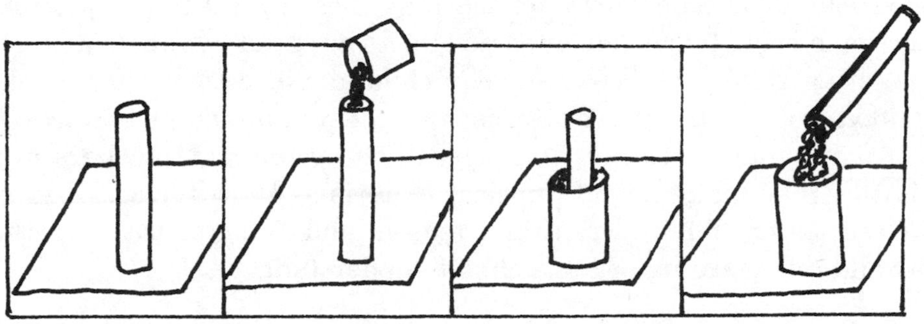

For learning to occur, three conditions are necessary: **maturity**, **physical experience**, and **social interaction.** The process of equilibration coordinates these three conditions.

Maturity: The older children are, the more likely their mental structures will act in coordinated ways. Young children shown a group of objects frequently claim there are a greater number when the objects are spread out, but older children no longer make this error. Younger children report what they perceive; older children have reached a level of mental maturity that allows them to understand that the number of objects does not change when the objects are repositioned. A child who does not see the contradiction between perception and reality is not in a state of disequilibrium.

Physical Experience: The more experiences children have with physical objects in the environment, the more likely related understanding will develop. Firsthand experimentation is needed. Merely looking at a soft drink can does not reveal the relationship between its height and its circumference. Testing an idea with physical materials provides valuable feedback for understanding relationships.

Social Interaction: The more opportunities children have to interact with peers, parents, and teachers, the more they hear other viewpoints that help them gain perspective on their own ideas. Social interaction stimulates children to think through their own ideas and to approach objectivity. This type of interaction is also an important source of information about social customs and conventions.

What are the teaching implications of these conditions for learning? A key factor in making instructional decisions is to consider the **source of the learning** of any new concept or skill. Mathematics relies on logical structures, and learning mathematics calls for making sense of these structures. The source of learning to understand mathematical ideas is **internal**. Being aware of children's maturity levels, providing experiences with physical materials, and supporting social interaction are all important aspects of helping children think, reason, and make sense of mathematical ideas.

Social knowledge, however, is also an aspect of mathematics. The symbolism that we used to represent ideas — the numerals we write to represent quantities and the symbols that we use to describe relationships — are social conventions that help us communicate about mathematical ideas. The source for learning these conventions is **external** and can be another person, a book, television, or some other source outside the child.

A teacher, another child, or a book can set a child in a direction, offer some information, or explain an idea, but children have to construct understanding for themselves in order to make sense of mathematics. Rather than "teaching by telling," teachers must structure learning activities that make use of physical materials, allow for social interaction, and provide opportunities for children to think, reason, and make sense of mathematics. You cannot talk a child into learning or tell a child to understand.

Managing the Classroom for Problem Solving

When considering how to organize math instruction based in problem solving and responsive to how children learn mathematics, teachers should look carefully at both the teaching and learning aspects of the classroom. In much of classroom practice, the teacher is the key person, providing information, explaining concepts or skills, giving examples. Students interact with the teacher, and with each other, but it is the teacher who directs the instruction, leads discussions, prompts responses, and paces the lesson. The primary focus in the class is on the teacher.

A problem-solving curriculum, however, requires a different role from the teacher. Rather than directing a lesson, the teacher needs to provide time for students to grapple with problems, search for strategies and solutions on their own, and learn to evaluate their own results. Although the teacher needs to be very much present, the primary focus in the class needs to be on the students' thinking processes.

Problem solving also requires a shift in students' attitudes. In order to become successful problem solvers, students must develop the following characteristics:

- interest in finding solutions to problems
- confidence to try various strategies
- willingness to risk being wrong at times
- ability to accept frustrations that come from not knowing
- willingness to persevere when solutions are not immediate
- understanding of the difference between not knowing the answer and not having found it *yet*

This is not a casual list of qualities. Teachers need to model these attitudes in order to help students develop them. To this end, students must feel that their teacher values problem solving. It's not enough for a teacher to provide problem-solving experiences in the classroom. Teachers also need to present themselves as problem solvers, as active learners who are seekers, willing to plunge into new situations, not always knowing the answer or what the outcome will be. There's no place for "Do as I say, not as I do" in problem-solving lessons.

Teachers need to emphasize the importance of working on problems, not merely on getting the right answers. Errors should be viewed not as unfortunate mistakes but as opportunities for learning. The classroom should be a safe place in which new ideas can be tried out and in which children can feel free to risk making mistakes. In solving problems, persistence, not speed, needs to be valued. Putting the value on quick right responses does not help establish a classroom where the process of solving problems is encouraged.

Teachers need to urge students to find ways to verify their solutions for themselves, rather than rely on the teacher or the answer book for verification. This may be difficult for teachers to demand; answer keys have long been a part of the teacher's domain in teaching mathematics. In considering this issue, however, teachers may find it helpful to take a careful look at real-life problems. There is not necessarily one correct solution to real problems. At times, several possible solutions exist. Often, an exact solution isn't even required and being close enough is sufficient. Most important, in real life, it's up to the problem solver to decide when a solution is "right" or "best." In light of those issues, providing answers does not enhance students' critical thinking skills. On the contrary, giving answers can result in stopping the thinking process. Evaluating solutions is an important aspect of problem solving.

Along with not providing answers, teachers need to encourage students to explain their approaches and results, even when they're totally correct. Often, teachers nod and affirm a child's correct response and question the child when there's an error. If teachers only question children when their responses are wrong, they soon catch on. Instruction should be structured so students describe their methods and solutions not only to the teacher but to their classmates as well. Time for discussions is needed, and students should be encouraged to listen, question, and learn from each other.

It's important to remember that developing problem-solving skills is not a lesson objective, but a long-range goal. Time is often a concern for teachers — they've got just a year to teach an enormous amount of material. Natural learning, however, doesn't happen on a time schedule and often requires more time than schools are organized to provide. Problem-solving experiences take time. It's essential that teachers provide the time that's needed for children to work through activities on their own and that teachers not slip into teaching-by-telling for the sake of efficiency.

COOPERATIVE PROBLEM SOLVING IN THE CLASSROOM

One way to organize the classroom to establish an environment that is safe and supportive for problem solving is to have children work in small groups. A small-group structure has the potential to maximize the active participation of each student and to reduce individuals' isolation. It provides a setting that values social interaction, a necessary element of children's learning. When organized into small groups, more students have the opportunity to offer their ideas for reaction and to receive immediate feedback. Organizing a class into small groups requires reorganizing the classroom physically, redefining the students' responsibilities, and considering the teacher's role.

Let's consider the physical reorganization first. The classroom needs to be organized so that small groups of two to five students are seated together. Getting the students into small groups is easy enough. If tables are available, each group can be seated at a table; if not, desks can be moved into clusters.

It's beneficial for students to have the opportunity to work with everyone over the course of time. To this end, teachers should assign groups randomly and change them regularly. Playing cards work well to accomplish this. The teacher can label the tables or clusters — Ace, 2, 3, 4, and so on — and then can select out the corresponding cards. By shuffling the cards and distributing them, the teacher can form groups of four by asking all the Aces to go to the Aces' table and so forth. Using the cards is a fair system that mixes groups effectively with each reshuffle. It removes the responsibility from the teacher of deciding who works with whom and communicates the message that students need to learn to work with all their classmates.

Three rules are in operation when students work in small groups:

1. You are responsible for your own work and behavior.

2. You must be willing to help any group member who asks.

3. You may ask the teacher for help only when everyone in your group has the same question.

The rules need to be explained to the class and discussed at least the first half dozen times students work in groups. The rules are only as useful as they are understood and practiced in actual operation. The first rule is not new for any student. Even so, it helps to clarify it with further explanation: You have responsibilities in this class and your job is to meet them. If you don't understand something, your first option is to ask your group for help. On the other hand, if you do understand, don't take over and give answers; listening to others' ideas is also a part of your individual responsibility. Sometimes, although you are sitting with your group, you will have an individual assignment to complete. Other times, your group will have an assignment to complete jointly, and then your responsibility is to contribute to the group effort.

Two comments help clarify the second rule: Notice that the benefit of this rule is that you have willing helpers at your disposal at all times, with no waiting for help. Also, remember that you are to give help "when asked." Students need to be cautioned not to be pushy, to wait for group members to ask, and to help, not merely by giving answers, but by trying to ask questions that would help someone focus on the problem at hand.

Rule three eliminates many procedural concerns, such as: What are we supposed to do? When is this due? Can we take this home? This rule directs students to seek help from each other first, relieving the teacher of the tedium of having to give the same directions or information over and over again. When a teacher is talking to the entire class, it's rare to have everyone listen attentively. Small groups help enormously. Chances are good that at least one out of each group is listening at any one time. Talking to eight groups of four offers better odds than talking to thirty-two individuals.

Staying true to rule three may seem uncomfortable at first. It's typical during initial small-group experiences for individual children to ask questions or to make requests. When this occurs, children should be directed to check with their group and should be reminded that when all hands are raised, the teacher will come and discuss with the entire group whatever problem there is. Responding in this way is not contrary to being a responsive, sensitive, helpful teacher; it motivates children to rely more on themselves. As teachers watch children become more confident and independent, they become convinced that this is an invaluable learning experience.

One benefit to students from working collaboratively in groups is that they have more opportunity to voice their thinking and to respond to others' ideas. This system also provides students with an organized way to get support from each other, rather than depending solely on the teacher's feedback. It builds students' independence, which, in turn, can free teachers to provide attention to individuals.

The benefits of this system can be realized only if enough time and attention are given to implementing it in the classroom. There is no guarantee of instant success from seating students in small groups and explaining the rules. Students need practice, encouragement, and discussion to learn to work together successfully. Although students may have heard much about cooperation, functioning cooperatively is not a skill they've necessarily put into practice. And although they've always been told they're responsible for their own work and behavior, meeting that responsibility independently doesn't come naturally. Teachers may intellectually accept the benefit of responding to students in small groups rather than to individuals, yet they may need to break long-standing teaching habits. In order for the system to best serve teachers and students, careful planning of instruction that utilizes this organization is important.

TEACHING THE COOPERATIVE PROBLEM-SOLVING LESSON

When tackling a problem, students first need to understand the problem, then to apply some strategy toward solving it, and finally to evaluate their solutions. It's helpful to think of teaching the cooperative problem-solving lesson in these categories:

> *Introducing*
> *Exploring*
> *Summarizing*

Introducing

During this part of the classroom lesson, the goal is for the students to understand the problem, the scope of solutions possible, and the guidelines established for recording results. At this stage, some or all of these teaching steps will be needed:

1. **Present or review concepts.**
2. **Pose a part of the problem or a similar but smaller problem for your students to try.**
3. **Present the problem to be solved.**
4. **Discuss to make sure students understand what they are to do.**

Before the problem is introduced to the class, it is helpful to have students seated in the small groups in which they will work and to have materials readily available or already distributed. This is not the time to deal with individual problems that do not relate to the class understanding of the problem. The focus should be on whole class interaction, using examples or having other students restate the problem.

Exploring

Once the problem has been introduced, exploring begins. In this stage, students work cooperatively toward a solution. While the groups are working, the teacher has three responsibilities:

1. **Observe the interaction, listening for use in later discussion to groups' ideas, strategies, and work procedures.**
2. **Offer assistance when needed, either when all members of a group raise their hands or if a group is not working.**
3. **Provide an extension for groups that finish more quickly than others.**

When offering assistance, the teacher has a goal of getting the group working productively and independently. To that end, teachers need to determine the nature of the problem, offer assistance, and move on once the group gets going. There are two types of problems that occur with groups, each calling for a different type of intervention.

One problem is difficulty with the activity itself. The group either is stuck or is pursuing an incorrect line of thought. If they're stuck, the teacher can assist by helping students restate what they know so far, posing a simple example for them to solve, and explaining concepts again if needed. Once they can do an example successfully and can restate the problem, they should return to work. If students are pursuing an erroneous idea or have made an error, it helps to point out a contradiction that illustrates their erroneous thinking or to ask them how they arrived at a certain conclusion. Teachers should avoid telling correct answers and should leave a group when the students are aware of their mistake.

However, the difficulty may be with the group rather than with the problem. Groups bog down for different reasons. For instance, the group may lack the needed impetus to get started. This may be obvious because of lack of materials — paper, pencil, blocks, whatever. If this is the problem, it helps for the teacher to join the group for a short time, to suggest that someone do what's necessary to get started, and, when a student in the group accepts that responsibility, to leave them. Groups may also need help with focusing. You may hear the *What are we supposed to do?* or *Didn't the teacher say to do it this way?* kind of question. Offer the needed clarification.

Other problems may arise. Sometimes, one person takes over and ignores the others' ideas. At times, a member of the group does not contribute or does not understand what the group is doing. In these kinds of situations, teachers should point out to the group what they observe and should restate that the group's job is to work together. In these instances, it is helpful to give the group more specific guidelines. Following are some examples:

- To make sure that everyone has an equal chance to speak, after you've spoken, wait until everyone else has offered a thought before you speak again.

- Find a way that everyone can contribute some part to the solution of the problem.

- We all need encouragement, so tell each other when someone offers an idea that is helpful.

Remember that when groups are working well, it's best not to interrupt or intervene but rather to listen and to observe as students work. This is helpful for assessing how students are thinking and learning.

During the exploration stage, it's necessary to have some extensions of the problem to offer groups who complete their work early. Extensions may be given verbally or with written directions. The latter method is second best; students respond best to personal interaction.

The exploring stage should continue until most groups have completed their solutions of the problem. It's helpful to structure the class so that groups move on independently to other work after they have checked with the teacher for completeness. That way, groups have the maximum time possible to finish their work.

Summarizing

Three goals are important when summarizing:

1. **Have groups report their processes, both group procedures and strategies used.**
2. **Have groups present solutions.**
3. **Generalize from the solutions.**

The following questions are useful for helping groups report about their experiences: How did you organize the work in your group? What problems did you encounter? Was your method effective or can you think of a better way to have worked? For a discussion of groups' problem-solving strategies, ask: What strategy did your group use? Did any group use a different strategy? Allow enough time for all groups to present their methods.

When presenting solutions, groups should state their findings and, whenever possible, display their work. Ask: How did you decide if your findings make sense? How can you check your solution?

Generalizing a solution involves extending it to other situations not necessarily dependent on the specific limitations of the problem. The following questions are effective in eliciting generalizations: Are there patterns or relationships you can see from your solution? Can you think of another problem you've solved that this reminds you of? How are the two problems alike and different? Another help is to give the students an altered version of the problem and to ask how their solution or methods of solution would change.

Before they summarize, all the students should have ended their explorations and should be ready for a class discussion. Having children come together in a gathering place helps them focus. Other classroom hints: Have students speak one at a time; direct groups to choose a spokesperson to report to the entire class; encourage students to respond to each other's comments; record data on the chalkboard as it's presented.

Extensions should not be summarized at this time unless all groups have had a chance to tackle them. They can be discussed later with the appropriate groups. Posing additional challenges at this time is one way to extend the problem for the more interested or able students.

As teachers use these techniques, they become more comfortable teaching with them. Only from direct experience with their own class and with different activities can teachers learn what time is required in each of the three stages. In some situations, it is possible for a class to complete all three stages within one math period. Other situations may require that summarizing be delayed until all have had sufficient exploring time or because time has run out on a particular day. Sometimes a teacher may pose several problems, even a week's work, and groups work at their own pace. These differences are not significant as long as students understand generally what is expected of them in problem-solving situations.

Note: A lesson does not imply a one-day experience. The investigation of a problem can extend for two, three, or more days. All groups should have adequate time to explore so that they can contribute to the summarizing. Also, summarizing is very important and should not be skipped or shortened for lack of time. It's valuable for students to reflect on their learning, to hear from others, and to connect others' experience to their ideas.

A SAMPLE LESSON — THE CONSECUTIVE SUMS PROBLEM

A good beginning problem-solving activity for children is *The Consecutive Sums Problem*. It reinforces a skill children have practiced — addition with sums to 25 — and extends this skill in a way that promotes cooperative group work. Following are directions for teaching this lesson.

Introducing

1. Present or review concepts.

Consecutive numbers are numbers that go in order, such as 1, 2, 3, 4 or 11, 12, 13. Each comes right after the other without skipping. Ask students for sequences of three or four consecutive numbers. Ask them to explain why 15, 16, 18, for example, are not consecutive.

2. Pose a part of the problem or a similar but smaller problem.

Ask: Who can tell me a way to write the number 9 as the sum of consecutive numbers? The usual response is $4 + 5$. Record this on the chalkboard. Underneath this, write $9 = 2 + 3 + 4$. Ask them to verify if this is true. Tell the class that this shows that it's possible to write 9 as the sum of consecutive numbers in at least two different ways. Try another example if you think it's needed.

3. Present the problem to be solved.

Ask the students, in their groups, to find all the ways to write the numbers from 1 to 25 as the sum of consecutive numbers. (For younger children, finding the sums for the numbers from 1 to 15 may be sufficient.) Tell them that some of the numbers are impossible; challenge them to see if they can find the pattern of those numbers. Direct them to search for other patterns as well, such as how many different sums there are for different numbers.

Provide groups with large paper for recording, and ask them to put their group label on their recording (Ace, 2, 3, etc.) as well as their group members' names. On their record, they should also write statements that describe the patterns they find.

4. Discussion.

Ask for questions. Review the guidelines for group work if you think that's necessary.

Exploring

1. Observe the interaction.

Notice work procedures. Some groups divide up the numbers so that one person does 1 to 6, the next does 7 through 12, and so on. In other groups, individuals work on whichever numbers they choose and add their findings to a group chart. Some groups have one person do all the recording; others share that job among the members. Recording formats differ as well. Some groups list the numbers from 1 to 25 and write the sums next to each. Other groups organize the numbers by how many different sums they found for each, so all those that could be written in only one way are in one column, those that could be written in two ways are in another, and so on.

2. Offer assistance when needed.

Sometimes a group will summon you to ask a procedural question, such as whether they should orient the paper the long way or the short way. Let them make those decisions for themselves; tell them they'll see later what other groups decided. Keep in mind that although it may seem like a minor decision to you, it isn't so for children. Organizing work on paper is a skill students need to acquire; group decisions can help them do so.

Groups sometimes make erroneous generalizations. For example, when they find it's impossible to write 2 and 4 as the sums of consecutives, they may conclude that 6 would fit the pattern and also be impossible. In such a situation, confront them with a contradiction. Ask the group to consider $1 + 2 + 3$. When they realize that the sum of those numbers is 6, leave them to rethink their hasty generalization.

You may notice a group bogged down in a way not related to the problem itself but to some procedural issue. For example, the group isn't keeping a group record. Join that group. Ask: How are you supposed to record your results? (This way you find out if they understood your instructions about which paper to use.) Then ask: Who will get the paper for your group? (This may prompt someone to do so.) Or ask: What do you need to do in order to get started?

Sometimes, a group has written all the sums they can find and calls you over to announce they've finished. However, when you look at their recording, you see that they haven't written any statements about patterns they've found. The usual response is that they can't think of any. Ask probing questions to kindle their thinking: Can you see a pattern to the numbers that are impossible? How could you describe that pattern in a summary statement? What do you notice about all the numbers that had three possible sums? Which numbers had only one possible sum? When the students have begun to consider some of your questions, leave them to write statements. Help them word one if you feel they need more support.

3. Provide an extension.

If a group has completed work to your satisfaction, offer a challenge. Can you find a way to predict how many ways 36 can be written as the sum of consecutive numbers? Can you predict for any number?

Summarizing

1. Have groups share their processes, both group procedures and strategies used.

Ask groups to report how they divided up the work. Ask if they thought their method was a good one or how they would change it if they had to extend this exploration to include the numbers up to 50.

Discuss strategies used. Usually, some took a number, such as 12, and used the *Guess and Check* strategy to find sums that worked. Others worked the other way, using the *Work Backward* strategy, starting with the sums and then writing them under the appropriate total. Younger children may have used counters to help — the *Use Objects* strategy. Most groups use the *Look for a Pattern* and *Make an Organized List* strategies. The different methods are important to discuss so students become aware that there are a variety of ways to approach problems. Also, such discussions can provide valuable insights into students' approaches to learning.

2. Have groups present solutions.

If possible, have groups post their recording sheets for the others to see. Discuss any differences and similarities in solutions. Ask groups how they were sure they had found all the possible ways to write any particular number.

3. Generalize from the solutions.

Review the summary statements, being sure that when incorrect generalizations appear, you provide counter examples to help students reconsider their ideas. Ask about the "impossible" numbers, drawing out as many different descriptions as possible. Encourage children to explain in their own words: "Start with 1, and multiply by 2." "They're doubles." "They're powers of 2." Ask for the patterns for numbers that were written two ways, three ways, etc. Ask older children to examine the primes and describe what they notice. Present the challenge of finding a way to predict how many ways any given number could be written.

INDEPENDENT PROBLEM SOLVING — THE MENU

Children also benefit from independent problem solving. One way to provide opportunities for independent problem-solving experiences in the classroom is to use menus.

A menu is a collection of activities for students to do. A menu may provide classwork for several days, a week, or for a longer period of time. The number of tasks on a menu can vary according to the topic and the age of the children. In general, the tasks on a menu are not hierarchical and do not conceptually build upon each other. Rather, menu activities pose problems, set up situations, and ask questions that help students interact with one or more mathematical ideas.

Teachers report different ways for managing the use of menu activities. Some write directions for each task on a 12-by-18-inch sheet of tagboard or construction paper. They post the tasks and orally introduce them to the class, discussing the directions. When students need clarification, they refer to the posted directions. Students take the materials they need from a general supply and return them when they finish their work or at the end of the class.

Rather than post tasks, other teachers duplicate about half a dozen of each, mount them on tagboard, and make them available for students to use. Children take copies of the tasks to their seats along with the materials they need. Some teachers prefer to assign different locations in the classroom for tasks, putting the task and materials needed in a container that is placed at the defined location.

Each of these systems encourages children to be independent and responsible for their learning. They are allowed to spend the amount of time needed on any one task and to make choices about the sequence in which they work on tasks.

A posted list of the menu tasks provides a class assignment pad for all the students to see. Some teachers also post a class list and label a column for each task so that children can indicate when they complete each activity. Others have students copy the list of menu activities and use it to keep track of tasks they've completed. Whatever the system, it's important that it be clear to the students and provide information about their progress.

Introducing a new menu requires explaining the activities to the entire class. If special materials are necessary, they should be made available. Due dates should be clear. It may take as long as one class period to introduce a long menu. Or teachers may prefer to introduce a few tasks, have the students begin work, and then introduce the others a few days later.

Make sure you are clear with the students about whether activities are cooperative or individual. Menu tasks can fit into both categories. Whether activities are designed for individual or cooperative work, students should have the support of their groups. It's important that classroom procedures be clearly set and discussed with the students as often as necessary so that the work time is as productive as possible.

Summarizing needs to be done for each activity. However, it's not advisable to do all the summarizing at one time. Stagger it, making sure that all students have had the opportunity to complete an activity before you begin a class discussion.

Using menus has several advantages for students. It provides them with the opportunity to make choices, to learn to manage their own time, and to work on problems at their own pace. Although they have to complete their menu work in a specified time, there are no rigid time limitations for any particular problem. Within a menu, students are able to make choices, both about the order in which they tackle the problems and about which of the optional tasks, if any, they choose to do.

The menu has advantages for you as well. It's possible to work with individuals or small groups and have discussions that give valuable insights into students' understanding. If you are absent, the children have ongoing work that they can do with the supervision of a substitute teacher.

SAMPLE CLASSROOM MANAGEMENT PLANS

The following descriptions present ways that teachers at different grade levels use the menu in their math programs. None of these solutions may fit all teachers' needs. That's not their purpose. They're meant to provide alternatives for consideration and to give a sense of the range of possibilities.

Carol teaches fifth and sixth graders. Her program is structured so that children do a week-long menu of problem-solving activities for three out of four weeks. Children are randomly placed into groups of four and change groups weekly. Each week's menu presents problems from each of the strands and includes both cooperative and individual work. During the fourth week, Carol specifically focuses on arithmetic and uses manipulative materials as the primary instructional tools for whole numbers, fractions, and decimals.

In Donna's sixth-grade class, the menu serves as the overall curriculum organizer for all subjects. Each Monday, she posts a clean piece of chart paper and lists assignments. Some assignments are new for the week and some are carried over from the previous week. Also, additional work may be added to a menu during the week and some assignments will be crossed off as due dates pass. For math, students keep a "math lab" book that they construct using construction paper for the cover and newsprint for the inside. Their books are kept in a class mailbox. Donna works with small groups while the other students work on menu tasks; she schedules whole group instruction as needed, to introduce new concepts or to discuss completed work.

Bonnie uses a similar system with her third graders. However, she uses the menu just for math. She introduces a new menu on Mondays and often spends that math time in whole group instruction, teaching any skills that the children will need in order to do the tasks. For example, if the children are to do a spinner experiment, she'll teach how to make a spinner. If she plans to have them make 0–99 number puzzles, she'll introduce coloring patterns on the 0–99 chart. During menu time, children may work alone or with others, but they must ask three other people for help before asking the teacher. Bonnie varies instruction by intermittently providing cooperative problem-solving lessons.

Doris teaches eighth and ninth graders, five classes a day, each for a 50-minute period. She groups all her classes into groups of four and changes groups every two weeks. She uses this organization for both her general math classes and her algebra classes and has students correct homework assignments and quizzes in their groups. Doris varies the instructional time among cooperative problem-solving activities, menus, and whole group instruction. Working on menus allows Doris to maintain ongoing work in the classroom; although work is interrupted by the end-of-the-period bell, the next day students pick up where they left off.

Barbara teaches first grade. She devotes about three times a week to menu time, which is structured without written tasks. Barbara has established eight work areas in the room and has a box designated for each area into which she puts the materials needed for an activity. She introduces each activity to the entire class. On a given day, there may be one or two new activities, with the rest familiar ones. The children learn to distribute the materials, carrying the boxes designated to each space and returning them to storage at the end of the work period. Each area is set up to accommodate a fixed number of children, and children are free to go to an area as long as space is available. Whole group instruction for various purposes (such as introducing a new activity or teaching word problems or doing a graph) occurs for short periods of time, two to four times weekly. These instructional periods may precede menu time on a given day or may use the entire math time. Barbara does small group instruction during the menu time when a classroom aide is available to supervise the rest of the children. Barbara also structures cooperative problem-solving activities intermittently, about once every few weeks, usually for 20 to 30 minutes.

ORGANIZING THE INSTRUCTIONAL PROGRAM

Organizing the math program into units of instruction is one way of structuring the content of a problem-solving mathematics curriculum. A unit is a collection of activities that deals with mathematics that is important for children to study and appropriate for their grade level. A unit can have one main focus or deal with several mathematical ideas, but it should include activities that engage students with ideas from all strands, so that students can see connections among the different areas of mathematics.

For example, as well as providing number experiences, a unit on fractions can involve students with geometry, measurement, logical reasoning, and graphing and interpreting statistical data. In this way, a topic that is usually relegated to the number strand with a focus on arithmetic skills can be taught in a way that more fully integrates mathematical ideas.

Although topics for units may be similar to chapter titles in traditional textbooks, the format of instruction is much different. Rather than providing a sequence of experiences that guide students toward mastery of a concept or skill, a unit is a collection of experiences that offer students a variety of ways to think about an idea. A unit of instruction can last from two weeks to five or six weeks. All activities in a unit should require and encourage children to think, to reason, and to solve problems.

Components of Units

When thinking about the organization of a unit, teachers will find it helpful to consider the following components:

UNIT OF STUDY

I. Directed Lessons
Present concepts and language
Introduce procedures and materials

II. Independent Explorations (Menu)
Present problem-solving activities
Integrate math ideas and language
Make activities nonsequential and nonhierarchical
Use individual and cooperative activities

III. Whole Class Discussions
Summarize and interpret results
Have children share thinking
Focus on relationships and connections

IV. Assessment

    Do before, as part of instruction, and after

    Focus on several aspects of student learning:

        understanding of ideas

        problem solving

        reactions to learning

    Use children's writing

Directed Lessons

Directed lessons are problem-solving lessons that introduce the mathematical ideas in the unit for the whole class to explore together. Activities in these whole class lessons introduce the procedures, materials, and language that the children need for tasks they will pursue as independent explorations. The section *Teaching the Cooperative Problem-Solving Lesson*, which begins on page 32, gives specific information about teaching these lessons.

Independent Explorations (Menu)

Independent explorations offer the children a collection of activities, all of which provide experience with the mathematical focus of the unit. Through these explorations, children have opportunities to use the mathematical ideas and language introduced in the whole class lessons. The activities may be for children to work on alone, with partners, or in small groups, and students in a class can work on different activities during the same math class. All tasks are problem-solving activities that promote mathematical thinking and reasoning, involve the children with various manipulative materials, incorporate writing, and encourage communication. For more information, see *Independent Problem Solving — The Menu*, the section that begins on page 37.

Whole Class Discussions

Whole class discussions are held after the children have had time to explore a particular activity or idea. Teachers use these discussions to summarize and interpret results from explorations, have children share their thinking and ideas, focus children on mathematical relationships, and help children make connections between and among the activities.

Assessment

Assessment should be an integral part of instruction, before, during, and after the unit. Assessments should focus on children's understanding of ideas, problem-solving abilities, and reactions to their learning. A teacher can assess from listening in whole class discussions, observing during small group work, and reading students' writing.

It's important to note that the separation of the components of a unit does not imply a sequence for instruction. For example, all the directed lessons are not meant necessarily to precede the independent explorations, nor do whole class summarizing discussions need to wait until the children have completed all the independent explorations. It's possible, for example, to teach one or two of the directed lessons and then introduce several independent explorations. The children might then work with the independent explorations for several days before you do another whole class directed lesson or introduce more of the menu activities. Also, it might be advisable on a particular day — because of the weather or a school event that disrupts the schedule or causes excitement — to take time out, change the pace, and switch to a quieter activity.

It isn't expected that every child will complete every activity in a unit. Some may do so and even continue with additional explorations. Others, however, may get involved in depth with a few activities on the menu and be purposefully engaged with the mathematics. Still others may need encouragement or prodding to get involved with what the menu offers.

GETTING STARTED

A note to teachers: It makes sense to start slowly, beginning with the current system and trying new ideas and ways of organizing the curriculum and the students within the structure of what you usually do. Rather than a massive restructuring, ease into changes with moderation. Think about instituting changes as your own professional research project. Decide to do something, try it, and then evaluate it. Try something new several times before making a decision. (Remember, the larger the statistical sample, the more valid your decisions based on that sample will be.) Things rarely work as smoothly the first time as they do the second. The third time will be even more comfortable. The more you work with a new idea, the more opportunity you have to internalize parts of it, which frees you to consider other aspects. This is how learning occurs best, for teachers as well as for students.

PART II

Problem-Solving Activities in the Strands

Introduction

*I*n this section, mathematics activities are presented for each of the following areas:

Measurement
Probability and Statistics
Geometry
Logical Reasoning
Patterns, Functions, and Algebra
Number

The ideas presented are not meant to be comprehensive. They are meant to serve as examples of the kinds of activities recommended for students' problem-solving experiences. Grade levels are not indicated. Teachers should read through each section and choose activities that are suitable for students.

The sections are organized in the following way:

1. **Introduction**. Background information about the strand is presented to explain its importance to the elementary math program.

2. **A Sample Activity.** For each of the strands, except for *Patterns, Functions, and Algebra,* a cooperative problem-solving experience is outlined in detail. The *Patterns, Functions, and Algebra* strand describes a sequence of activities for introducing pattern instead of presenting one model lesson. Activities for all strands are suitable for a wide span of grade levels. Two sample activities are included for *Number* — one for primary children and one for the intermediate grades.

3. **Activities.** Most of the activities are suitable for independent explorations and are well suited for students to work on cooperatively in small groups; the directions for these activities are written for students. Some activities are marked "Whole Class" because they are more appropriate for whole class investigations, and the directions are written to the teacher. Whole class activities often prepare students for similar and related independent explorations.

Measurement

INTRODUCTION

Concepts and skills in the *Measurement* strand of the math curriculum all deal with making comparisons between what is being measured and some suitable standard of measure. Key to the development of skills in measurement is ample experience with measuring activities. Children acquire measuring skills through firsthand practice. Also important is the reality that measurement is never exact, that even the most careful measurements are approximations. Children need to learn to evaluate when their measurements are "close enough." Children also need practice making estimates in measurement.

Why Teach Measurement?

Measurement tools and skills have a variety of uses in everyday adult life. Being able to measure connects mathematics to the environment. The ability to use measuring tools — rulers, thermometers, measuring cups, scales, and the like — and to estimate with these tools are necessary skills for children to develop.

Instruction in measurement intersects with other strands of the elementary math curriculum. Measuring gives children practical applications for the computation skills they are learning. It also provides a way to tie basic geometric concepts to number concepts. In addition, measurement offers opportunities for interdisciplinary learning in subjects such as social studies, geography, science, industrial arts, home economics, art, and music.

What Concepts in Measurement Should Be Taught?

In the organization of classroom measurement activities, four successive stages in learning need to be considered:

1. Making comparisons between objects by matching.

Children compare objects by matching, without the use of other tools of measurement. They order things by this method of comparison.

2. Comparing objects with nonstandard units.

Children use a variety of objects for measuring — parts of the body, straws, cubes, books, and whatever else is readily available.

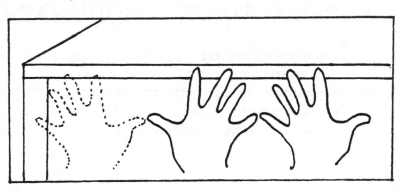

3. Comparing objects with standard units.

Standard units should emerge as a convenient extension of nonstandard units, useful for the purpose of communication. It makes sense that children become comfortable with both the metric and English systems. We live in a "bilingual" measurement world, and children need to be familiar with both ways of measuring.

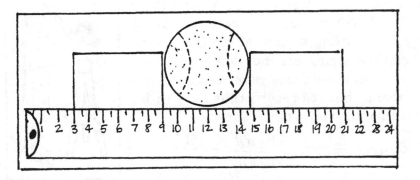

4. Choosing suitable units for specific measurements.

Children learn to select the appropriate standard units of measurement needed for specific applications.

Instruction should progress through these four stages in each of the areas of measurement: length, time, weight/mass, volume/capacity, temperature, area. Within each of these areas, students need to learn to use standard units and tools of measuring and to develop the ability to estimate. Also, underlying all areas of measurement is the idea that the physical act of measuring produces, at best, an approximate measure. The concept of "rounding off" becomes meaningful when applied to measuring procedures.

It's not possible to say precisely when children are ready to function in each of the stages. However, a general guideline is that before third grade, children spend their time most profitably using direct comparisons and nonstandard units to make comparisons. After the third grade, more emphasis can be placed on using selected standards of measure. It's also important to check children's abilities to conserve in each of the different measurement areas.

A SAMPLE ACTIVITY — BODY RATIOS

This is an activity that uses nonstandard measurements to explore body ratios. In addition to the measuring experience, it provides a way to introduce the concept and symbolic notation of ratios. For younger children, however, the ratio notation is inappropriate. A more suitable activity would be to cut a string equal to one body measure and to use that string to find things in the room that are longer, shorter, or the about the same length.

Materials

string
scissors

Introducing

1. Present or review concepts.

Ask the students to estimate how many times a piece of string equal to their height would wrap around their head as a headband. When they've done this, have a student assist you in cutting a piece of string equal to your height. Wrap the string around your head. Your height is equal to about three times your head measurement. Show students how to record that as a ratio, using either or both of the two symbols shown:

$$\text{head} : \text{height} = \frac{1}{3} \qquad \frac{\text{head}}{\text{height}} = \frac{1}{3}$$

(**Note:** There is often confusion about whether to write this ratio as 1:3 or 3:1. Substituting the actual measurement values for head and height into the ratio shows where the smaller and larger numbers belong.)

2. Pose a part of the problem or a similar but smaller problem.

Ask: What do you think the ratio is between my foot and my height? How could I find out? Demonstrate this for them. Your height should be about six or seven times your foot length. Record: foot/height = 1/6. Also show with your string that your foot and your forearm are just about the same length. Record that as well: foot/forearm = 1/1.

3. Present the problem to be solved.

Tell the class: First cut a piece of string equal in length to your height. Help each other do this. Individually, with your height string, explore ratios on your body. Record at least ten ratios using the notation shown. Then, in your groups, compare all the ratios you individually found, and see how many you can find that are true for all of you. Be prepared to report group ratios back to the class.

4. Discuss the results.

Ask for questions. It might be a good idea to reinforce the notation, helping the students see how to decide which number goes where in a ratio. This notation is totally arbitrary, as is all mathematical notation, but is the conventional way to record ratios.

Exploring

There shouldn't be much for you to do. Circulate, encouraging groups to stop and compare their individual ratios when a reasonable time period has elapsed. No extension is needed; students can find more ratios.

Summarizing

Discuss the group processes. Ask students to compare working individually and working cooperatively in their groups — which was easier, more enjoyable, etc. Ask groups to report what they did if they found they hadn't explored the same ratios individually when they compared ratios in their groups.

List the groups' common ratios on the board. See if any were the same for everyone (or almost everyone).

Ask: Which ratios would be different for babies and why? If any of your students have infant brothers or sisters, send a note home asking their parents to help the students measure the baby's height and head circumference.

Extensions

Are You a Square?

Have students compare their heights with their reaches, both arms outstretched. Post a graph for them to record their names in the proper place. Squares have equal heights and reaches. Tall rectangles have heights that are longer than reaches. Wide rectangles have longer reaches than heights.

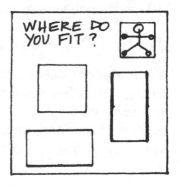

A Half-Size "Me"

Tell students: Fold your height string in half and cut a length of butcher paper that is equal to that measurement. This is the height of a half-size you. Measure the length of your head with your string. Fold it in half, and measure down from the top of the paper. That shows where your chin will be. Continue measuring this way, using string to find half the width of your face, half the length of your neck, half the width of your shoulders, and so forth. The more measurements you take, the more accurate your drawing will be. When you've drawn yourself, color the drawing to show how you're dressed today. Post your portrait.

Index Card Portrait

Follow the procedure for the previous activity, but this time you have to fit your drawing on a 5-by-8-inch index card. Calculate how many times you'd have to reduce your dimensions so your drawing will fit. Then do it.

The Statue of Liberty Problem

(This activity is suitable for older or more able students.) The Statue of Liberty's nose, from bridge to tip, measures 4 feet, 6 inches. This information is available in an almanac or encyclopedia. How could you use your string and your own body to figure out how long her right arm is, from shoulder to finger tip? (The Statue of Liberty's right arm actually measures 42 feet.) If students' answers are far off, ask them to surmise why.

A SAMPLE ACTIVITY — INTRODUCING THE METRIC SYSTEM

This sequence of activities is a plan for introducing children to the metric system, focusing mainly on length. Give children a 12-by-18-inch piece of construction paper to make a folder in which they will keep their recordings. Have children title the booklet: *My Metric Length Book.* At the end of the unit, children take the booklets home to share with members of their family.

Materials

white and orange Cuisenaire Rods, one each per student
a train of 10 orange Cuisenaire Rods taped on a table
string and scissors
tagboard strips, 5-by-25 centimeters, one per student
12-by-18-inch construction paper for folders, one piece per student

Initial Concrete Experience

Each student needs a white rod, an orange rod, and a piece of string equal in length to 10 orange rods. Set out a train of 10 orange rods on a table for students each to measure and cut their own string. Their task is to find at least five things that are the same length as each of these three measures. They record on three sheets of paper as shown. Draw facsimiles of the measures on the board for them to use as models.

You may need to discuss a procedure with your students for cutting the string so they all don't bunch up around the table. Also, discuss the fact that measurement is never exact, and give examples of objects that are "close enough" in measurement for their lists.

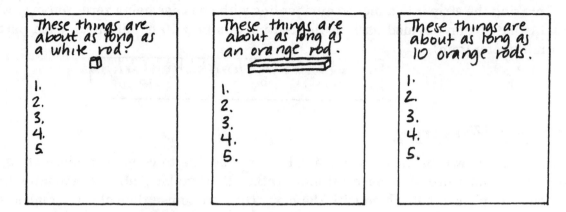

Connecting to the Metric Labels

Tell the students that there are other names for the measuring tools they've been calling "the white rod," "the orange rod," and "the string." They're also called "1 centimeter," "1 decimeter or 10 centimeters," and "1 meter or 10 decimeters or 100 centimeters." It helps some students to relate this to the fact that they may call their parents "mom" and "dad," but some people call them by their first names or by "Mr." and "Mrs." These are all labels for the same people.

When a new concept is taught, it's important to connect the correct mathematical language and symbolic notation to the students' concrete experience with the concept. For this reason, have the students first measure without introducing the names for the metric measures. Then write the following sentences on the board and have the students record them at the bottom of the appropriate sheets.

> The white rod is 1 centimeter long. (1 cm)
> The orange rod is 10 centimeters or 1 decimeter long. (10 cm = 1 dm)
> The string is 1 meter or 10 decimeters or 100 centimeters long.
> (1 m = 10 dm = 100 cm)

Relating to Body Measures

Have students find some measure on their bodies that matches the three lengths so they'll always have a reminder of those measurements with them. Record on a page like this:

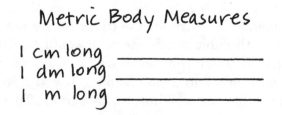

Making a Metric Ruler

Give each student a 5-by-25-centimeter strip of tagboard to make their own centimeter ruler. They use their white and orange rods to make the marks. It helps to tell them to think of making the strip into a metric number line with one edge being zero. You may wish to explain that if they divided each of the centimeters into 10 equal parts, each part is called 1 millimeter (mm).

Practicing Measuring

Draw the chart shown below on the board for the students to copy on a piece of paper. Advise them to measure after each estimate rather than making all the estimates first. Then each example can help them with the next. They are to use the ruler they made and their string.

	Estimate	Measurement	How Far Off ?
Length of Hand			
Length of Foot			
Around your wrist			
Around your head			
Length of arm			

An Extension into Language

Have students write a story titled: "If I Were 1 Centimeter Tall."

An Extension into Volume and Capacity

Have each student construct a 10-centimeter cube from heavy paper or tagboard. Bring in empty milk cartons in quart and half-gallon sizes. Have students compare their cubes with the cartons to see that the cubes are about half of the half-gallon carton. This means a cube would hold about 1 quart. If you have a plastic 10-centimeter cubic container, you can demonstrate this.

Tell the students the metric measure for the cubes they made. One cube holds 1 liter by metric measure. If filled with cubic centimeters, it would hold 1000 of them. Also, if you filled this liter container with water, that much water would weigh 1 kilogram. Metric measures are all related to each other in a tidy fashion. If you have balances and containers, students can benefit from exploring weights and capacities. There is no substitute for first-hand experience.

ACTIVITIES

Foot Cutout

You need: construction paper
scissors

Trace your left foot (with your shoe off) on construction paper. Cut it out. Record your name, shoe size, and the length of your foot in centimeters. Compare your shoe size and foot length with those of others. Do longer feet always have larger shoe sizes?

Foot Figuring

You need: a partner
your cutout foot

Make two guesses:
  1. How many of your feet equal your height?
  2. How many of your feet equal your standing broad jump?
Then find out. Record the information on the back of your cutout foot as shown.

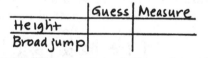

	Guess	Measure
Height		
Broad jump		

Foot Area and Perimeter

You need: your cutout foot
string
centimeter squared paper (see blackline masters)

Trace around your cutout foot on centimeter squared paper. Figure the area of your foot in square centimeters and record. Cut a piece of string equal to the perimeter of your foot. Measure it in centimeters. Can you find someone with the same length perimeter? Are your foot areas the same?

Extension: Cut a piece of string half as long as the perimeter of your foot. Use it to make a foot shape on centimeter squared paper. Compare this area with the area of your foot.

Squaring Up

You need: string and foot area (from *Foot Area and Perimeter*)
centimeter squared paper (see blackline masters)

Tape the string that is equal to the perimeter of your foot to a
piece of centimeter squared paper in the shape of a square.
Answer these questions:
1. What is the area of the square?
2. How does this compare with the area of your foot?
3. Why do you think the areas are different?

Extension: *Giant Foot.* Draw a giant foot that is about twice the size of yours.
Compare the length and perimeter of this giant foot with the length and
perimeter of your cutout foot.

Book Measuring

You need: five books
measuring tapes or string
scale

Choose five books and label them A, B, C, D, and E. Order them from largest to
smallest in the ways listed below. For each, predict first before measuring.

	1st	2nd	3rd	4th	5th
weight					
thickness					
height					
width					
size of cover					

The Perimeter Stays the Same

You need: centimeter squared paper (see blackline masters)
scissors

Draw three different shapes on centimeter squared paper following three rules.
Record the area inside each shape.
1. Stay on the lines when you draw.
2. You must be able to cut your shape out and have it all in one piece.
3. Each shape must have a perimeter of 30 centimeters.
Record the area on each shape. Cut out the one that has the greatest area and
the one with the least. Tape them on the class chart.

Your Height in Money

You need: nickels
quarters
measuring stick

Which would you rather have: your height made of quarters laid end to end, or your height made as a stack of nickels? How much is each worth? Estimate first. Then figure.

How Thick Is Paper?

How thick is a sheet of paper in this book? Devise a way to find out and then do it. Compare your result with others' results.

Extension: Try the same investigation for paper in other books.

Box Measuring

You need: centimeter squared paper, several sheets (see blackline masters)
scissors

If you had a piece of 20-by-20-centimeter squared paper, you could cut a square the same size from each corner and fold up what's left to make a box.

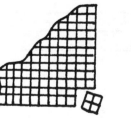 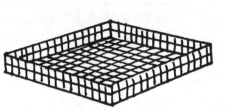

1. How many different size boxes could you make using this method, making each from a different piece of 20-by-20-centimeter squared paper. Do it.
2. Which of these boxes holds the most? Figure the volume of each to find out.

Round Things

Look for circular shapes in the class and around school. For each one, measure its diameter and its circumference. Record your results on a chart. Do this for at least 10 objects. What pattern can you find when you examine the relationship between the diameter and circumference of each?

Obj.	Diam.	Circum.

Wrap-Around

Make a measuring tape that, when wrapped around a tree or pole or other circular object, tells you the diameter of that object.

How Long Is a Minute?

You need: a partner
a way to time 1 minute

How many times can you do each of the things listed in the chart below in 1 minute? Make a guess for each and then have your partner time you. Record on a chart as shown. Take turns timing each other.

	Guess	Count
Bounce a ball.		
Write your name.		
Say "six sick sheep."		
Count by threes to 30		

Ratio with Cuisenaire Rods

You need: Cuisenaire Rods

Measure across your desk using only light green rods. Then figure out how many rods it would take to measure the same distance if you used only red, only white, or only blue rods. Explain your answer; then test by measuring with the rods.

Extension: Do the same for the other color rods as well.

Double the Circumference

You need: a small circular object to trace (jar lid, cup, etc.)
string
centimeter squared paper (see blackline masters)
tape

Trace around the circular object onto the centimeter squared paper. Figure the area in square centimeters and record it inside the circle.

Use string to measure the circumference of this circle. Cut a piece of string double the circumference of the circle and use it to form a new circle on the paper. Tape it in place. What is the area inside the new circle? Predict first and then figure. Write a sentence that describes the relationship between the circumferences and areas of the two circles.

What will the area be for a circle with a circumference equal to half the original circle? Predict first and then find out.

Extension: When the circumference of a pizza pan doubles, should the price double? Explain your reasoning.

The Area Stays the Same

You need: two 5-by-8-inch index cards
scissors
centimeter squared paper (see blackline masters)

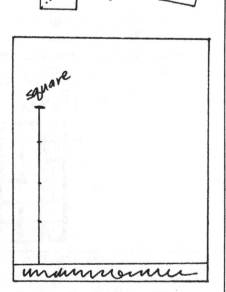

Cut a square that measures 5 centimeters on each side from a corner of one of the index cards. Use this shape to make other different shapes. You can do this by cutting the square on the diagonal into two triangles and putting them together in various ways or by cutting the square in other ways and arranging the pieces together.

Trace around the different shapes you make, cutting each from the index cards. You will need at least five shapes, including a 5-centimeter square. All of your shapes will have the same area.

Draw a line segment equal in length to the perimeter of each shape. (You can use the actual shapes and trace around each edge.) Label each line segment with the shape.

How do the perimeters compare? Record and make a statement about your findings.

Yarn Shapes

You need: yarn or string
Color Tiles
tape

Cut a piece of yarn or string 50 centimeters long and tie the ends together so you have a loop. Make a shape with your loop. Predict how many Color Tiles will fit inside your shape. Then fill it. Use 10 tiles of each color to make counting easier. You may want to tape your loop in several places to hold it while you fill it. Make a sketch of your shape and record how many tiles filled it.

Repeat for four more shapes, making them as different from one another as you can. Examine the shapes that held the *most* and *least* numbers of tiles. Write what you notice about these shapes.

Perimeter with Cuisenaire Rods

You need: Cuisenaire Rods
centimeter squared paper (see blackline masters)

Use one red rod, two light green rods, and one purple rod. Arrange the rods into a shape on centimeter squared paper in such a way that when you trace around it, you draw only on the grid paper lines. Also, you must be able to cut out the outlined shape and have it remain in one piece. (Corners touching are not allowed.) Make several different shapes in this way. Trace each and record its perimeter. Experiment to find how to arrange the rods to get the longest perimeter and the shortest perimeter.

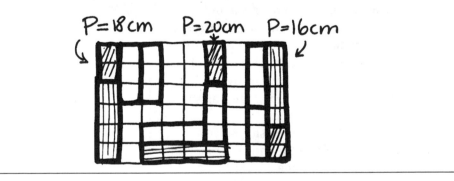

INTRODUCTION

Statistics is the science or study of data. Statistical studies require collecting, sorting, representing, analyzing, and interpreting information. The information is then used for predicting, drawing inferences, and making decisions. There is always some degree of uncertainty with data that is collected. This means that statistics is most often concerned with using information in the face of uncertainty. Probability gives a way to measure uncertainty and is therefore essential to understanding statistical methods.

Why Teach Probability and Statistics?

Recent technological advances have made more statistical information available to us than ever before. In conversation, on television, and in newspapers, we are flooded with data that demands an increasing understanding of statistics for us to understand its use. What is the effectiveness of seat belts and should you wear them? What can you do to protect yourself against the rising cost of living? Is there a justifiable connection between smoking and disease? Which money market or retirement fund makes the most sense? What does a particular advertising claim really mean? Is the death penalty a deterrent to crimes of murder? How do you weigh the benefits of birth control pills against their dangers? Should a certain food dye be banned because it has caused cancer in rats under some conditions? What effect will the rate of population growth have on our lives? How should the increased number of older people in our society affect social decisions? For all of these questions, and many others, probability and statistics concepts are integral for making decisions.

Statistics has never enjoyed a terrific reputation. It's been said that you can prove anything with statistics. To some, statistics and lies are often synonymous. Many people have been hardened against statistics by claims of politicians and advertisers. However, our society is increasingly making use of ideas found in statistics and probability. Students need to develop skills that enable them to live in this statistical society so they will not be misled or blinded by statistics. Without these skills, they will have an incomplete understanding of the world they live in.

Learning probability and statistics provides real applications of arithmetic. When basic computational skills are used in a context, students have the opportunity to see the advantages and limitations of their calculations. Most everyday applications of arithmetic are statistical, done with variability in mind and with some degree of uncertainty — estimating costs, calculating the amount of wallpaper or floor covering needed, figuring time for trips or cooking. The simple arithmetic done is valuable only in the context of its application. To understand those applications, probability and statistics are needed and therefore are essential elements of students' basic number skills.

Studying probability and statistics also helps students develop critical thinking skills. In carrying out experiments in probability and statistics, students develop ways to cope with uncertainty as they search for the truth in a situation and learn to report it faithfully. Approaching situations statistically can make students face up to prejudices, think more consistently about arguments, and justify their thinking with numerical information. This approach has applications in all areas of life — social, political, and scientific.

What Concepts in Probability and Statistics Should Be Taught?

The teaching of probability and statistics should stem from real problems. A theoretical or abstract approach is not appropriate for the elementary grades. The approach should be based on experiments that draw on children's experience and interests. Children's intuition needs to be challenged first. Once they sense what "should happen" in a situation, then it's timely for them to carry out an experiment to test their predictions. Not only will such experiments provide firsthand experience in collecting, organizing, and interpreting data, but they will also reinforce computational skills. Basic to probability and statistics are the following ideas:

1. Collecting Data.

Students need experience gathering both factual data and data that involves opinions. The latter requires that students consider how to collect data in a way that avoids biased responses.

2. Sampling.

In real life, even though information is often needed about an entire population, it may only be possible to sample a part of the population. That information from the sample is then used to infer characteristics about the total population. Students need to learn the difference between random and nonrandom samples and the importance this difference makes in statistical studies. For example, to determine the percentage of people in the general population who are left-handed, you would not poll professional baseball players as a random sample. (Why?)

3. Organizing and Representing Data.

Students need experience organizing data and representing it graphically in a variety of graphs, tables, and charts.

4. Interpreting Data.

Students should learn to read graphs, making quick visual summaries as well as further interpretations and comparisons of data through finding means, medians, and modes.

5. Assigning Probabilities.

Initial experiences with measuring uncertainty should be informal and should include discussion of whether a result is possible or likely, or whether outcomes are equally or not equally likely. Assigning probabilities gives further information for making a decision in the face of uncertainty. The probability of an event can be represented by a number from 0 to 1. For example, the probability of rolling a 4 when rolling a die is 1/6. The probability of rolling an even number when rolling a die is 3/6. The numerator of the fraction represents the number of outcomes you're interested in; the denominator represents the total number of possible outcomes.

6. Making Inferences.

Students need to draw conclusions based on their interpretation of data. They should learn to justify their thinking using numerical information they've collected and analyzed.

A SAMPLE ACTIVITY — SPINNER EXPERIMENTS

Spinner experiments provide a good beginning probability and statistics experience for children of all ages. They give students the opportunity to make individual predictions, to collect data using a graph, and to compare their individual results with a larger class sample. Younger children benefit from the practice of writing numerals; older students can be challenged to extend the experiment into a more formal analysis of the probability involved. Making the spinners gives all students practice in following directions. (Young children may need more assistance with this part of the task.)

Materials

5-by-8-inch cards, one per student
paper clips, one per student
plastic straws, one 1/4-inch length per student
scissors
tape
squared paper for graphing, one per group (see blackline masters)

Introducing

1. Present or review concepts.

Describe and show how to make a spinner, following the directions on the next page. (You may choose to give students who prefer to make them from the directions themselves the opportunity to do so.)

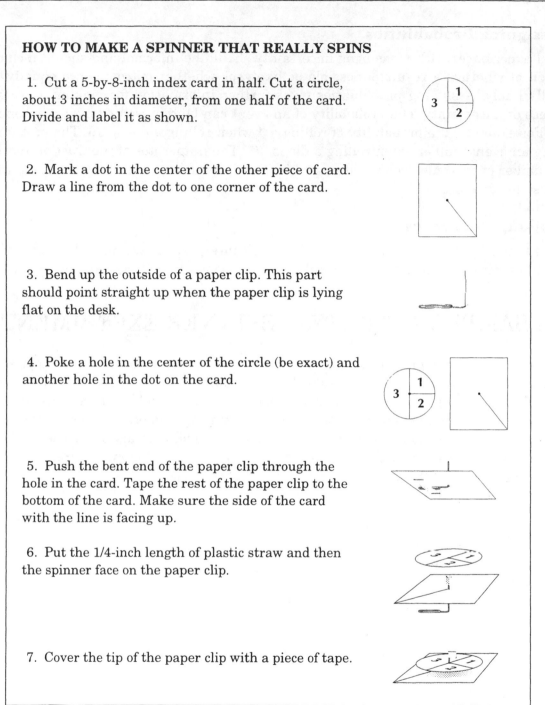

HOW TO MAKE A SPINNER THAT REALLY SPINS

1. Cut a 5-by-8-inch index card in half. Cut a circle, about 3 inches in diameter, from one half of the card. Divide and label it as shown.

2. Mark a dot in the center of the other piece of card. Draw a line from the dot to one corner of the card.

3. Bend up the outside of a paper clip. This part should point straight up when the paper clip is lying flat on the desk.

4. Poke a hole in the center of the circle (be exact) and another hole in the dot on the card.

5. Push the bent end of the paper clip through the hole in the card. Tape the rest of the paper clip to the bottom of the card. Make sure the side of the card with the line is facing up.

6. Put the 1/4-inch length of plastic straw and then the spinner face on the paper clip.

7. Cover the tip of the paper clip with a piece of tape.

2. Pose a part of the problem or a similar but smaller problem.

Ask: When you spin the spinner, is any number more likely to come up than any other number? Why do you think so? Explain: You can keep track of spins on a graph recording sheet that is 3 squares by 12 squares. Demonstrate for the class how to spin and record on the graph. After three or four spins, ask: What do you think the entire graph will look like when one number reaches the top of the paper?

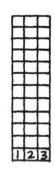

3. Present the problem to be solved.

Explain: Each of you needs to make a spinner and a graph record sheet, and try the experiment. When one of the numbers reaches the top, you've completed the experiment. Then post the paper to show which number "won." (You should provide bulletin board or wall space with sections labeled 1, 2, and 3.) When everyone in your group has finished the experiment, let me know and I'll start you on another.

4. Discuss the results.

Ask for questions.

Exploring

Circulate and clarify as needed for groups whose members all have the same confusion. Usually, there are no major problems. The most common error in constructing the spinner is that students are too neat with their washers. The washers need to be crimped for the spinner face to be raised from the base and spin freely.

Extension

This is called *Two-Person Spin.* Students work in partners. If they spin their spinners and add the numbers that come up on each, there are five possible sums: 2, 3, 4, 5, and 6. Each pair of students makes a graph record sheet that is five squares wide. First, partners should predict which sum they think will come up most often. Then they spin their spinners and take turns recording the sum of the two numbers that appear. When one sum reaches the top of their graph record sheet, they post their results.

Summarizing

Discuss the class results. Most likely, 3 was the winning number on most of the graph record sheets, but there will be instances of 1 or 2 as winner. Ask the students how they might find out if the number 3 actually came up in half of all the spins. Ask for volunteers to add up the total number of spins for each number and report back to the class later.

Although the number 3 is twice as likely to come up as either 1 or 2, there is no guarantee that 3 will come up twice as often when you do the experiment. Very few of the graph record sheets (if any) will actually reflect that result. The mathematical theory of probability says that the more times you spin a spinner, the closer the results will match the theoretical distribution.

If enough of the class has completed *Two-Person Spin,* summarize it. If not, wait until more of the students have posted results. Also, refer to the additional spinner activities in this section for more investigations.

ACTIVITIES

WHOLE CLASS: Tiles in the Bag (Version 1)

You need: a paper bag
　　　　　Color Tiles in two colors

This is an introductory activity for all grade levels. Place 10 tiles in a bag, some of two different colors. Tell the students what you've done (without telling them how many of each). Go around the class, asking individual students to draw out a tile without looking, to note its color, and then to replace it. (This is called taking a sample with replacement.) Have a student record the color on the board.

Do this for 10 draws, and then ask groups to look at the information and decide whether they are willing to predict what is in the bag, or if they need more information. Have groups share their opinions.

Then do 10 more draws again, and again have groups discuss and share. Repeat as many times as needed for most of the class to feel they're willing to predict what is in the bag. (For younger children, the question might be: Which color do you think there's more of in the bag?)

Suggestions for recording:

Extensions:

1. Change the colors and the quantity of the tiles.

2. Choose a group to decide on the tiles to put in the bag. The group must tell the rest of the class the total number of tiles in the sack before they start the activity.

For some children, this experiment is an exercise in guessing, with a smattering of some intuition and a lot of hopeful predicting. For others, some notions of ratio and proportion are useful for predicting. Taking 50 or 100 draws (if the students are interested) makes predicting easier and more valid.

WHOLE CLASS: *Tiles in the Bag (Version 2)*

You need: three paper bags filled with Color Tiles in this way:
> 25 red, 5 blue
> 20 red, 10 blue
> 10 red, 20 blue

Write this information on the board. Have a student choose one bag at random so that even you do not know which it is. Then, in the procedure described in Version 1, make 25 random samples with replacement. Record each to have a list of the samples in order. Compute the percentage of red tiles for each of these: the first 5 samples, the first 10 samples, the first 15 samples, the first 20 samples, all 25 samples.

Have groups answer these questions:

1. Which bag do you think you used?

2. Which bag would you have chosen if you had based your decision on 5 samples? 10? 15? 20? How many samples do you think you needed?

WHOLE CLASS: *Sampling Bean Populations*

You need: one bag of white beans and three bags of brown beans. Mix all beans together. (Choose beans that are about the same size.)

Have each student take a small handful of beans and sort them. Then ask the children in each group to pool their samples and to organize them into rows.

Ask each group to predict which of the following they think they would most likely get if they were to take 4 beans from the bag with their eyes closed:

> 3 white and 1 brown
> 2 white and 2 brown
> 1 white and 3 brown
> 4 white
> 4 brown

Have groups present their predictions and their reasoning.

Return all the beans to the bag. Then have each student pick out, without looking, 4 beans. Have students record on a class graph the number of each color bean they picked. Discuss the results.

Divide the beans among the groups and have the students actually count the number of brown and white beans. Compare these totals to the samples of handfuls and the samples of 4 beans.

WHOLE CLASS: The 1-2-3-4 Activity

You need: a slip of paper with the numbers *1 2 3 4* for each student

In the *San Francisco Chronicle* on November 30, 1980, the following item appeared: "Write the numbers 1, 2, 3, and 4 on a piece of paper. Ask somebody to circle any one of these numbers. Four out of five so asked will circle the 3." Try an experiment to test this.

    1. Distribute slips with *1 2 3 4* on them. Ask each child to circle a number and turn the slip face down, with no discussion.

    2. Have each child write his or her answer, individually, to these questions: Do you think any one number will be circled lots more than any other and, if so, which one? Why do you think that?

    3. In their groups, ask students to come to consensus about the questions and choose one person to report back to the class.

    4. List the numbers 1, 2, 3, and 4 on the board. Have students tape their papers next to the number they circled to graph the class data.

    5. Analyze the results. Do they match the newspaper prediction? Would the results change with a larger sample?

Extensions:

1. Have each student take home three additional slips for others to circle a number. Have them predict how these additional samples will affect the graph.
2. What if the numbers had been in a different order? What if the slips had *a b c d* on them instead? What about other letters or shapes? Have interested students devise and carry out their own investigations.

Design Your Own Spinner

You need: a spinner
               a graph record sheet cut from squared paper (see blackline masters)
               a notebook-sized sheet of paper

In this activity, you design your own spinner and test what happens. Follow the directions:

    1. Design and make a spinner.
    2. Make a graph record sheet.
    3. Make a prediction and record it.
    4. Do the experiment, recording on your graph record sheet.
    5. Write the actual results.
    6. Post your work.

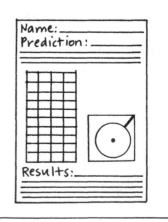

WHOLE CLASS: *Alphabetical Probability*

This investigation uses probability and statistics techniques to analyze the frequency of letters in the English language.

    1. Have students decide, individually, what they think are the five most commonly used letters in the English language. They should list their predictions, starring the letter they think is the most common.

    2. Ask students to share their individual predictions in their groups and to arrive at one group prediction.

    3. Then have each student pick a sentence from a book and tally how many times each letter appears in the sentence. Have groups compile their individual results and put their results on a class chart. Analyze the class chart and list the letters of the alphabet in the order of frequency according to the students' findings.

    4. Compare the class results with their predictions and with the actual order of frequency in the English language:

    E T A O (N I) S R H L D C U (P F) M W Y (B G) V K (Q X) (J Z)
    (Those bracketed have the same frequency of occurrence.)

Extensions:

1. Would this be the same for other languages? Find out.

2. What is so strange about these three sentences?— THIS IS ODD. DO YOU KNOW WHY? TRY AND FIND OUT.

3. A language exercise: Have students write, or talk, without using one of the common letters.

4. Each letter in the cryptogram below stands for another letter in the alphabet. Can you figure out what it says?

    AB CD EDDF AG FXD HIJY,
    A CAKK LMN NZM IG AWD WJDIE WZGD.

Here's another clue to help you: The most frequently used words in the English language are "the," "an," "a," "and."

5. Examine the games of Scrabble, Boggle, and so forth to see how they used the information about frequency of letters.

6. Buy some transfer lettering from a stationery or art store. Analyze the frequency of the letters provided.

7. When Christopher L. Sholes invented the type-writer in 1867, he purposely scrambled the letters so typists couldn't type too quickly and jam the keyboard. (Your two most agile fingers rest on rarely used "j" and "k," while your left pinky is used for "a.") Have students design a keyboard that makes use of this mathematical investigation. Then compare their keyboard with the one pictured. This was designed by August Dvorak in 1930 to make better use of the frequency of letters. (See "Tangled Typing," *Science 81*, May issue, and a reply in the "Letters to the Editor" column in the July 1981 issue from a Dvorak user.)

The Left-Handed Experiment

By taking a sample of some people in your school, can you determine approximately how many right-handed people there are for every left-handed person? Follow this procedure:

1. Find out how many people there are in the school.

2. Decide how many people you'll sample. Pick a place to ask this number of people whether they're right-handed or left-handed.

3. From this sample, figure out how many right-handed people there are for each left-handed person.

4. Now take a census to find out how many right-handed and left-handed people there actually are in the school. Visit each class and take a poll. Compile your results. How many right-handed people are there for each left-handed person in the entire school?

5. Compare the results of your sample with the census. Are they similar? Were you satisfied with your sampling procedure? If not, how would you improve the way you sampled? Write a report.

Extension: The procedure outlined in *The Left-Handed Experiment* can be used by individuals or small groups of students to investigate a variety of topics:

By sampling, determine approximately how many red-, blond-, brown-, and black-haired people there are in your school.

By sampling, decide how many people there are with each eye color.

Use sampling to learn about students' weekly allowances.

Use sampling to determine the favorite TV show of students in your school.

Tile Trading

You need: two paper bags, labeled A and B
Color Tiles
15 red and 15 blue (or any two colors)

Place 15 red tiles in bag A and 15 blue tiles in bag B. Without peeking, put one tile from A into B. Shake B. Then put one from B into A. Shake A. Then move one from A into B. Continue until you have moved 30 tiles, but first predict how many of each you'll have in each bag after doing this:

A _____ red _____ blue
B _____ red _____ blue

Now do it. What was the outcome?

A _____ red _____ blue
B _____ red _____ blue

Try the experiment several more times. Discuss with others what you think "should happen." **Note:** You may want to move fewer tiles or more tiles.

Shake and Spill

You need: six Two-Color Counters

If you spill the counters and record how many red sides and yellow sides come up each time, do you think you'll get one result more often than the others? If so, what will it be? Why do you think that? Try it, spilling the counters at least 25 times. Record your prediction and your actual results.

Extension: Try the experiment with other numbers of counters.

Two-Coin Toss

You need: two different coins

Toss two coins together 25 times. After each toss, record what comes up — two heads, two tails, or one head and one tail. What do you think will result?

Prediction: two heads ___ two tails ___ one head/one tail ___

Outcome: two heads ___ two tails ___ one head/one tail ___

Note: If you toss just one coin, there are two possibilities: heads and tails. If you toss two coins, there are four equally likely possibilities.

The Birthday Twins

If you asked people to tell you their birthdays (the month and the day), how many people do you think you'd have to ask before you'd find two that were birthday twins?

Prediction: ____ people

Now try it and see. Take a poll. List each person's birthday. Stop when you get a match.

Outcome: ____ people

Note: Mathematicians say that in a group of 30 people, there is a better than 50-50 chance there will be a pair of birthday twins. In a group of 100, there is a 97 percent chance! How do your results relate to this theory?

Got a Match?

You need: a partner

           two spinners that are the same

You and your partner are to spin your spinners 24 times. Each time, compare to see if you have a match. Predict on how many spins you think your results will match. Then do the experiment, recording what comes up each time. Figure out how many matches you had. Record the outcome.

How Many Rolls to Get a 1?

You need: one die

Roll a die until a 1 comes up. Record how many rolls it took. Do this five times. Put your five results on the class chart, such as the one shown.

HOW MANY ROLLS TO GET A 1?
Use tally marks to show your results.

1	11	21
2	12	22
3	13	23
4	14	24
5	15	25
6	16	26
7	17	27
8	18	28
9	19	29
10	20	more

Extension: How many rolls to get a 6? Would the results be similar or different? How could you find out?

Shake and Peek

You need: a partner

           one shake-and-peek box (a small box containing 10 beads or marbles of two colors, taped shut, with a corner cut out for viewing)

Shake the box, peek through the open corner, and record the color you see. Repeat many times. Stop when you and your partner feel you have a sufficient number of samples to predict what's in the box. (Hint: The box has 10 beads.)

The X-O Problem

You need: three cards the same size marked as follows:
  one with an X on both sides
  one with an O on both sides
  one with an X on one side and an O on the other
a paper sack

Play the following game with the materials: Draw one of the three cards at random from the sack and look at what is marked on just one side. Predict what you think is on the other side. Check your prediction. Score a point each time you predict correctly.

Decide what would be a good strategy for predicting so that you would score the most points possible. Then test your strategy by playing the game 30 times, recording your prediction and outcome each time. How many points did you score? Are you satisfied with your prediction? Try another strategy if you like.

What's the Record?

You need: a pair of dice

Who can set a record for the most rolls of two dice without getting doubles? Try the challenge. Roll two dice and tally the number of rolls you make before getting doubles. Who set the record in your group? On the class chart, record how many rolls the winner made.

The Game of Pig

You need: a pair of dice
  a partner or small group

This is a game for two or more players. The goal of the game is to be the first to reach 100. On your turn, roll the dice as many times as you like, mentally keeping a running total of the sum. When you decide to stop rolling, record the total for that turn and add it to the total from previous turns.

The catch: If a 1 comes up on one of the dice, the player's turn automatically ends and 0 is scored for that round. If 1s come up on both dice, not only does the turn end, the total accumulated so far returns to 0.

After becoming familiar with the game, write a strategy.

How Many Throws?

You need: a partner
two dice of two different colors
two charts as shown

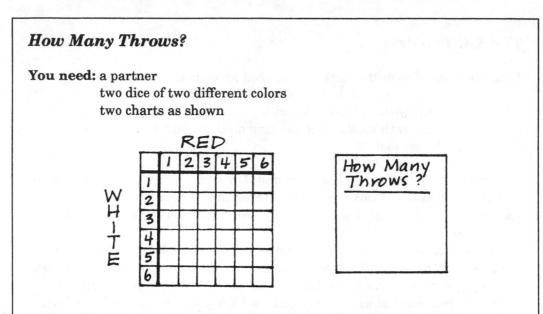

Here are the jobs for each partner: One rolls the dice and makes a tally mark on the *How Many Throws?* chart for each roll. The other enters the sum that comes up on each roll on the chart (unless it was already entered before). The colors are important. For example:

Red 3 and White 2 gives 5;

Red 2 and White 3 also gives 5;

BUT ... they go in different boxes. So there are 36 possible sums.

Discuss with your partner how many throws you think it will take to complete the chart of sums. Then roll and record until all the sums have been entered. **Note:** When there are only five blanks left on the chart, write in the missing sums.

Extension: On class charts, post the number of throws it took to roll all sums and the last five sums you entered. Discuss what the information posted reveals about two-dice sums.

> How Many Throws?
> Write the number.

> Last Five Sums
> Make tally marks.
>
> 2
> 3
> 4
> 5
> 6
> 7
> 8
> 9
> 10
> 11
> 12

How Many Ways?

You need: a chart as shown

Complete the chart. As in *How Many Throws?*, *3, 1* is a different outcome from *1, 3*. After you complete the chart, answer the questions.

Possible Totals	2	3	4	5	6	7	8	9	10	11	12
			2,2 3,1 1,3								
Total Ways			3								

    1. Add across the *Total Ways* row on the bottom. Did you get 36? If not, there's a goof somewhere.
    2. List the *Possible Totals* in order, from the ones with most possibilities to the ones with least.
    3. The probability of rolling a 7 is 6 chances out of the 36 possible outcomes. Mathematicians write this as 6/36 or 1/6. Why?
    4. What is the probability of rolling each of the other sums?
    5. Add up the probabilities for all the sums. What is the total? Explain why this total makes sense.

The Two-Dice Sum Game

You need: a partner or small group
              11 counters for each player
              a pair of dice

This is a game for two or more players. Each player makes a number line from 2 to 12, with spaces large enough for the counters to fit on the numbers. Place your 11 counters on your number line in any arrangement. (You may put more than one counter on some numbers and none on others.) Take turns rolling the dice. On each roll, every player removes one counter that is on the number that matches the sum on the dice. (If players have more than one counter on a number, they may remove only one.) The winner is the first player to remove all 11 counters.

    Decide on the best winning arrangement of counters on the number line. Explain your thinking.

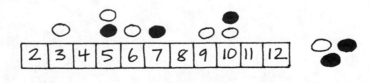

Fair Game 1

You need: a group of four

Play the paper, scissors, rock game with three players and one recorder. All players make a fist and on the count of four, each player shows either:
  paper (by showing four fingers)
  scissors (by showing two fingers)
  rock (by showing a fist)
Decide who is player A, B, and C and play 20 times with these rules:
  Player A gets a point if all players show the same sign.
  Player B gets a point if only two players show the same sign.
  Player C gets a point if all players show different signs.
Tally the winning points:

Player	Tally	Total
A		
B		
C		

Is this game fair? Which player would you rather be? How could you make the game more fair?

Fair Game 2

You need: a partner
              a pair of dice

Take turns rolling the two dice. Player A scores a point if the sum is even. Player B scores a point if the sum is odd. Is the game fair? If not, how could you make the game fair? Explain your reasoning.

Play the game again, this time figuring the product. Player A scores a point if the product is even. Player B scores a point if the product is odd. Is the game fair? If not, how could you make the game fair. Explain your reasoning.

The Popcorn Problem

You need: 10 each of six colors of cubes
a paper sack

A popcorn company found that sales improved when prizes were put in the popcorn boxes. They decided to include a felt-tip pen in every box and to use pens in six different colors. The company bought equal numbers of pens in each color and were careful when shipping popcorn to stores to send boxes with the same number of each color pen. When you buy a box, you have an equal chance to find any one of the six colors of pens inside.

About how many boxes of popcorn do you need to buy to have a good chance to get a complete set of six different color pens? Explain your reasoning.

Try the following experiment to simulate the situation: Put six cubes in a sack, one each of six colors to represent the pens. Reach into the sack and, without looking, draw a cube. Note its color and replace it. Continue until you have drawn out one of each color, keeping track of the number of draws you make. (How many draws do you think will be needed?)

Repeat the experiment. Then compile results from other class members.

Discuss the popcorn problem in light of the information gathered from the simulations.

Extension: Repeat the simulation, this time putting 60 cubes in the sack, 10 each of six colors. Compare the results with the first simulation.

GRAPHING IN THE CLASSROOM

Graphing is a way to present data in a concise and visual way that makes it possible to see relationships in the data more easily. In order to learn to interpret graphs and use them as a problem-solving tool, children need to make their own first. Making graphs requires collecting and then sorting and classifying data. Such experiences can be provided at all grade levels.

Introducing Graphs to Young Children

For younger children, graphing experiences best begin concretely. For example, have everybody take off one shoe, then sort all the shoes into two rows: with laces, without laces. This creates a concrete graph. A pictorial representation of that relationship can be introduced at a later stage; still later, a symbolic graph could be made. The possibilities for things to graph should be taken from the interests of the children and experiences that occur in the classroom.

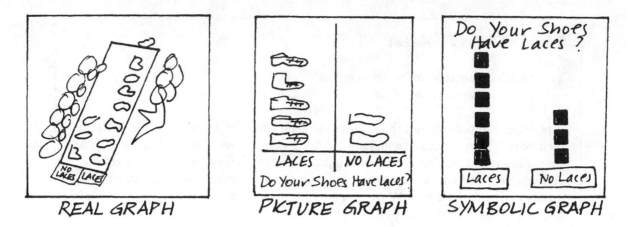

REAL GRAPH   PICTURE GRAPH   SYMBOLIC GRAPH

Real graphs use actual objects to compare and build on children's understanding of more and less. Some examples include: Is your pencil dull or sharp? Which paste jars need filling and which don't? Are the bottoms of your shoes smooth or bumpy?

Picture graphs use pictures or models to stand for real things. Children can draw pictures to represent objects, or they can cut pictures from magazines. Some examples include: a rubbing of the bottom of their shoes, a picture of the cookie they like best, a picture of a pet.

Symbolic graphs are the most abstract because they use symbols, such as a colored square or tally mark, to represent real things.

An important aspect of a graphing activity is the discussion and interpretation of the information. Progress made by students is directly related to the time spent on discussion. The following are the kinds of questions that can be asked about graphs, whether they are real, picture, or symbolic.

Which column has the least?
Which column has the most?
Are there more _____ or more _____ ?
Are there fewer _____ or fewer _____ ?
How many more _____ are there than _____ ?
How many fewer _____ are there than _____ ?
How many _____ are there altogether?

After children become more familiar with graphs, they should be able to draw conclusions from the information without being prompted with questions.

Attendance Graphs

Using a daily attendance graph is one way to provide regular graphing experience. When the children enter the room in the morning, they mark themselves on the graph. The graph can be concrete, pictorial, or symbolic. There are three categories of graphs: graphs that ask for opinions, graphs that require factual reporting of information, graphs that require some processing before the information needed can be recorded.

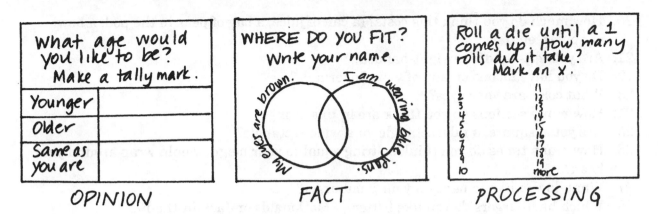

OPINION   FACT   PROCESSING

Process the graphs in the following ways:

1. Use the graphs to write arithmetic equations that show the relationships reported. In the *What age would you like to be?* graph, you can write an addition sentence to show the number of children who would like to be a different age than they are now: 17 + 4 = 21.

2. Write generalizations from graphs. For example: Most students in our class wish they were older. Less than one-fourth of the students are content with their present age.

3. Write questions that can be answered from the graph. Children can answer them individually or in groups. In this way, graphs give a ready supply of word problems that relate to information from the students. For example: What percent of our class has brown eyes? What fraction of the class would like to be older?

4. Have groups take responsibility for writing the questions for everyone to answer. Eventually, have pairs or groups of children prepare attendance graphs.

Ideas for Graphs

1. Do you have a library card?
2. Is your Halloween costume scary or not scary?
3. How many scoops of rice do you think will fill the jar?
4. How much allowance do you get?
5. What time did you go to sleep last night?
6. At what age do you think you'll be a grownup?
7. How many glasses of milk do you drink each day?
8. What's your favorite TV show?
9. How many pencils are there in your desk?
10. Which do you think there are more of on the U.S. flag — long red stripes, long white stripes, short red stripes, or short white stripes?
11. How many letters are there in your first name?
12. Is your last name longer, shorter, or the same length as your first name?
13. Are your ear lobes hanging or attached?
14. On what day of the week were you born?
15. Who decides when you get your hair cut?
16. How many doors are there in your house?
17. Do you have a middle name?
18. What's your favorite ice cream flavor?
19. Do you have a younger brother or sister?

20. How much do you think this costs? (a can of juice, a bag of peas in the pod, a bowl of apples, etc.)
21. Are you left-handed or right-handed?
22. Do you have moons on any of your fingernails?
23. What color are your eyes?
24. How many sections do you think are in this orange?
25. Are you a square, a tall rectangle, or a wide rectangle?
26. How many times do you think a string equal to your height would wrap around your head?
27. What do you like to have on your hamburger?
28. Which hambúrgers do you like better — McDonalds or Jack-in-the-Box?
29. What do you call your mother—mother, mom, mommy, something else?
30. Do you like spinach?
31. Will you buy your lunch today?
32. How many cubes can you hold in one hand?
33. Have you ever visited another country?
34. How many of your feet equal your height?
35. Does your last name begin with a letter in the first half of the alphabet or the last half?
36. How do you like to eat eggs — scrambled, hard-boiled, soft-boiled, fried, other, not at all?
37. What is your birthday month?
38. If a = $.01, b = $.02, c = $.03, and so on, how much is your first name worth?
39. Is your hair straight, curly, or wavy?
40. Which holiday do you like best — Thanksgiving, Halloween, or April Fool's Day?
41. How many glasses of milk do you drink on an average each day?
42. How many televisions are there in your house?
43. Do you think children should have to earn their allowances?
44. Do you like to rollerskate?
45. Should children choose their own bedtime?

INTRODUCTION

*I*n the elementary grades, experiences in geometry should provide for the development of the concepts of shape, size, symmetry, congruence, and similarity in both two-dimensional and three-dimensional space. Experiences should begin with familiar objects and should utilize a wide variety of concrete materials to develop appropriate vocabulary and to build understanding. In middle school instruction, more formal generalizations in geometric relationships can be stressed. The activities provided in this section are designed to provide problem-solving experiences in geometry that help students develop understanding of geometric properties and relationships.

Why Teach Geometry?

Young children have considerable experience with geometry before entering school. They spend a great deal of time exploring, playing, and building with shapes. In their play experiences, children encounter relationships among shapes naturally. They sort and resort objects, make discoveries about how different blocks fit together, and learn about shapes that roll, slide, or do neither.

These initial investigations should be nurtured and extended in children's school learning of mathematics. In their classroom experiences, children should have opportunities to explore shapes and the relationships among them. They benefit from problem-solving situations that lead them to investigate patterns and structures in shapes and to develop reasoning processes in spatial contexts. They need experiences that relate geometry to ideas in measurement, number, and patterns. Through these kinds of activities, students grasp how mathematics adds to their understanding of the world.

Although elementary mathematics textbooks include sections on geometry, it's not uncommon for teachers to treat these sections as optional and to skip them or to present them to the children as if they were less important. There are several explanations for this. Because the major emphasis in elementary mathematics has been on the teaching of arithmetic skills, some teachers think that geometry in math instruction is not as significant for elementary students. Also, many teachers remember geometry as a high school subject that dealt mainly with formal proofs and complicated terminology. However, geometry is a significant branch of mathematics, the one most visible in the physical world.

Developing spatial ability has applications in everyday life, a fact that any adult encounters when having to figure quantities for wallpaper, floor covering, paint, fabric, lawn needs, or a myriad of other home projects. Geometric concepts and relationships are also essential to many branches of industry, the building trades, interior design, architecture, as well as other work situations. Geometry should be included as an integral part of the mathematics program.

A SAMPLE ACTIVITY — PENTOMINOES

The emphasis in this geometry activity is on informal, concrete experience, not on the symbolism and formal definitions that are the focus in many textbooks. *Pentominoes* calls on a different kind of reasoning than is needed for numerical tasks. In the classroom, children who are not generally considered to be good math students often enjoy success in these kinds of spatial experiences.

There are two aspects to this activity. One is searching for possible arrangements of squares, a geometric visualization task. The other is deciding when all possible arrangements have been found, which requires the use of logical reasoning.

Materials

square tiles (about 1 inch on a side), five per student
paper ruled into squares the same size as the tiles, two sheets per group

Introducing

1. Present or review concepts.

Three points need to be presented here. First, demonstrate the rule for making shapes in which one whole side of each square touches at least one whole side of another. Draw the following examples on the board or overhead:

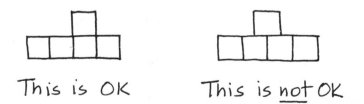

Second, explain how to decide if two shapes are the same or different. Cut the two shapes in question out of paper and move them about to see if one fits exactly on the other. You might have to flip one over, or rotate one, but if they can be made to fit, they are called *congruent* and are considered to be the same.

Finally, discuss the derivation of the word *pentomino*. Draw a picture of a domino on the board or overhead. It's made of two squares. A pentomino is a five-square version. A three-square version is a triomino; a tetromino is made from four squares.

2. Pose a part of the problem or a similar but smaller problem.

Ask: Suppose you were trying to find all the different arrangements of three squares. What shapes could you make? Have students try this. There are only two triominoes: ⬜⬜⬜ and ⬛. Have them try the same with four squares. (There are five possible tetrominoes.)

3. Present the problem to be solved.

Ask groups to investigate different ways to arrange five squares. Direct them to cut each of the pentominoes they find out of the graph paper provided.

4. Discuss the results.

Ask for questions.

Exploring

Two situations typically arise during the exploration. Some groups cut out two shapes that are the same but believe they are different. In that case, comment that you notice that two of their shapes are the same, and leave them to find the congruent shapes.

The second situation arises when a group has found all they can. Usually they'll ask you if they have them all. Tell them that is for them to decide and encourage them to find some way to analyze their arrangements to see if they think their collection includes all that are possible. Also tell them this issue will be discussed after all the groups in the class have finished the activity.

Extension

Direct the group to sort their shapes into two sets, those that will fold into a box and those that will not. Demonstrate with the shape that looks like the Red Cross symbol: ⬛ Ask: Can you see how you could fold up the sides of this shape so that it would be a box without a lid? Which side do you think would be the bottom of the box, opposite the open side? Mark that with an X. Now try folding it to check your prediction. With each of the other shapes, predict whether or not you think it will fold into a box, marking with an X the side that will be the bottom.

Summarizing

Discuss their group processes. Ask students to report how they found different shapes and decided who would cut out the pieces.

Discuss how they knew when they had found all the pieces possible. This is a good opportunity to discuss the issue of answers. If you had told them in advance that there were 12 shapes, you would have limited their opportunity for problem solving. Students benefit from hearing you reinforce the importance of problem solving. The goal in this activity is not just to find all the shapes; it is also to know when you've found them.

In classrooms, children often learn to depend on the quicker thinkers to provide answers. They also learn to depend on the teacher for finding out if they are right or wrong. It's valuable for children to learn to become self-reliant in their thinking processes. You can support this by keeping the emphasis on the problem-solving process and by not providing answers.

Discuss the challenge if all groups have had a chance to explore it. If not, discuss it at a later time, after students have had sufficient time to tackle it.

Extensions

The Pentomino Game
Students each make a set of pieces from sturdy paper and a gameboard that is a 5-by-12 squared sheet, with squares matching the size of the squares they used for the pentominoes. As an individual puzzle, they try to fit all 12 pieces onto the board. As a two-person game, players take turns placing pieces on the board. The object is to be the last player to play a piece, making it impossible for the opponent to fit in another. In this second version, all the pieces do not have to be used.

The Factory Box Problem
Someone in a factory bought lots of cardboard that measured five squares by four squares. They figured that each sheet of cardboard could be cut into four pieces so each piece would fold into a topless box. How could the sheet be cut?

Milk Carton Geometry
Save school milk cartons. (Rinse them well!) When you've got enough so each student can have several, let them cut the tops off so all are topless boxes. Then students try to cut them so they lie flat in the different pentomino shapes.

Pentomino One-Difference Loop
Arrange the pentomino pieces into a loop, so that only one square needs to be moved to change a shape into the one next to it.

ACTIVITIES

WHOLE CLASS: *The Tangram Puzzle*

You need: 6-inch squares of construction paper, one per student
scissors, one pair per student

The Tangram is cut from a square. Having children each cut their own is a good lesson in following directions. Also, children are then convinced that the pieces truly go back together to make a square. The directions below show how to cut the square into the seven pieces: two pairs of congruent triangles, one middle-sized triangle, one square, and one parallelogram.

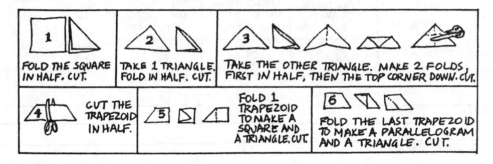

Using just the three smallest triangles, make a square. Then use those same pieces to make a triangle, a rectangle, a trapezoid, and a parallelogram. Then use the five smaller pieces (all but the two large triangles) to make the same shapes. Repeat with all seven pieces. Record on a chart as shown.

	▢	◸	▱	▱	▱
3 small triangles	◹				
5 small pieces					
all 7 pieces					

Extensions:

1. *Area and Perimeter.* Compare the areas of the square, the parallelogram, and the middle-sized triangle. Then compare their perimeters.

2. *Tangram Puzzle Cards.* Have children explore making shapes using all seven pieces. When they find ones that please them, have them draw around the outline of the shape on drawing paper. They then name it, sign it, and put it in a class Tangram box so others can try to fit their pieces into that shape. Students sign their names on the backs of each other's puzzles as they solve them.

3. *Using All Seven.* There are 13 different convex shapes you can make with the seven pieces of the Tangram. Find them.

4. *Making Squares.* You can show a square with just one piece of the Tangram or by using all seven. What about using two, three, four, five, or six? One of those is impossible. Which is it, and why isn't it possible?

That's Just Half the Story

You need: a small rectangular mirror

Some letters have mirror symmetry. That means when you place the mirror on them, you can see the whole letter — half on your paper and half in the mirror. Which letters work this way? Which work more than one way? Record the uppercase letters on a chart. Put in dotted lines to show where you placed the mirror.

These work one way.	These work more than one way.	These do not have mirror symmetry.
A	X	F

Interior Regions

Which uppercase letters have interior regions? That means if you built a fence in the shape of that letter, it would keep your dog inside. Record on a chart as shown.

YES	NO
P	E

Straight or Curved?

Which uppercase letters have only straight line segments? Which have only curves? Which have both? Record like this:

STRAIGHT	CURVED	BOTH
A	C	B

Then put your results on a Venn diagram, like this:

No-Lift Letters

It's possible to draw this shape ⊠ without lifting your pencil and without retracing any line. Try it. Then investigate the alphabet. Which uppercase letters can you write without lifting your pencil and without retracing any line? Record.

More No-Lift Letters

You can tell if a letter will work by looking at the points where line segments meet or end (the vertices) and by seeing how many of these points have an odd number of line segments meeting there (odd vertices).

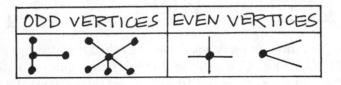

ODD VERTICES	EVEN VERTICES

Count the odd vertices for all the letters than can be written without lifting your pencil or retracing. What's the pattern?

LETTER	B	C	D		
ODD VERTICES	2	2	0		

Extensions:
1. Try all the activities with lowercase letters.
2. Some letters have rotational symmetry. That means they are the same when turned upside down. Make a list of these.

Geometry Building

You need: a partner or small group
an identical set of materials for each person — blocks, toothpicks, squares, etc.
walls (from books or binders) so each person has a working space that no one else can see

One person builds a structure using some or all of the materials and then describes it so the others can build it. The others can ask questions at any time. Finally, lift your walls to see if the structures you built are the same. Try it again so all students have a chance to be the describer. Discuss the language used, focusing on what was useful and what was not.

Pool Hall Math

(Adapted from *Mathematics: A Human Endeavor* by Harold Jacobs, Freeman Publishing Company)

You need: centimeter squared paper (see blackline masters)

A pool table is a rectangle or square of any dimensions. The ball always starts at the lower left corner. It moves by going to the opposite corner of each square it enters and keeps moving until it reaches a corner. Examples:

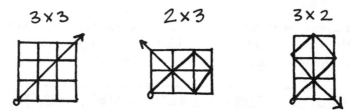

If the ball goes through *every* square on the table, then that pool table is **INTERESTING.** If the ball doesn't go through every square, the table is **BORING.** Find 10 interesting and 10 boring pool tables. Record. Can you find a pattern for predicting whether a pool table is interesting or boring before you test it?

Extensions:

1. *Exit Corners.* Examine where the ball leaves each pool table. Some go out at A; others at B or C. Find 10 different pool tables for each exit corner. Can you find a way to predict the exit corner?

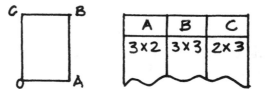

2. *Paths.* The ball takes different paths on different tables. Find all the different patterns for the paths the balls take.

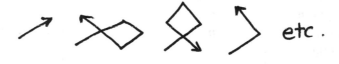

Area and Perimeter

You need: a partner or small group
a sheet of shapes as shown, duplicated on tag (see blackline masters)
a large piece of chart paper
scissors

Cut out the shapes on the Area and Perimeter sheet. Use these pieces to do the following:

1. Order the pieces according to their areas.

2. Then compare the perimeters of the pieces.

3. Display results to show the relationships between the areas and perimeters.

4. Write statements that describe what you discovered.

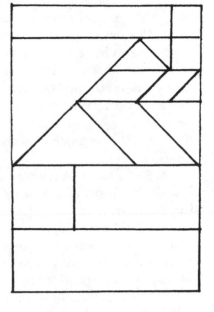

Extensions:

1. *Sorting by Shape.* Compare the areas and perimeters of each of the triangles, and then of the squares, and then of the rectangles and parallelograms. Write statements that describe what you discovered.

2. *Similar Shapes.* Similar shapes have the same shape but are different sizes. You can informally test to see if two shapes are similar by "sighting" with one. Here's how. Place the large square on the table. Stand up so you're looking down on it. Hold the small square in one hand, close one eye, and move the square up and down until it exactly covers the larger square. Because it can cover it exactly, they are similar. Will all squares be similar? Test the triangles, parallelograms, and rectangles the same way. Which are similar and which are not?

3. *Arrangements.* All of the pieces on the sheet fit perfectly into a rectangle. Could all of them be arranged into a triangle? A square? A parallelogram? Find ways to arrange them into other shapes.

Mirror Cards

You need: three 3-by-5-inch index cards
          a small piece of yarn or string
          markers
          mirrors
          a hole punch

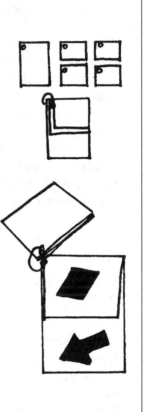

Follow the directions to make mirror cards:

1. Cut two of the index cards in half.
2. Punch holes in the same corner of the four half-cards and in the card that wasn't cut. Put the stack of cut cards on top and tie all five cards together with a piece of yarn. Write your name on the back of each card.
3. On the bottom half of the uncut card, make a design.
4. Put a mirror anywhere on the design, and draw on the half-card what you see both on your design and in the mirror.
5. Flip that half up. Move the mirror and draw what you see now on the second half-card.
6. Continue until you've drawn five designs in addition to your original one.
7. Try to solve others' cards, using the mirror to figure out where the creator placed it to get the design drawn. Write your name on the back of the uncut card to show you've solved the set. If you have trouble solving one, talk with the person who drew it.

The Fold-and-Cut Investigation

You need: scissors

Fold a piece of paper in half. Cut out a small shape on the fold. Try to draw what the paper will look like when you unfold it. Then unfold and compare. Do this at least five times. **Note:** Try deciding on a shape first and then cutting to see if you get it.

Try the same activity, but fold the paper twice before cutting.

Square Partitioning

Draw nine squares on a sheet of paper. Number them as shown. Then divide each square into the number of smaller square regions written beside it. Examples:

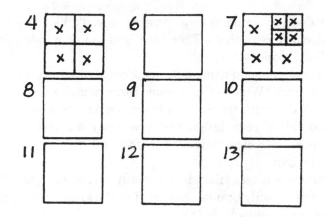

Extensions:
1. *There's More Than One Way to Cut a Square.* Find all the different ways you can partition a square into a given number of smaller squares.
2. *What's Wrong with 5?* Notice that 5 was omitted. How come?
3. *Going Further.* Continue the activity for larger numbers.

The Banquet Table Problem

You need: Color Tiles
 squared paper, centimeter or half-inch (see blackline masters)

A banquet hall has a huge collection of small square tables that fit together to make larger rectangular tables. Arrange tiles to find the different numbers of people that can be seated if 12 small tables are used. Do the same if 24 are used. Record on squared paper.

Extensions:
1. *The 100 Table Problem.* If 100 small square tables are arranged into a large rectangular table, find the most and least numbers of people that can be seated.
2. *Banquet Cost.* If the banquet hall charges by the number of square tables used, what's the least expensive way to seat 16 people? 50 people? 60? 100? Any number?

Introductory Explorations with Pattern Blocks

You need: Pattern Blocks

Try the following introductory explorations to become familiar with Pattern Blocks.

1. Make a floor, covering as large an area as you'd like. Try this using blocks that are different kinds. Then see if you can do it using only one kind of block. Will all blocks work?

2. Make a straight road using only one kind of block. Can you do this with each different block? Which of your roads can you make turn a corner?

3. Make a design with the Pattern Blocks on a piece of heavy paper. Trace around the outside of your design. List how many of each block you used. Exchange papers with classmates to see if you can fit the proper pieces into each others' designs.

4. Try building a larger triangle using only green triangles. Try building a larger square using only orange squares. Try the same with each of the other pieces. Which work and which do not?

5. Try building a shape exactly the same as (congruent to) the yellow hexagon using only green triangles. Try this with each of the other pieces. Which work and which do not?

6. If the area of the green triangle has the value of one unit, find the value of the area of the blue, red, and yellow pieces. Do the same with the area of the blue diamond as one unit, and then again with the red and yellow pieces as one unit.

7. Compare the areas of the orange and white pieces. Convince a friend of your comparison.

Hexagon Fill-In Puzzle

You need: Pattern Blocks
large hexagon shape drawn with each side double the length of the yellow hexagon (see blackline masters)

You need 6 blocks to fill the hexagon shape with as few pieces as possible — 3 yellow hexagons and 3 blue parallelograms. (Try it.) To fill it with as many blocks as possible, you would use 24 green triangles. Explore the following:

1. Can you find ways to fill the hexagon shape with each number of blocks from 6 to 24 (7, 8, 9, 10, etc.)? Record.

2. For each of the numbers possible, find different ways to fill the shape. Record. (A different way means a different collection of blocks, not a different arrangement of the same blocks.)

Extension: In how many different ways can the hexagon shape be filled using Pattern Blocks?

Hexiamonds

You need: green triangles from the Pattern Blocks
Pattern Block triangle paper (see blackline masters)

Hexiamonds are shapes made from six equilateral triangles arranged so that each triangle touches at least one other. Whole sides must touch. Use the green triangles to find all the different (noncongruent) hexiamonds. Cut them out of the triangle paper to verify that they are different. Record your solutions. Explain how you know you have found them all.

Angles with Pattern Blocks and Hinged Mirrors

You need: Pattern Blocks
hinged mirrors
5-by-8-inch index card with a dot and line on it, as shown below

The size of an angle is a measure of rotation, and degrees are used to measure angles.

Part 1. Figure out how many degrees there are in the angles formed by the corners of each Pattern Block. Use the following procedure:

    1. Place a corner of a block in the hinged mirrors.
    2. Close the mirrors so the corner nestles snugly.
    3. Use Pattern Blocks to build the design.
    4. Sketch or trace it.
    5. Figure the degrees in the nestled corner by dividing the number of blocks in the design into 360 degrees. Label your drawing to show the number of degrees in each angle.

Part 2. Construct other-size angles using the Pattern Blocks, hinged mirrors, and index card. Experiment with the following procedures:
    1. Use combinations of Pattern Blocks. For example, the orange square and blue parallelogram can be put together to make an angle that is 90 degrees plus 60 degrees.
    2. Use the hinged mirrors and the index card. For example, place the hinged mirrors so you see five dots and a pentagon. Trace along the base of the hinged mirrors to draw the angle created. Divide 360 degrees by 5 to figure the size of the angle traced. Label the angle.
    3. Combine to make angles from blocks and mirrors.

Extension: What size angles cannot be constructed using Pattern Blocks and hinged mirrors?

Explorations with Four Toothpicks

You need: a partner or small group
flat toothpicks, about 80
toothpick dot paper (see blackline masters)

Investigate all the different ways to arrange four toothpicks by following two rules:

1. Each toothpick must touch the end of at least one other toothpick.
2. Toothpicks must be placed either end to end or to make square corners.

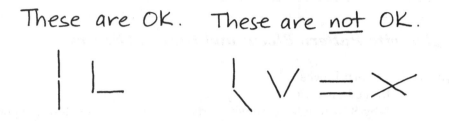

If a shape can be rotated or flipped to look like another shape, both shapes are the same. It's helpful to draw the shape in question on a piece of paper, flip it, and hold it up to a window to see if it's the same as another shape.

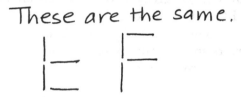

Record your shapes on dot paper. When you find all 16 shapes, cut your dot paper to make a set of cards.

Play a game. You need your cards and four toothpicks. Choose a starting card and make the pattern with the toothpicks. Deal the remaining cards to each player. (Discard extras so each player has the same number of cards.) Players place their cards face up so all are visible. In turn, each plays a card that shows a pattern that can be made from changing the position of exactly one toothpick on the pattern shown. Players help each other with moves and discuss patterns. Players pass if they can't play. The player who uses all his or her cards first is the winner for that round.

Extension: *The Put-in-Order Problem.* Arrange the cards so that each pattern can be made from the previous pattern by changing the position of just one toothpick. Can the cards be arranged in a continuous loop? Can they be arranged in more than one way?

WHOLE CLASS: *The Four-Triangle Problem*

You need: 3-inch squares of construction paper in two colors
scissors
tape or paste
newsprint

In this investigation, children explore shapes made from construction paper triangles. Begin by showing children how to cut a square in half on the diagonal to make two triangles. Have them explore the different ways to put the triangles together, following the rule that two edges the same size must be matched. Discuss the possibilities with the class. (There are three — square, triangle, and parallelogram.) Then continue with the following explorations:

1. Have children, in pairs, investigate the different shapes they can make using four triangles. They should tape the triangles together or paste them on newsprint. Have many squares available for their exploration.

2. On a class chart called *Polygons,* organize the shapes the children found. To introduce the standard vocabulary, label columns: *triangle, quadrilateral, pentagon,* and *hexagon.* Have children post their shapes.

3. Have children choose one four-triangle shape. Using two triangles of each color, they make the shape with different arrangements of the colors.

Extension: *Rotating Shapes.* Children choose a four-triangle shape, trace it on tagboard, and cut it out. They draw a dot near the middle of a 12-by-18-inch sheet of drawing paper. They place a corner of their shape on the dot and trace. Then they rotate the shape and trace again. They continue rotating and tracing.

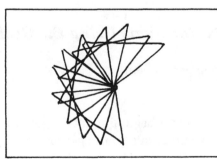

Penticubes

You need: interlocking cubes (Snap or Multilink cubes)
squared paper, the same size as faces of the cubes (see blackline masters)
isometric dot paper (see blackline masters)

This activity extends the pentomino exploration into three dimensions. Penticubes are three-dimensional shapes made from five cubes each. See how many you can construct. The following are ideas for follow-up explorations.

1. *Penticube Jackets.* Using paper ruled into squares the same size as the faces of the cubes, cut a jacket to fit a penticube. (Jackets are nets that fold to cover exactly all faces of the penticube.)

2. *More Penticube Jackets.* Take one penticube and find different possible jackets. (Is the number of possible jackets the same for each penticube?)

3. *Surface Area.* Compare the surface area of different penticubes. What do you notice about the shapes of penticubes with different surface areas?

4. *Penticube Riddles.* On squared paper, draw three views of a penticube — top, bottom, and side. Staple the drawings to a paper bag that holds the actual penticube. Others try to build the shape from the drawings and check their construction with the structure in the bag.

5. *Perspective Drawing.* Use isometric dot paper to draw penticubes.

6. *Building Rectangular Solids.* Put together several of the same or different penticubes to make rectangular solids. Investigate which dimensions of rectangular solids are possible to build.

WHOLE CLASS: Explorations Using the Geoboard

You need: geoboards, one per student
rubber bands

The following ideas are useful for beginning investigations.

1. Have children make numerals on the geoboard.

2. Have children make their initials. Ask them to make other letters.

3. Ask children to make something that can fly. Have students show what they made. Discuss. For example: Joe made a rocket. Did anyone else make a rocket? How are the rockets alike? How are they different?

4. Ask children to use just one rubber band and to make a shape that touches four pegs with one peg inside. It helps to describe this as making a fence that has four fenceposts and one tree inside the fence. Have children check with their neighbors to see that everyone has done it correctly and if there are different solutions. Continue: Make a shape that touches five pegs with zero inside; make a fence with five fenceposts and two trees inside, etc.

5. Ask children to use one rubber band and to make a shape that is not a square and looks the same on whichever side the geoboard rests. Ask: How many different shapes did we make in the class?

Explorations Using the Geoboard

You need: a partner or small group
geoboards
rubber bands

Each student finds a solution for the first direction. In your group, check each other's solutions, compare results, and discuss similarities and differences. Then continue with the next direction.

1. Make a shape that touches five pegs. (Think of the rubber band as a fence, and the pegs it touches as fenceposts.) Then try shapes that touch six and four pegs.

2. Make a shape that has three pegs inside. (That means if the shape is a fence the pegs inside are trees inside the fence.)

3. Make a shape that has ten pegs outside it, not touching the rubber band. (Think of them as trees growing outside the fence.)

4. Make a shape that has five fenceposts with three trees inside. Then try six fenceposts with two trees inside and three fenceposts with two trees inside. A challenge: Are there any combinations of fenceposts and trees that are not possible?

5. Use two rubber bands. Use each to make a line segment so the two line segments touch a total of nine pegs.

a line segment

6. Repeat item 5 again, this time finding different ways to make the line segments (a) parallel, (b) intersecting, (c) perpendicular, (d) the same length.

7. Make a triangle with one square corner and no two sides the same length.

8. Make a four-sided polygon with no parallel sides.

9. Make a four-sided polygon with all sides different lengths.

10. Make a four-sided polygon with no square corners but with opposite sides parallel. (What is this polygon called?)

11. Make a four-sided polygon that is not a square, not a rectangle, not a parallelogram, and not a trapezoid.

12. Make two shapes that have the same shape but are different sizes and are not squares.

WHOLE CLASS: Sorting Shapes on the Geoboard

You need: geoboards, one per student
rubber bands

Each student makes a shape using one rubber band. Have eight to twelve students prop their geoboards on the chalkboard tray. Sort them in some way, separating groups by moving them on the tray. Have the students discuss in small groups how you sorted them. When a group thinks they know, they bring up a different shape and add it to the category it fits. After a while, have someone describe how the shapes were sorted. Repeat.

Some ways to sort shapes include:

> do or do not have at least one right angle
> touch a corner peg or not
> have zero or one or two, etc., pegs inside
> have three, four, five, etc., sides
> are or are not symmetrical

Extension: Have groups brainstorm different ways to sort shapes and choose one to try on the class. The group sorts the shapes and the rest of the class, teacher included, try to guess.

Square Up

You need: a partner
a geoboard
one rubber band
12 Unifix cubes or game markers in two colors with holes in each

This game is for two players. Each takes twelve cubes in one color. Take turns putting one cube of your color on an empty peg. When you think four of your cubes mark the corners of a square, say, "Square up." Then your partner says, "Prove it." Prove it by stretching a rubber band around the pegs you've marked.

Geoboard Line Segments

You need: a geoboard
one rubber band

Find the next to the longest line segment you can make on the geoboard. Explain why you are sure your answer is correct.

Extension: How many different length line segments are there on the geoboard? Find a way to record them and order them from shortest to longest.

Areas of Four on the Geoboard

You need: a geoboard
         rubber bands
         dot paper (see blackline masters)

The square made by stretching a rubber band around four pegs with no pegs inside has an area of one square unit. Find other shapes with an area of four square units. Record them on dot paper. Choose one shape, copy it on large size dot paper, cut it out, and post it. (**Note:** Post a shape that is different from those already posted.)

Shape Construction on the Geoboard

You need: a geoboard
         rubber bands
         dot paper (see blackline masters)

Construct shapes that fit each of the following. Can you find more than one solution for any of these?
     1. A rectangle with area of two square units
     2. A triangle with area of two square units
     3. A triangle with area of three square units
     4. A parallelogram with area of three square units
     5. A hexagon with area of four square units
     6. A rectangle and square with the same area (Which has the smaller perimeter?)

Geoboard Square Search

You need: a geoboard
         rubber bands
         dot paper (see blackline masters)

Find all the different size squares you can make on the geoboard. (Hint: There are more than four.) Record on dot paper.

Geoboard Triangle Search

You need: a geoboard
         rubber bands

Find triangles with areas of five and seven square units.

Pick's Theorem

There is a function called Pick's Theorem (named after the mathematician who discovered it) that enables you to find the area of any shape on the geoboard from the number of pegs on the perimeter of the shape (P) and the number of pegs inside the shape (I). The following sequence of activities suggests a way to find this theorem.

1. The square with an area of 1 has four pegs on its perimeter and zero pegs inside. Investigate other shapes with four pegs on the perimeter and zero pegs inside. Compare their areas. What about shapes with four pegs on the perimeter and one peg inside? Two pegs inside? Three? Four? Five? Etc.? Write a formula that describes the relationship.

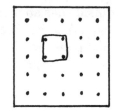

Remember: P = pegs on the perimeter
           I = pegs inside
           A = area of the shape

P	I	A
4	0	1
4	1	
4	2	
4	3	
4	4	
⋮	⋮	

2. Do the same investigation for shapes with other numbers of pegs on the perimeter.

P	I	A
3	0	
3	1	
3	2	
3	3	
⋮	⋮	

P	I	A
5	0	
5	1	
5	2	
5	3	
⋮	⋮	

P	I	A
6	0	
6	1	
6	2	
6	3	
⋮	⋮	

3. Now investigate patterns for the areas of shapes when the number of inside pegs stays constant and the number of pegs on the perimeter varies. For example:

P	I	A
3	0	
4	0	
5	0	
6	0	
7	0	
⋮	⋮	

P	I	A
3	1	
4	1	
5	1	
6	1	
7	1	
⋮	⋮	

P	I	A
3	2	
4	2	
5	2	
6	2	
7	2	
⋮	⋮	

etc.

4. Finally, can you find a master formula that allows you to figure the area (A) for any combination of pegs on the perimeter (P) and pegs inside (I)? That's Pick's Theorem.

Just to check your formula:

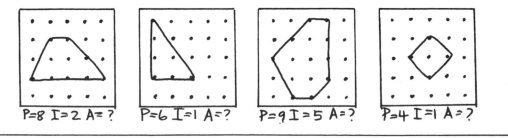

P=8 I=2 A=?   P=6 I=1 A=?   P=9 I=5 A=?   P=4 I=1 A=?

Area on the Geoboard

You need: a geoboard
                rubber bands

Find the area of each shape.

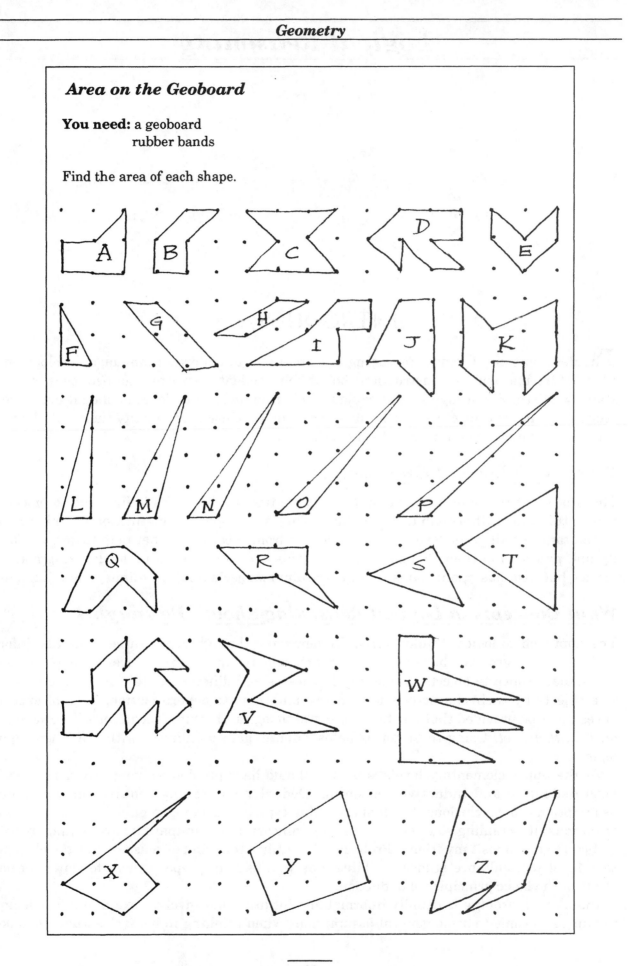

Logical Reasoning

INTRODUCTION

The development of logical reasoning is closely tied to children's language development. Elementary mathematics instruction should help students learn to organize ideas, understand what they're studying, and explain their thinking. Math lessons should encourage students to make conjectures, generalizations, and conclusions; to justify them with logical arguments; and to communicate them to others.

Why Teach Logical Reasoning?

The process of reasoning is basic to all mathematics. Mathematics is first and foremost a way of thinking, rather than a body of facts. This is an important distinction for children to understand. At all grade levels, children benefit from experiences that help them gain clarity and precision in their thought processes. This is not only essential for learning mathematics but also has applications in all curriculum subjects and in ordinary life situations.

What Concepts in Logical Reasoning Should Be Taught?

The approach to logical thinking from kindergarten through grade three should be informal. At these grades, there should be many opportunities for children to explore and manipulate concrete objects, to identify likenesses and differences, to classify and categorize objects by their characteristic features, and to state generalizations. Verbal experiences must be provided that use terms integral to logical thinking, including *all, some, and, or, if ... then, not*. Using these terms helps children gain familiarity with the language of logic.

At the upper elementary levels, students should have problem-solving experiences with both deductive and inductive reasoning. Deductive reasoning requires moving from assumptions to conclusions. Students use this type of reasoning regularly in daily living situations: It is raining so I need to wear my raincoat. My grandparents are coming to visit so I can't go and visit my friend. Problems that utilize this kind of reasoning at the elementary level will enhance students' abilities as well as help prepare them for later formal study of the basic principles of deduction.

Inductive reasoning is usually informal and intuitive and involves examining particular instances to come to some general assumption. When thinking inductively, students make hypotheses, extend thought patterns, use analogies, and make reasonable conclusions from examining what appears to be a large enough body of evidence. Again, students do this regularly in ordinary life situations: Mom never lets me go to movies during the week, so she probably won't let me go this time, either. If I get good grades on the next two quizzes, I think I'll get an A in the class. Students benefit from problem-solving activities that require the use of these thinking skills.

A SAMPLE ACTIVITY — THE GAME OF POISON

The Game of Poison is a version of the game of Nim. It provides an opportunity for logical reasoning at several levels and, so, can be used beneficially at all grade levels.

Materials

thirteen objects for each pair of students

Introducing

1. Present or review concepts.

The Game of Poison is a game for two people. For a first game, use thirteen objects. Players take turns removing one object or two objects. Play until all objects have been taken. The last object to be removed is considered to be the poison. Whoever gets stuck taking it loses.

2. Pose a part of the problem or a similar but smaller problem.

Play the game once with a volunteer. To enable the class to observe the game, use objects on an overhead or draw marks on the chalkboard.

3. Present the problem to be solved.

Give these directions: You need to play five games with each member of your group. After you've done this, as a group discuss what you noticed about the game. Your group task is to try to find a winning strategy for avoiding the poison. Write down statements that describe your thinking. If your group thinks you have a winning strategy, raise your hands so you can try to poison me.

4. Discuss the results.

Ask for questions. It is useful to reinforce the idea that the group's task is to cooperate in finding a winning strategy, not to focus on competitive play.

Exploring

Circulate and observe. Encourage groups to stop playing and to discuss strategies if they seem to be lagging. If you're called over by a group to "be poisoned," be sure that the entire group is involved and that they all understand the strategy being used. If you suspect that one person is doing all the thinking and has not communicated with the others in the group, ask one of the others to play. This helps focus students in a group on sharing their thinking. For a group that has a winning strategy and is able to poison you, offer the first extension and, if there is additional time later, the others.

Extensions

1. *Changing the Number of Objects.* Add one more object to the pile and play again. Try playing with other numbers of objects.
2. *Changing the Number You Can Remove.* Change the rules so it's possible to remove one, two, three, or some other number of objects on a turn.
3. *Making the Poison a Treat.* Play the game so the person who removes the last object wins. How does this affect your strategies?

Summarizing

Explain that the game of *Poison* has a winning strategy. This means the game will never end in a draw, as *Tic-Tac-Toe* can. Someone will always win, and figuring out how requires logical thinking. Encourage students not to reveal the winning strategy if they know it so that others have a chance to continue their thinking. Encourage them, however, if they have a strategy to test their thinking by varying the number of objects used in the game or the number a player can take on a turn. **Note:** It's possible to find a master strategy for playing with any number of objects and being allowed to remove any number of them on a turn.

ACTIVITIES

King Arthur's Problem

This is a fictionalized historical problem. King Arthur wanted to decide who was most fit to marry his daughter. He chose the following method. When all his knights were seated at the Round Table, he entered the room, pointed to one knight, and said, "You live." The next knight wasn't so fortunate. "You die," said King Arthur, chopping off his head. To the third knight, he said, "You live," and to the fourth, he said, "You die," chopping off his head. He continued doing this around the circle, chopping off the head of every other knight, until just one was left. The remaining knight got to marry the daughter, but, as the legend goes, he was never quite the same again.

   The problem is to figure out where you should sit in order to live. Do this for different numbers of knights. Find a pattern so you can predict where to sit no matter how many people are seated in the circle.

WHOLE CLASS: *Junk Sorting*

You need: a collection of objects for each group (keys, jar lids, fabric swatches, buttons, nuts and bolts, postcards, shells, polished rocks, etc.)

Give the groups a chance to inspect their collections. Then ask them to sort their materials into two sets. Have them do this several different ways. Have them sort their collections into three sets. Then have them decide on one way to sort their collection for other groups to analyze. Have them follow these directions:

1. Groups sort materials into two, three, or four sets, making loops of string to keep the sets separate.

2. On a piece of paper, groups write down the attributes of each set and place the paper face down on the table.

3. Groups rotate to a different table where they try to figure out how another group has sorted its material. When they think they know, they turn over the papers to check their predictions. Then they sort the materials in a different way, writing the new attributes under the old ones, and move to another table.

4. Groups continue to rotate as long as there is interest. Then they return to their original tables and examine the different ways their materials were sorted as listed on the papers.

Note: For young children, give a small group a collection of similar materials to explore. After they have had time to explore the collection freely, ask for a volunteer to tell one thing he or she noticed about the objects. For jar lids, for example, a child may offer, "Some are white." Then the group can sort them into two piles — the lids that are white and the lids that are not white. Then ask for something else someone may have noticed, and sort again. Continue until the children have exhausted all possibilities.

Difference Trains

You need: a partner or small group
Attribute Blocks or Attrilinks

Start with one block. Arrange the blocks or links into a train so each piece is next to another that is different from it in just one way. Try to use all the pieces. (This may take some rearranging.) Then try to join the ends of the train to make a continuous loop. (This most likely will necessitate more rearranging.)

Guess My Rule

You need: a partner or small group
         Attribute Blocks or Attrilinks
         loops
         label cards

One person is "It" and sets up a Venn diagram with one, two, or three loops, selecting (secretly) a label card for each loop. The label cards are placed, face down, on the loops they describe. Your partner or group members take turns choosing a piece and asking to which sets it belongs, then placing it in the proper place. Take turns being "It."

Difference Puzzle

You need: puzzle cards
         Attribute Blocks or Attrilinks

To make puzzle cards, first decide how many pieces you'd like to use and draw that many circles. Put a piece in each circle and then draw lines connecting circles to show the number of differences between the shapes in the joined circles. For example, if the pieces are both large and red, but one is a square and the other is a triangle, they differ in only one way — shape. If the pieces have different shapes and sizes but are the same color, they have two differences. Remove the pieces. You now have a puzzle with at least one solution.

    Then have others place pieces in the circles so that they have the number of differences as described by the lines.

———————————————————— one difference

════════════════════ two differences

≡≡≡≡≡≡≡≡≡≡≡≡≡≡≡≡≡≡≡≡ three differences

Record as shown in the example.

RECORDING SYSTEM

L: Large   R: Red   C: Circle
S: Small   Y: Yellow   D: Diamond
          B: Blue   S: Square
          G: Green   T: Triangle

LYT: Large Yellow Triangle

SAMPLE

LYT — LBS
| |
SRC — LRT

The Prison Problem

There was a jail with 100 cells in it, all in a long row. The warden was feeling very jolly one night and told his assistant that he wanted to give all the prisoners a wonderful surprise. While they were sleeping, he wanted the assistant to unlock all the cells. This should be done, he told the assistant, by putting the key in each lock and turning it once.

Following the order, the assistant unlocked all the cells and then came back to report that the job was done. Meanwhile, however, the warden had second thoughts. "Maybe I shouldn't let all the prisoners go free," he said. "Go back and leave the first cell open, but lock the second one, by putting the key in and turning it once. Then leave the third open, but lock the fourth, and continue in this way for the entire row."

The assistant wasn't very surprised at this request. The warden often changed his mind. After finishing this task, the assistant returned, and again the warden had other thoughts. "Here's what I really want you to do," he said. "Go back down the row. Leave the first two cells as they are, and put your key in the third cell and turn it once.Then leave the fourth and fifth cells alone and turn the key in the sixth. Continue down the row this way."

The assistant again did as instructed. Fortunately, the prisoners were still asleep. As a matter of fact, the assistant was getting pretty sleepy, but there was no chance for rest yet. The warden changed his mind again, and the assistant had to go back again and turn the lock in the fourth cell and in every fourth cell down the row.

This continued all through the night, next turning the lock in every fifth cell, and then in every sixth, and on and on, until on the last trip, the assistant just had to turn the key in the hundredth cell.

When the prisoners finally woke up, which ones could walk out of their cells?

The Three Sacks Problem

You need: three sacks with cubes as described in the problem

There are three sacks with red and blue cubes in them. One is labeled *Red*, one is labeled *Blue*, and the third is labeled *Red and Blue*. There's one thing you know for sure — each of the three sacks is mislabeled. The problem is to figure out which sack really is which. You can't look into any of them, but you can reach into any one sack and remove one cube at random. Which sack would you reach into?

WHOLE CLASS: Decision Making

You need: one die

Teach the game by asking each student to set up a blank addition problem as shown. Roll the die five times. Each time, call out the number that comes up. Students have to write the number in one of the five blanks. Once they write the number down, they cannot change its position. The goal is to place the numbers to produce the largest sum possible. Play the game several times until you're sure all the students understand it.

Then assign the group task. Groups are to write one procedure that the entire group will follow in playing the game as a team. They may write this decision-making strategy any way they like, as long as it is clear to all group members and accounts for all possible rolls.

When groups have completed their procedures, play five rounds of the game. See if any group's strategy produced more wins than any other.

Have groups post their procedures to compare the different ways the procedures were written and the different strategies the groups used.

Sally and the Peanuts

On the way home from school, Sally McCrackin likes to eat peanuts. One day, just as she was reaching into her sack, a hideous, laughing creature jumped into her path, identified itself as a pig eyes, and grabbed her sack. It stole half of her peanuts plus two more. A bit shaken, Sally continued toward home. Before she had a chance to eat even one peanut, another horrid creature jumped into her path and also stole half of her peanuts plus two more. Upset, she continued on. (What else could she do?) But, before she had a chance to eat even one peanut, another of these tricksters jumped out and did the very same thing — took half her peanuts plus two more.

Now there were only two peanuts left in Sally's sack. She was so despairing that she sat down and began to sob. The three little pig eyes reappeared, feeling some sense of remorse, and told her they would return all her peanuts to her if she told them how many she had altogether when she started.

How many peanuts had been in Sally's sack?

Extension: Suppose Sally had been left with three peanuts? Or there had been four nasty pig eyes? Can you find a way to predict how many peanuts Sally had in her sack to start with regardless of how many she was left with or regardless how many pig eyes stole peanuts from her?

Number Sorting

You need: cards or slips of paper numbered from 1 to 30

Sort the numbers in these ways:
1. into two groups
2. into three groups
3. into four groups

Record how you did this as shown in the example. Trade your paper with a classmate. Each of you tries to figure the rule the other used for sorting.

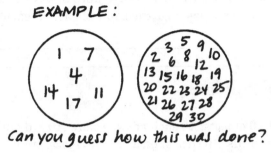

EXAMPLE:

Can you guess how this was done?

Latin Squares

You need: sixteen Color Tiles, four of each color
squared paper (see blackline masters)
crayons or markers

Try each of the following:
1. Start with nine tiles, three each of three different colors. Arrange them into a square with one of each color in each row and each column. Record on squared paper.
2. Use all sixteen tiles and build a four-by-four square following the same rules. Record.
3. Repeat each, making the long diagonals contain one of each color also.

Your Choice Tic-Tac-Toe

You need: a partner

Play on a regular tic-tac-toe board. On your turn you can put down either an X or an O, changing your mind on each turn if you wish. The winner is the one who finishes a row with either all X's or all O's in it.

The Orange Juice and Water Problem

Suppose you have two glasses that are the same size and shape. One has water in it. The other has orange juice in it. The glasses have the same amount of water and juice.

Now suppose you take a spoonful from the glass of orange juice and put it in the glass of water. Mix it up. Then you take a spoonful from the glass of water (with the orange juice in it) and put it in the glass of orange juice. Mix it well. Once again, put a spoonful from the orange juice glass into the water glass and then a spoonful from the water glass back into the orange juice glass.

Now for the problem. Is there more orange juice in the water glass than there is water in the orange juice glass? Or the same of each in each?

The Two-Color Problem

You need: a set of 20 objects, 10 each of two colors (10 red and 10 black
playing cards, 10 tiles of each of two colors, etc.)
two paper bags

Separate the objects by color and put each set of 10 in a paper bag. Reach into one bag and remove 3 objects. Put them in the other bag. Mix the contents of the second bag, and then reach in and remove 3 objects (at random) and put them in the first bag. Repeat this process three more times. Now examine the contents of each bag.

Consider the following questions:

How is this problem like *The Orange Juice and Water Problem?*
How is it different?
How would the activity change if you moved 5 objects each time or some other number?
What if you kept changing the number of objects you moved on each turn, rather than keeping it the same for the entire process?

The Card Problem

You need: 10 cards, numbered 1 to 10

Arrange the cards this way: the top card is a 1 and should be placed face up on the table; put the next card on the bottom of the deck; place the third card, which should be a 2, face up on the table; move the next to the bottom of the deck. Continue until all the cards are in order on the table top.

Logical Breakfast

Steven, Doreen, and Jay each ate something different for breakfast. One had granola, one had scrambled eggs and toast, one had a banana split. (The last one was allowed because the parents were away on vacation and there was a very lenient babysitter.)

Jay did not have scrambled eggs and toast or a banana split. Doreen did not have scrambled eggs and toast.

Whose parents were on vacation?

Guess My Word

You need: a partner

One player thinks of a three-letter word for the other to guess. Whenever the person guesses, the player who thought of the word tells whether the guess comes before or after the word in the dictionary.

WHOLE CLASS: Riddles with Color Tiles

You need: Color Tiles
          small paper bags

Students use clues to figure out the Color Tiles in a bag. For the first riddle, it's helpful to present each clue separately, giving the students a chance to use the Color Tiles to make a combination that might be in the bag. The second riddle can be done in the same way, or you can give students the first three clues to analyze together. After students are comfortable solving riddles, they work in pairs to make up their own riddles for others to solve.

Riddle 1
Clue 1:   I have 12 tiles.
Clue 2:   I used 3 colors.
Clue 3:   There are no red tiles.
Clue 4:   There are the same number of green and blue tiles.
Clue 5:   I have 4 yellow tiles.

Riddle 2
Clue 1:   There are fewer than 10 tiles.
Clue 2:   I used 2 colors.
Clue 3:   I have no green or red tiles.
Clue 4:   I have twice as many blue tiles as yellow tiles.
Clue 5:   I have 2 yellow tiles.

A Mathematical Tug-of-War

(Adapted from *Math for Smarty Pants* by Marilyn Burns; Little, Brown & Company)

The problem is to use the information given to figure out who will win the third round in a tug-of-war.

Round 1: On one side are four acrobats, each of equal strength. On the other side are five neighborhood grandmas, each of equal strength. The result is dead even.

Round 2: On one side is Ivan, a dog. Ivan is pitted against two of the grandmas and one acrobat. Again, it's a draw.

Round 3: Ivan and three of the grandmas are on one side and the four acrobats are on the other.

Who will win the third round? Write an explanation of your reasoning.

Digit Place

(Adapted from *Make It Simpler* by Carol Meyer and Tom Sallee, Addison-Wesley Publishing Co., Inc.)

You need: a partner

Each person picks a three-digit number with no two digits the same. They take turns guessing each other's number. Each time someone guesses, the other person tells how many digits in the guess are correct and how many of the correct digits are in the correct place. A chart is useful for keeping track of the information:

Do not tell *which* digits are correct or in the correct place, just *how many*. Whoever guesses the other player's number first wins that round.

Guess	D	P
293	0	0
356	1	1
296	0	0
⋮	⋮	⋮

Race for 20

You need: a partner

Take turns. On your turn, you may count one or two numbers. So the first person says: "1" or "1, 2." And the second continues with one or two more numbers. The player who says "20" wins.

Four-in-a Row

You need: a partner or small group
inch squared paper (see blackline masters)
Color Tiles

This game can be played by two to four players. The squared paper is the playing board. Each player chooses a different color and uses the tiles of that color. On each turn, a player places a tile on a square. The first to get four-in-a-row — horizontally, vertically, or diagonally — wins.

After students are familiar with the game, have them discuss and write about their strategies. **Note:** Unlike the game of *Poison*, it is possible for this game to end in a draw.

Color In

You need: a partner
playing board (as shown)
crayons or markers

Color in ▢, ᗺ, or ▭▭

Each player, in turn, colors one square or two squares with a common side. Whoever colors in the last square wins.

Odd Number Wins

You need: a partner
fifteen counters

Take turns. On your turn, you can pick up one, two, or three counters. Whoever has an odd number of counters when all have been picked up is the winner.

Patterns, Functions, and Algebra

INTRODUCTION

Patterns are key factors in understanding mathematical concepts. The ability to create, recognize, and extend patterns is essential for making generalizations, seeing relationships, and understanding the order and logic of mathematics. Functions evolve from the investigation of patterns and make it possible to predict results beyond the information at hand. Functions are useful for solving problems in mathematics and in many other fields of study — including science and economics. Algebra makes it possible to represent patterns and functions and study and understand them further.

What's Important About Patterns, Functions, and Algebra?

Studying patterns, functions, and algebra involves students in investigating numerical and geometric patterns; describing them verbally; representing them symbolically in several ways, including in tables, with symbols, and graphically; using them to make predictions and generalizations; and exploring properties of our number system. By studying patterns, functions, and algebra, students learn about the various uses of variables and how to solve equations.

INTRODUCING PATTERNS

Looking for patterns is natural for young children, and early experiences should focus on recognizing regularity, identifying the same pattern in different forms, and using patterns to make predictions. For example, introduce a repeating pattern like *clap, snap, clap, snap, clap, snap, ...* and have children join in. Give them materials with which they can represent the pattern — by making a train of interlocking red-blue-red-blue-red-blue-... cubes, for example. Represent the pattern with letters, in this case *ababab....* Also, ask children to predict what comes later in the sequence. In the pattern above, for example, the twelfth element will be *snap, blue,* or *b.* Mix easy patterns with more complicated ones:

clap, clap, snap, clap, clap, snap, clap, clap, snap, . . .

□ □ △ □ □ △ □ □ △ □ □ △ . . .

a a b a a b a a b a a b . . .

Number sequences, like *2, 4, 6, 8, ...* and *1, 2, 4, 8, 16, ...*, also provide patterns for children to investigate. Growth patterns like these are **recursive patterns**; that is, each number is found from the previous number by repeating some process. Students benefit from examining such sequences and figuring out how to determine subsequent terms — for example, *adding 2* or *doubling*.

What comes next ?
1, 4, 7, 10, 13, 16, . . .
0, 2, 6, 14, 30, 62, . . .
2, 12, 22, 32, 42, 52, . . .

DEVELOPING UNDERSTANDING OF FUNCTIONS

Looking for patterns in the relationships between two sets of numbers is a key way to develop students' understanding of functions. For example, we know that one tricycle has three wheels and two tricycles have six wheels. How many wheels do three tricycles have? four tricycles? *n* tricycles? The number of wheels is a function of the number of tricycles. This means that since each tricycle has three wheels, we can use the rule of multiplying the number of tricycles by 3 to determine the number of wheels for any number of tricycles. One way to describe this relationship between tricycles and their wheels is as a set of pairs of numbers: (1,3), (2,6), (3,9), (...,...) (one tricycle and three wheels, two tricycles and six wheels, and so on). This set of pairs of numbers form what is called a **function.**

Younger children can have beginning experiences with functions by exploring number patterns that describe relationships that exist in the real world. For example, have children come to the front of the room and count their eyes. One child has two eyes, two children have four eyes, three children have six eyes, and so on. The number of eyes depends on the number of children and therefore the number of eyes is a function of the number of children. Children can record the eyes pattern as shown below. Then have then predict beyond the information they have recorded.

Other patterns to investigate with young children in this same way include fingers, thumbs, toes, noses, the number of points on any number of five-pointed stars, the amount of money for any number of nickels or dimes, the number of children needed to turn any number of jump ropes, and so on.

Older students should be introduced more formally to the concept and standard notation of functions. A function is defined as a set of ordered pairs, such as in the tricycle-and-wheels example of (1,3), (2,6), (3,9), (...,...)., in which no two pairs have the same first number. Note that the order of the numbers in each pair is significant: (3,1) would mean that for three tricycles there is one wheel, and that's not true. Also, for any number of tricycles, there is only one correct number of wheels; it's not possible to have a different pair of numbers beginning with 1, 2, 3, or any other number.

An important first step for students is to describe patterns like these verbally. An important goal of mathematics instruction is for students to learn to represent functions in the following three forms:

1. Table
2. Formula
3. Graph

Table. For the tricycle example, using T to represent tricycles and W for wheels, you can represent the function in a table. You can think of T as the *input* and W as the *output*.

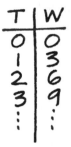

T	W
0	0
1	3
2	6
3	9
⋮	⋮

Formula. The relationship between tricycles and wheels can also be represented in an algebraic equation using T and W as variables: $$T \times 3 = W$$ Because the number of wheels depends on the number of tricycles, mathematicians often refer to W, the quantity of wheels, as the dependent variable, determined by a rule that is applied to T, the independent variable.

Graph. Coordinate geometry makes it possible to represent functions graphically. Graphing a function calls for using the ordered pairs to place points on a coordinate graph. The standard way to do this is to start where the two heavy lines (the *axes*) meet. This point is called the origin. Use the first number in each pair to count over from the origin, the second number to count up, and place a dot. Young children can learn this system of placing points without much difficulty. Notice that the dots for the tricycles and wheels function are in a straight line, indicating that it is a linear function.

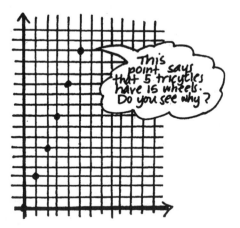

USES OF VARIABLES

Representing functions algebraically calls for the use of variables, as T and W were used to represent the function about tricycles and wheels. However, variables serve other purposes as well. Young children typically first learn about using variables as place holders for unknown numbers; for example, $\Box + 3 = 10$ or $5 + n = 12$. In these situations, variables represent answers — specific, nonvarying numbers that can be determined by solving the equation.

Later, students learn that variables can be used not only for specific unknown quantities, but also for a wide range of values. Equations that use variables in this way can generalize arithmetic properties. For example, $\Box + 0 = \Box$ is true for any value of $\Box$ because we know that adding zero to a quantity results in the same quantity. Zero is called the *additive identity*. Similarly, $n \times 1 = n$ for any value of n; the number one is the multiplicative identity. Other examples of using variables to describe arithmetic properties include $a + a = 2a$, $\Box \times 0 = 0$, and $x + y = y + x$. Each of these equations is true for any values of a, o, x, or y.

Variables are also used in formulas; for example, $A = lw$, with A, l, and w representing varying quantities of area, length, and width.

A SAMPLE ACTVITY — PAINTING TOWERS

Suppose you build a tower of interlocking cubes that is 99 cubes tall. And suppose you paint every square on all four sides of the tower, as well as the top. (You don't have to paint the base of the tower.) How many squares do you have to paint? What is the relationship between the height of the tower and the number of squares to paint?.

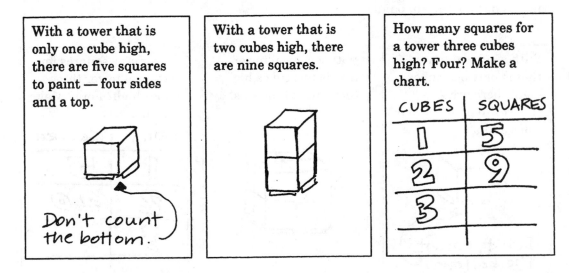

> With a tower that is only one cube high, there are five squares to paint — four sides and a top.
> Don't count the bottom.

> With a tower that is two cubes high, there are nine squares.

> How many squares for a tower three cubes high? Four? Make a chart.
>
> | CUBES | SQUARES |
> |-------|---------|
> | 1 | 5 |
> | 2 | 9 |
> | 3 | |

Painting Towers is a sample of the kinds of problems that follow. Each problem presents a situation that you can investigate geometrically, numerically, and algebraically. For each, continue the table started until you can identify a pattern. Then think about how to solve the problem without continuing the pattern, but by looking for the functional relationship. Represent the function with a formula and graph enough of the pairs of numbers to describe the pattern made by the points.

ACTIVITIES

Paper Folding

Suppose you fold a piece of paper in half, and then in half again, and again, until you make six folds. When you open it up, how many sections will there be?

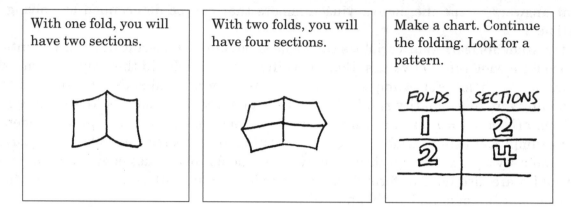

With one fold, you will have two sections.	With two folds, you will have four sections.	Make a chart. Continue the folding. Look for a pattern.

More Painting Towers

You need: interlocking cubes

Suppose you build a cubical tower that is 99 cubes tall. And suppose, as you did for *Painting Towers* on page 115, you have to paint every square on the four sides and the top of the tower. (You don't have to paint the base of the tower.) How many squares do you have to paint?

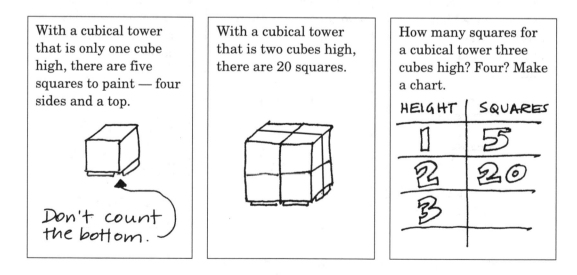

With a cubical tower that is only one cube high, there are five squares to paint — four sides and a top.	With a cubical tower that is two cubes high, there are 20 squares.	How many squares for a cubical tower three cubes high? Four? Make a chart.

Dot Connecting

Suppose you draw 10 dots on a circle. If you draw lines connecting every dot to every other dot, how many lines will you draw?

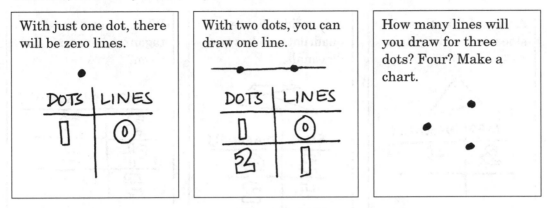

| With just one dot, there will be zero lines. | With two dots, you can draw one line. | How many lines will you draw for three dots? Four? Make a chart. |

Paper Tearing

Suppose you tear a piece of paper in half and give half to someone else. Then each of you tears your piece in half and passes half on to someone else. How many people will have a piece of paper after 10 rounds of tearing like this?

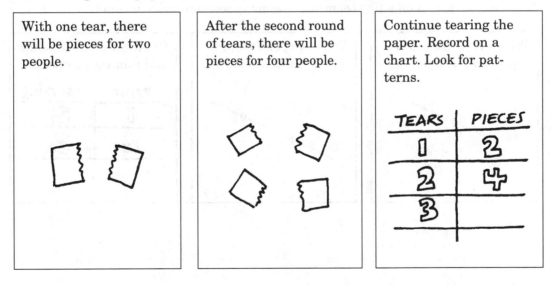

| With one tear, there will be pieces for two people. | After the second round of tears, there will be pieces for four people. | Continue tearing the paper. Record on a chart. Look for patterns. |

The Diagonal Problem

If you have a 12-sided polygon (a dodecagon), how many diagonals can you draw? Remember that diagonals connect the corners of shapes.

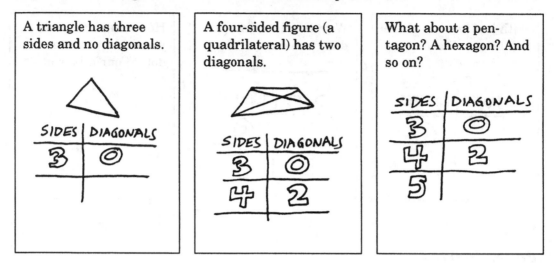

A triangle has three sides and no diagonals.	A four-sided figure (a quadrilateral) has two diagonals.	What about a pentagon? A hexagon? And so on?

Points Dividing a Line

If you put 20 points on a line segment, how many sections can you count?

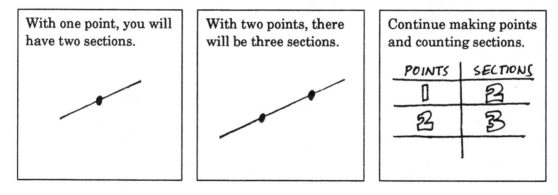

With one point, you will have two sections.	With two points, there will be three sections.	Continue making points and counting sections.

The Ice Cream Cone Problem

If an ice cream shop sells 31 different flavors of ice cream, how many different double-dip cones can they make? Hint: Use different color interlocking cubes for flavors and build the cones.

| If the shop has only one flavor, there will be only one possible double-dip cone. | With two flavors, there are three combinations for double-dip cones. | How many double dips are possible with three flavors? Four? Make a chart and look for patterns. |

FLAVORS	DOUBLE DIPS
1	1
2	3

Extensions:

1. If you count vanilla on top and pistachio on the bottom as different from pistachio on the top and vanilla on the bottom, how will your result change?

2. Try the same problem for triple-dip cones.

Squares from Squares

If you build larger and larger squares from small squares, how many squares will you need to build one that measures 12 on a side?

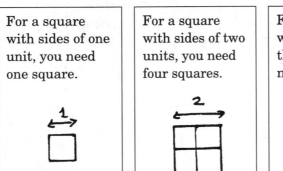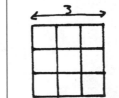

| For a square with sides of one unit, you need one square. | For a square with sides of two units, you need four squares. | For a square with sides of three units, you need nine squares. | Continue the pattern. |

LENGTH OF SIDE	SQUARES
1	1
2	4
3	9

More Squares from Squares

If you build squares as in *Squares from Squares,* what will be the length of the perimeter of a square that is 12 on a side?

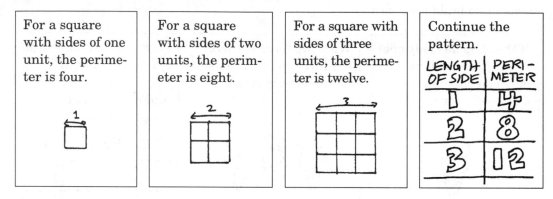

For a square with sides of one unit, the perimeter is four.	For a square with sides of two units, the perimeter is eight.	For a square with sides of three units, the perimeter is twelve.	Continue the pattern.

Continue the pattern.

LENGTH OF SIDE	PERIMETER
1	4
2	8
3	12

Rod Stamping

Imagine the white Cuisenaire Rod is a rubber stamp that stamps 1-centimeter squares. How many stamps would it take to cover each of the other rods? What is the pattern?

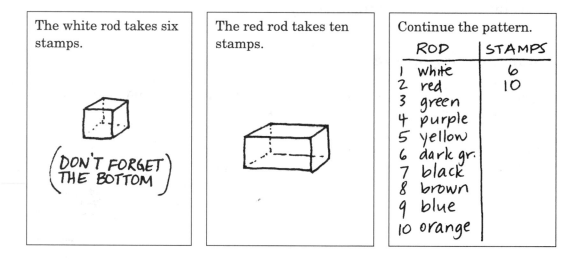

The white rod takes six stamps.	The red rod takes ten stamps.	Continue the pattern.

(DON'T FORGET THE BOTTOM)

Continue the pattern.

	ROD	STAMPS
1	white	6
2	red	10
3	green	
4	purple	
5	yellow	
6	dark gr.	
7	black	
8	brown	
9	blue	
10	orange	

More Rod Stamping

Suppose you take rods of one color and pretend to glue them together as the picture shows. Figure out how many stamps are needed for each and look for the pattern.

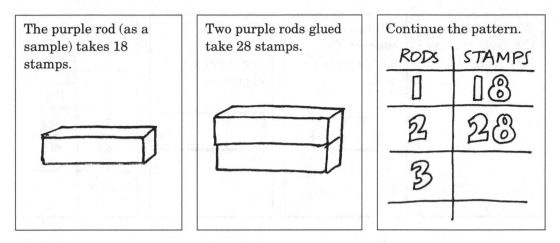

The purple rod (as a sample) takes 18 stamps.	Two purple rods glued take 28 stamps.	Continue the pattern.

RODS	STAMPS
1	18
2	28
3	

Extension: Suppose you glue the rods together offsetting each 1 centimeter as the picture shows. Make a chart of the stamps needed and look for the pattern.

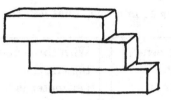

A Row of Triangles

If you line up 100 equilateral triangles (like the green triangles from the Pattern Blocks) in a row, what will the perimeter measure? (You may think of this as a long banquet table made from individual triangular tables. How many people can be seated?)

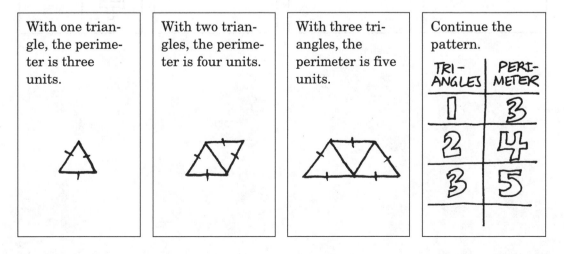

With one triangle, the perimeter is three units.	With two triangles, the perimeter is four units.	With three triangles, the perimeter is five units.	Continue the pattern.

TRI-ANGLES	PERI-METER
1	3
2	4
3	5

A Row of Squares

If you line up 100 squares in a row, what will the perimeter measure? (As in *A Row of Triangles*, you may think of this as a long banquet table made from individual square tables. How many people can be seated?)

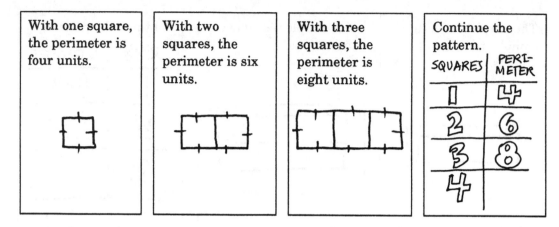

| With one square, the perimeter is four units. | With two squares, the perimeter is six units. | With three squares, the perimeter is eight units. | Continue the pattern. |

SQUARES	PERIMETER
1	4
2	6
3	8
4	

A Row of Pentagons

If you line up 100 regular pentagons in a row, what will the perimeter measure?

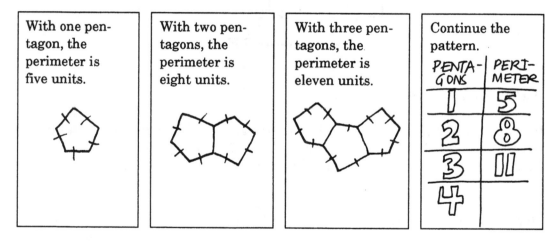

| With one pentagon, the perimeter is five units. | With two pentagons, the perimeter is eight units. | With three pentagons, the perimeter is eleven units. | Continue the pattern. |

PENTAGONS	PERIMETER
1	5
2	8
3	11
4	

A Row of Hexagons

If you line up 100 regular hexagons in a row, what will the perimeter measure?

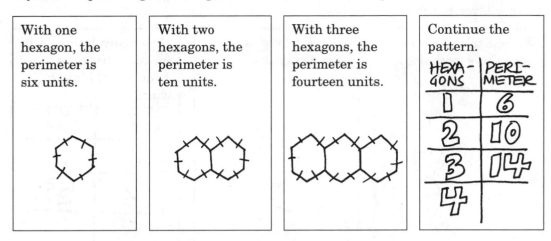

With one hexagon, the perimeter is six units.	With two hexagons, the perimeter is ten units.	With three hexagons, the perimeter is fourteen units.	Continue the pattern.

HEXA-GONS	PERI-METER
1	6
2	10
3	14
4	

Note: There is a way to figure out the pattern for a row of any regular polygon. Try it if you're interested.

Interlocking Trains

If you make trains ten cubes long using two colors of interlocking cubes, how many different arrangements can you make? (**Note:** The order of the colors matters. For example, for a train that is three cubes long, red-red-blue and red-blue-red each count as a different arrangement.)

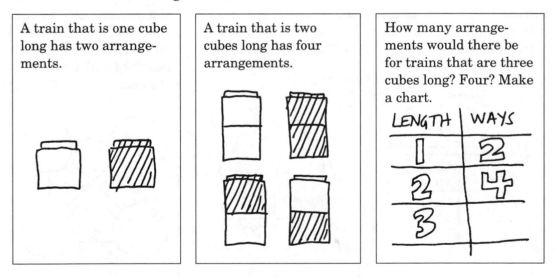

A train that is one cube long has two arrangements.	A train that is two cubes long has four arrangements.	How many arrangements would there be for trains that are three cubes long? Four? Make a chart.

LENGTH	WAYS
1	2
2	4
3	

Toothpick Building

If you continue the pattern shown to build a row of 100 triangles, how many toothpicks will you need?

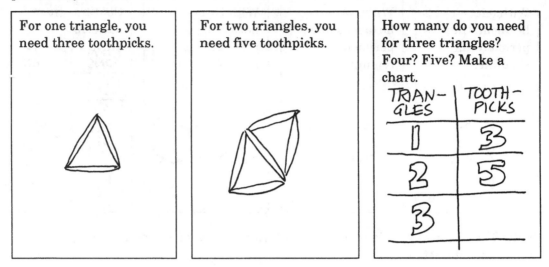

For one triangle, you need three toothpicks.	For two triangles, you need five toothpicks.	How many do you need for three triangles? Four? Five? Make a chart.

Extension: Try the problem for rows of squares, pentagons, and hexagons.

The Handshake Problem

Suppose everyone in this room shakes hands with every other person in the room. How many handshakes will that be?

With only one person in the room, there will be no handshake.	With two people, there will be one handshake.	How many handshakes will there be with three people? Four? Continue the chart.

Number

INTRODUCTION

*N*umbers are used to describe quantities, to compare quantities, to identify specific objects in collections, and to measure. Children must be able to make sense of the various ways numbers are used. They need to develop a sense of number that enables them to recognize relationships between quantities; to use the operations of addition, subtraction, multiplication, and division to obtain numerical information; to understand how the operations are related to one another; to be able to approximate and estimate when appropriate; and to be able to apply their understandings to problem situations.

What Concepts in Number Should Be Taught?

Children's math learning should emphasize the development of number sense, should help them see relationships among numbers, and should encourage them to examine the properties of numbers. Children should investigate the use of numbers in many situations so that they develop the confidence and flexibility to apply their understanding in new situations.

The study of patterns is valuable for helping children discover and develop generalizations about number. Investigating patterns in numerical relationships needs to be an ongoing part of the elementary mathematics program.

The nature of numbers includes such ideas as whether numbers are prime or composite, whether they are even or odd, what their factors and multiples are, and how numbers relate to other numbers. Experiences with these ideas help students develop understanding of our number system.

Students need to develop an intuitive understanding of the properties of the basic operations, including commutativity, associativity, and distributivity. Instruction should introduce these concepts in problem-solving settings rather than present their definitions abstractly.

The activities in this section require that students apply numbers in problem situations. These problem situations differ from traditional word problems for which specific skills are used to get single answers. The focus here is on the use of numbers in problems for which there are often a variety of solutions or a variety of possible ways to arrive at a solution. It is assumed that students have calculators available for their use at all times.

A SAMPLE ACTIVITY AT THE PRIMARY LEVEL — NUMBER SUMS

This activity requires that children can write sums for numbers less than 10. Although practice of basic addition facts is provided, the emphasis of the problem is to use the facts to find all the possible ways to represent sums.

Introducing

1. Present or review concepts.

Review with the children the fact that there are different ways to write sums of numbers. Use the number 3 as an example, showing the children the three ways to write 3 as a sum using addends greater than or equal to 1. Record on the board:

$$1 + 1 + 1$$
$$2 + 1$$
$$1 + 2$$

2. Pose a part of the problem or a similar but smaller problem.

Ask the children to help you find all the ways to write 4 as a sum. Remind them that if the addends are in a different order, the sum will be counted as a different way. Record the seven ways on the board:

$$1 + 1 + 1 + 1$$
$$1 + 1 + 2$$
$$1 + 2 + 1$$
$$2 + 1 + 1$$
$$1 + 3$$
$$3 + 1$$
$$2 + 2$$

3. Present the problem to be solved.

The groups' task is to find all the ways to write sums of the number 5.

4. Discuss the results.

Ask for questions.

Exploring

Circulate and observe. If a group calls you over to announce that they are finished, look at their sums. If you notice they've repeated any, tell them, but leave them the task of finding the repeats. If you know there are more ways to be found, ask them to continue to think about the problem. If they've found all 15 different ways, suggest that they try the investigation for the number 6.

Summarizing

Discuss the group processes. Ask how they organized themselves to work together. Ask how they decided when they had found all the sums. Have children report their findings.

Number	How many sums?
3	3
4	7
5	15
6	.
:	:

Look at the pattern in the number of ways there are to write the sums for 3, 4, and 5. Ask the children to predict how many ways there are to write 6. Assign the problem of finding the different ways to write sums of 6 to groups that did not get started on it during the exploration. Have the other children continue trying to figure out the pattern so they can predict how many sums there are for 7 and 8.

A SAMPLE ACTIVITY AT THE INTERMEDIATE LEVEL — PALINDROMES

This activity engages students in looking for number patterns, both visually and numerically.

Materials

0–99 chart, one per student (see blackline masters)
palindrome recording chart, one per student (see blackline masters)
crayons or markers

Introducing

1. Present or review concepts.

A palindrome is a number that reads the same forward and backward, such as 44, 252, or 8008. A number that is not a palindrome, such as 13, can be changed into a palindrome by using a particular procedure: You reverse the digits and add. Demonstrate on the board how to do this. Since it takes one addition, 13 is a one-step palindrome.

Some numbers take more than one addition. Demonstrate with 68.

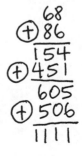

2. Pose a part of the problem or a similar but smaller problem.

Have the students try to change 48 into a palindrome. As they work, do it on the board so they can check their work. Then show the class how to record the results for 13, 68, and 48 on the palindrome recording chart.

3. Present the problem to be solved.

Each group is to investigate all the numbers from 0 to 99. First they should decide how to divide the work. Everyone is to keep individual records on the chart as demonstrated. Also, each person is to record on a 0–99 chart, coloring the numbers that are already palindromes with one color, coloring in one-step palindromes with another color, two-step palindromes with another color, and so on. As a group, they should agree on the colors to use. Direct them to look for patterns on both charts. Also, tell them not to tackle 98 and 89 unless they are ready for a serious bout with addition. (Each number takes 24 steps with a resulting palindrome of 8,813,200,023,188.)

4. Discuss the results.

Ask for questions.

Exploring

Problems do not generally arise during this exploration. Several class periods may be required for all groups to finish their work. Before beginning work on the second day, it may be useful to have a brief discussion about their progress so that students can hear from others about organizational tips, problems, etc.

Summarizing

Discuss the group processes. Ask groups: How did you divide the work? Was your system a good one? Did you change your system during the activity? What do you think would be the best way for a group to do this activity?

Ask about patterns that emerged on charts. Start a chart of the students' discoveries. Some groups, for example, notice that when the sum of the digits of a number is less than 10, the number is always a one-step palindrome. Others notice that all resulting palindromes are multiples of 11. Have the class look for other patterns such as these.

Ask if they categorized one-digit numbers as one-step, already palindromes, or neither. There is no right answer to this, but groups should be able to explain their ideas.

ACTIVITIES

WHOLE CLASS: *Investigations with Raisins*

You need: 1/2-oz. boxes of raisins, one per student
1 1/2-oz. boxes of raisins, one per group

Lesson 1

1. Show a 1/2-oz. box. Have the students guess how many raisins it contains.

2. Distribute the boxes. Each student opens a box, counts the raisins that are visible, and makes an estimate of how many raisins are in the entire box. (Be sure to remind them not to remove any raisins yet.) They then discuss their estimates in their groups, decide on a group estimate, and report it in writing, explaining their reasoning.

3. Each student counts the raisins in his or her box, arranging them on paper so it's easy to see how many there are. Record the counts on the board.

4. Based on the information recorded on the board, students predict what one number might be a good guess for how many raisins typically are in a box. Have them record individually and explain their reasoning, discuss their ideas in their groups, and finally report to the class.

5. Students figure how many raisins there are altogether in their group's boxes. They record and explain how they figured. Finally, they can eat their raisins if they wish, but have them save the boxes for the next lesson. Also, save the information you recorded about their actual counts.

Lesson 2

1. Give each group a 1 1/2 oz. box of raisins. Have them estimate how many raisins are in it and explain in writing how they did it. Have groups report to the class.

2. Have groups count the raisins in the box and then figure out how to share them equally. They write about how they solved this problem.

WHOLE CLASS: Coin Riddles

You need: four dimes and two pennies, concealed from the class

Present the clues to the class in the sequence given. After each clue, have groups discuss what they know for sure. Ask if they have sufficient information to guess the coins you have or if they need another clue. The coins can be guessed from the following clues.

Clue 1. I have six coins.
Clue 2. I have only dimes and pennies.
Clue 3. I have at least two pennies.
Clue 4. I have more dimes than pennies.

Simpler riddles are more suitable for younger children. Be sure to provide children with coins to use for figuring.

Riddle 1. I have two coins worth $.11.
Riddle 2. I have three coins worth $.27.
Riddle 3. I have four coins worth $.22.

Making Change

Find all the ways to make change for $.50.
Easier version: Find all the ways to make change for a quarter.
Harder version: Do the same for $1.00

Number Bracelets

Choose any two numbers from 0 to 9 and follow this rule: Add the two numbers and record just the digit that appears in the ones place in the sum. For example, if you start with "8 9," then the next number would be "7." Then add the last two numbers (the 9 and the 7) and record "6," the ones place of their sum. Continue until you get back to where you started: " 8 9 7 6 3 9 2 ...." How many numbers in your series until you get a repeat?

Answer these questions:

1. How many different possible pairs of numbers can you use to start?
2. What's the shortest bracelet you can find?
3. What's the longest bracelet?
4. Investigate the odd/even patterns in all your bracelets.

The 0–99 Chart

You need: worksheet of six 0–99 charts (see blackline masters)
crayons or markers

Have students follow these directions to color the 0–99 charts:
1. Color all the even numbers.
2. Color all the numbers with digits that add to 8.
3. Color the numbers with digits that differ by 1.
4. Color all the numbers with a 4 in them.
5. Color the multiples of 3.
6. Color the numbers with both digits the same.

How Many Sums?

If you add two or more of these numbers, find all the different possible sums you can get.

19   21   15   17   13

Pascal's Triangle

Figure out how to extend this pattern to include additional rows. Look for patterns in rows and diagonals.
Find out who Pascal was.

1
1 1
1 2 1
1 3 3 1
1 4 6 4 1
1 5 10 10 5 1

Change from a $10.00 Bill

If you spend $1.85 and pay with a $10.00 bill, you get $8.15 in change. Notice that the digits in your change are the same as the digits in the amount you spent. Try to find all the other amounts you could spend and get change with the same digits. Explain why you think you have found all of the possibilities.

Addition Table Explorations

You need: an addition chart

+	1	2	3	4	5	6	7	8	9	10
1	2	3	4	5	6	7	8	9	10	11
2	3	4	5	6	7	8	9	10	11	12
3	4	5	6	7	8	9	10	11	12	13
4	5	6	7	8	9	10	11	12	13	14
5	6	7	8	9	10	11	12	13	14	15
6	7	8	9	10	11	12	13	14	15	16
7	8	9	10	11	12	13	14	15	16	17
8	9	10	11	12	13	14	15	16	17	18
9	10	11	12	13	14	15	16	17	18	19
10	11	12	13	14	15	16	17	18	19	20

Describe general rules or shortcut methods to find the following:
1. The sum of any three horizontally adjacent numbers.
2. The sum of any three vertically adjacent numbers.
3. The sum of any two-by-two array of numbers.
4. The sum of any three-by-three array of numbers.
5. The sum of any ten-by-ten array of numbers.
6. The sum of any cross of five numbers.
7. The sum of any three diagonally adjacent numbers.
8. The sum of any four diagonally adjacent numbers.
9. The sum of any five diagonally adjacent numbers.

Invent at least three other problems like these and describe rules for them.

Multiplication Possibilities

Find as many ways as you can to fill in this problem so the arithmetic is correct:

```
   □ □ □
  × □
  ─────
   9 6 6
```

Where Does 100 Land?

If you write the counting numbers in rows of seven numbers each, in which column will 100 land? In which row?

```
1 2 3 4 5 6 7
8 9 10 11 12 13 14
15 16 17 ···
```

Write the counting numbers in rows of six numbers each. What's the location of 100 in this array?

```
1 2 3 4 5 6
7 8 9 10 11 12
13 14 15 16 ···
```

Write arrays with other length rows. Find a way to predict in which row and column 100 will land for any array of numbers.

Extension: *From Column to Column.* For each array, if you add a number from the second column to a number from the third column, in which column will the sum land?

WHOLE CLASS: The Border Problem

You need: 10-by-10 grid of centimeter squared paper, one per student

Students are asked to figure out how many squares there are in the border of a 10-by-10 grid. Record all the different ways reported by translating their verbal explanations to arithmetic notation. Then have students test their methods on a 5-by-5 grid.

Show the class a larger square grid, one for which they do not know the number of squares on a side. Ask them to describe how they would go about figuring the number of squares in its border. Show how to translate one of their methods into an algebraic formula. Have them work together to translate all their methods into formulas.

Which Day of the Week Were You Born?

Follow these directions to find out what day of the week you were born:

1. Write down the last two digits of the year you were born. Call this number *A*.

2. Divide that number (*A*) by 4, and drop the remainder if there is one. This answer, without the remainder, is *B*.

3. Find the number of the month you were born from the Month Table below. This number is *C*.

4. What day of the month were you born? This number is *D*.

5. Add the numbers from the first four steps: $A + B + C + D$.

6. Divide the sum you got in step 5 by the number 7. What is the remainder from that division? (It should be a number from 0 to 6.) Find this remainder in the Day Table. That tells you what day of the week you were born. (This method works for any day in the 20th century.)

Month Table		*Day Table*
January 1 (leap year is 0) July 0		Sunday 1
February 4 (leap year is 3) August 3		Monday 2
March 4 September 6		Tuesday 3
April 0 October 1		Wednesday 4
May 2 November 4		Thursday 5
June 5 December 6		Friday 6
		Saturday 0

The Postage Stamp Problem

You can combine different denominations of stamps to get the proper postage for a letter or package. In this problem, you investigate the postage amounts that can be made when you are restricted to using only certain stamps.

To begin, if stamps only came in 3¢ and 5¢ denominations, what amounts of postage would be impossible to make? Is there a largest "impossible" amount? Explain your answers.

Do the same investigation if there were only 8¢ and 5¢ stamps. Then continue with other combinations of two denominations of stamps. For each, investigate the following:

1. How many impossible amounts are there?

2. Is there a largest impossible amount and, if so, what is it?

Write an explanation for each of your answers.

Arrow Arithmetic

You need: a 0–99 chart (see blackline masters)

Look at the starter hints, using the 0–99 chart for reference. Then solve the others.

Starter hints: 18 →= 19 18 ←= 17 18 ↑ = 8 18 ↓ = 28

How about these? 18 ↗ = ? 18 ↖ = ? 14 ↙→ → = ? 76 ↘ ↑↑ = ?

True or false? 16 ↓↓ → → = 38

24 →↙↗↓ = 34

61 ↑ ↗ → = 42

24 ↓↓↓ = 67

83 ↑↑↑↑↖ = 22

Make up problems for others to solve.

Extension: How would you solve these? 9 → = ? 7 ↑ = ? 70 ← = ?

PART III

Teaching Arithmetic

Introduction

Arithmetic, as one of the time-honored three Rs, receives the largest share of attention and concern of all the topics in the elementary mathematics curriculum. The rationale for this is obvious — arithmetic skills are necessary life tools that people use regularly every day. A person who is not able to do arithmetic is handicapped in many situations.

However, while the importance of arithmetic has not diminished, the criteria for evaluating students' proficiency with arithmetic and the methods for teaching arithmetic have changed and broadened. Facility with standard paper-and-pencil algorithms is no longer the measure of arithmetic understanding and competence; students don't acquire all the knowledge they need by simply learning basics and practicing computation. Basic arithmetic skills extend beyond memorization and computational facility and include learning to use numbers to solve problems and developing number sense. An emphasis on computation done in isolation does not prepare children to use their skills to solve everyday problems. Nor does it help develop number sense so that students think and reason numerically, make sound numerical judgments, estimate, and see numbers as useful. Problem solving, number sense, and computation are all integral to arithmetic competence.

Paper-and-pencil skills and memorization are still important in children's arithmetic learning. However, memorizing basics, while essential for computation, should follow, not lead, instruction that builds children's understanding. Teaching algorithms as the primary emphasis of arithmetic instruction is not sufficient; other kinds of appropriate teaching practices are needed. The emphasis should be on using paper and pencil to keep track of numerical reasoning, not necessarily on using one particular procedure. The calculation method needs to be appropriate to the numerical situation and must efficiently produce an accurate answer.

For many calculations, including most of the arithmetic we do in our daily lives, we figure in our heads. Learning to compute mentally, too often shortchanged in school, is also an important aspect of arithmetic proficiency. When numerical problems are too complex or unwieldy to solve mentally, then students should be able to figure out answers with the help of paper and pencil, using methods that make sense for the problems at hand.

THE MISMATCH BETWEEN SCHOOL ARITHMETIC AND REAL-LIFE ARITHMETIC

Because arithmetic is a much-used life skill, it makes sense to look at real-life applications when making decisions about what children really need to learn. One way to begin is to identify the daily uses people have for arithmetic. (It would be useful to make a list of the actual occasions during the past month when you used arithmetic. Include as many situations as you can in which you had to add, subtract, multiply, or divide to arrive at an answer you needed.)

Adults who make such a list generally include the following types of situations: when I figure my checkbook balance; when I'm in the supermarket figuring how much I'm spending or doing price comparisons; when I want to know how much wallpaper or floor covering I need; when I need to determine the tip in a restaurant; when I want to know what mileage I'm getting on my car; when I need to figure how long a roast or turkey needs to cook; when I have to decide what time to leave to arrive at the movies on time.

A list of everyday applications of arithmetic is testimony to the usefulness of arithmetic. For further insights, two questions can be asked about any specific situation:

- What method is used most often to do the arithmetic calculation — a calculator, paper and pencil, or figuring mentally?
- Is it necessary to be accurate or is an estimate sufficient (or even preferable)?

When adults analyze the arithmetic methods they most often use, they find that they usually have relied on two methods — using a calculator and figuring mentally. (A study has reported that 93 percent of adults' uses of arithmetic do not involve paper and pencil.) When the lists are evaluated to determine how often accuracy is necessary and how often an estimate will suffice, there is generally a 50-50 split.

In classroom practice, however, teachers admit to spending more than 75 percent of their math time, and closer to 90 percent for many, on paper-and-pencil arithmetic skills, with students practicing the skills in isolation from any problem situations. Arithmetic exercises are usually provided on worksheets or textbook pages, neatly arranged and ready for children to apply the computation methods they've been taught. Estimating is often encouraged, but arriving at accurate answers is always required.

The mismatch between the work students are asked to do in school and the arithmetic needs they will have in real life is revealed even more clearly when we examine the typical uses of arithmetic. An example: finding yourself in a supermarket without your checkbook and with only $20.00. You need to keep track of the cost of the groceries you put in your cart to avoid arriving at the checkout counter with a grand total more than you can pay. A running total is required, and most likely you'll keep it mentally. (There are some supermarkets, however, that now provide shopping carts with built-in calculators!) Each time you select an item, you decide how much to add to your running total. If a chicken costs $2.37, you'll most likely add $2.50; if a sack of chips costs $.89, you'll probably add $1.00. Although you'll try to be fairly accurate with your calculations, it's sensible to estimate each item to avoid the unnecessary hassle of laborious computation. Not only is it more sensible to use estimates than accurate amounts, it's also advisable to overestimate each time, or at least enough of the time, to be sure not to be caught short. Your arithmetic calculations may help you decide, in order to keep within your limit, not to buy items that aren't absolute necessities.

Another example: tipping in a restaurant. The check for dinner shows a total of $33.92. You examine the check for accuracy, adding the amounts listed or, more likely, estimating to make sure the total is reasonable. Of the total, the amount for the meal was $32.00 and tax was $1.92. Suppose the food was good and the service prompt and cordial. What tip do you leave? How do you figure it? Standard protocol calls for at least 15 percent of the total without tax. You most likely do the calculation mentally and most likely by a method different from the standard multiplication algorithm you learned in school. Some people figure that 10 percent of $32.00 is $3.20, half of that is $1.60, and the amount together is $4.80. Still, how much do you leave? $4.80? $5.00? More? Less?

One more example: figuring gas mileage. Some people regularly check their gas mileage when filling the tank to check their car's performance. Suppose it takes 11.7 gallons of gas to fill the tank. The odometer indicates that you've traveled 253 miles since the last fill-up. How do you figure the miles per gallon? You know you have to divide. If you have a calculator handy, you may use it. If, however, you're figuring mentally, chances are you'll adjust the numbers to make them friendlier. Instead of 11.7, 12 will do; instead of 253, you use 250. Calculating mentally, you get a little more than 20 miles per gallon. That's close enough to know that your car doesn't need immediate attention. But suppose you had arrived at an answer of 8 miles per gallon. What would you do? Most likely you'd first recheck your calculations, since you know what a reasonable answer ought to be. Then you would decide if emergency car care was needed.

Contrast these real-life situations with the work children generally face in school. Most of children's arithmetic practice is separated from problem situations. They do not have to choose the operations nor decide on reasonable numbers to use. They are not asked to decide how to do a calculation but are expected to perform algorithms using pencil-and-paper procedures they were taught. Although encouraged to recheck their computations, most students are not motivated to do so. Since there is no context for the calculation, there is no way to readily notice when an answer is unreasonable or, in some cases, ridiculous.

Estimates for answers are generally not acceptable on children's arithmetic work. (A cartoon in a national magazine showed two students at the chalkboard, one struggling with 6 + 7. The struggling student commented to the other, "The problem is, they require such pinpoint accuracy.") Textbook directions often encourage students to estimate first for a ballpark figure against which to judge their answers. But students rarely do so. Why estimate when an accurate answer is required? Why do the work twice? Since there is no context for the calculations, students are not given opportunities to decide when accuracy is demanded and when estimates are sufficient. Their interest is very different from the interest an individual has when in the supermarket, the restaurant, or at the gas pump.

WHAT ARE THE BASICS IN ARITHMETIC?

The real-life situations people face that call for using arithmetic generally require that they do the following:

1. Choose the operation (or operations) needed.
2. Choose the numbers to use.
3. Perform the calculation, either using a calculator, paper and pencil, or figuring mentally.
4. Evaluate the reasonableness of the answer and decide what to do as a result.

The situations students face in school, however, most often require only the third step listed and allow only one option — using paper and pencil to perform the calculation as it was taught. An emphasis on this narrow aspect of arithmetic in no way provides even minimal arithmetic proficiency.

Why has pencil-and-paper arithmetic computation become the mainstay of the elementary curriculum? It seems clear enough to understand. The ability to do calculations has long been seen as essential for the successful use of arithmetic. This practice was in place and well entrenched long before calculators and computers removed the drudgery from computation. There was no way to arrive at arithmetic answers other than doing the calculations by hand. Because of the present availability of calculators, having students spend more than six years of their schooling mastering paper-and-pencil arithmetic computation is as absurd as teaching them how to ride and care for a horse in case the family car breaks down.

With or without calculators, however, learning to do paper-and-pencil arithmetic and practicing on isolated examples has never ensured that children learned to use these skills when needed. This deficiency is obvious to teachers when word problems are assigned and children repeatedly ask, "Do I need to add or subtract?" Arithmetic practice in isolation does not lead children to notice when they make a division error, such as omitting a zero in the quotient, and produce an answer that is 10 times too small.

This does not mean that children do not need to learn any arithmetic. Arithmetic skills are necessary life tools. Doing arithmetic mentally demands mastery of basic facts along with the ability to estimate. Using a calculator successfully and evaluating the answer requires an understanding of the necessary arithmetic processes and the ability to identify a reasonable solution. Being able to use paper and pencil to solve an arithmetic problem has its place. But there is no place in our schools for focusing on computation apart from problem situations and then claiming that children are being taught arithmetic. The very definition of teaching arithmetic needs to be revised. Arithmetic competence cannot be measured solely by evaluating students' mastery of computational algorithms. Mastery of arithmetic must include, as basic and integral, knowing which operations are appropriate to particular situations, which numbers are most reasonable to use, and what decisions can be made once the needed calculations have been done. It makes no sense to say that a child can do arithmetic but cannot apply it to situations. The basics of doing arithmetic must include being able to apply arithmetic operations to situations, as well as being able to calculate answers.

You would never say that a person who can only play scales knows how to play the piano. You would not assume that a person who can catch a football knows how to play the game. You would not make the judgment that a person who can saw a board knows how to build a bookcase. The rudiments are necessary, but they would be senseless to learn as ends in themselves.

The motivation for learning skills in life is their eventual use. Children who practice scales have heard music. Children who practice catching and throwing a football have seen football games. In school, however, children are expected to practice their arithmetic skills without any sort of mathematical bookcase to build. No wonder so many are not motivated to develop their proficiency. What sense does it make? Instead of seeing arithmetic skills as useful tools that save work, children often see them as making work, their only purpose the completion of pages of exercises.

142

The reality is that many children cannot apply arithmetic skills even to the simplest of word problems. Many students are not able to tell if it is cheaper to buy things two for a nickel or three for a dime. They are lost when asked if one-third of a cup and one-half more will give more or less than a full cup. However, when these same children can demonstrate proficiency with paper-and-pencil computation, it is common for teachers to say that, because the children can perform addition, subtraction, multiplication, or division calculations, they have mastered arithmetic.

The simplistic and useless definition of arithmetic competence that has resulted in the achievement of computational proficiency as the major mathematics goal of the elementary school must change. The definition of skills basic to arithmetic must broaden. Children must develop understanding of arithmetic concepts in problem-solving contexts. They must learn to calculate mentally, to use numbers comfortably to come to reasonable estimates, to develop understanding of relationships among numbers and operations, to be confident and competent in their number understanding, and to develop an appreciation and fascination for numbers.

RESULTS FROM CLASSROOM RESEARCH

Sandra Nye, a teacher in West Babylon, New York, asked her fourth graders to find the answer to 19×21. This was early in December. Sandra had done no instruction in multiplication that year but knew her children had had some experience with multiplication in the third grade. She put them into small groups of four or five students and asked each group to choose a recorder to write down everything the group did. As the children worked, Sandra circulated, reading what they were producing, and making notes on their papers to have them go further or to clarify their thoughts. Her goal was to get insights into the children's thinking, rather than merely to test their ability to do the computation. Following are actual reports of the written dialogue between Sandra and each group.

The Red Group

Children: *First we ✗'s one times nine. Next we ✗'s the one by the one. Then we go down a line and put a zero under the nine. Next we ✗'s the two by the nine and the two by the one. Now that we have two answers (one on top and one on bottom) we add them and get an answer of 399.*

$$\begin{array}{r} 19 \\ \times 21 \\ \hline 19 \\ 380 \\ \hline 399 \end{array}$$

Sandra: *Why did you go down a line? What do the two answers mean? Why did you add them?*

Children: *We changed lines because the rules are to change lines and the rules are also to put a zero in the beginning of the second line. The rules are that way because there is no way to get 399 with 380 on the same line as 19. We found this out in 3rd grade. We added them because that's the way we were taught and it gives a sensible answer.*

143

Sandra: *Now, can you explain each of the numbers in your answer?*
Children: *The 19 means that one times 19 equals 19. The 38 means that two times 19 equals 38. (Remember it's a rule to put a zero on the second line.) The 399 means 19 plus 380 equals 399. That's how we did this problem.*
Sandra: *Why is it a rule to put a zero on the second line? What's the purpose of the rule?*
Children: *Nobody in our group can remember why we put the zero on the second line. We told you above that it is a rule to put the zero on the second line.*

The Blue Group

Children: *This is how we solved our problem. First we times 19×21 and we got 389 and we found out it was wrong. The teacher put some answers on the board and told us they were wrong. The answers were 57, 3,819, and 389. Then about 5 minutes later we found out the real answer is 399. We added 21 19 times. We proved it by making a 21×19 rectangle. The way you set it up is*

$$
\begin{array}{r}
19 \\
\times 21 \\
\hline
19 \\
380 \\
\hline
399
\end{array}
$$

That is the way you set it up because any time you're timesing two digit numbers, first you put down the first answer and then you put down a 0 on the next line before you multiply.
Sandra: *How do you get the first answer? What does it mean?*
Children: *You get the first answer by timesing 1×19. It means that you have the first part done.*
Sandra: *Why do you "put down a 0" on the next line? What does the number on that line show?*
Children: *So it makes the number bigger. That line should be the larger number.*
Sandra: *Why should that line be bigger?*
Children: *So you get a reasonable answer.*
Sandra: *Why does 380 show? What numbers do you multiply to get 380?*
Children: *It shows 38 with a 0 on the end. You multiply 19×20 to get 380.*
Sandra: *Where is the 20?*
Children: *The 20 is the 21 without the one because you times the one already.*

The Purple Group

Children: *We wrote it this way:*

$$
\begin{array}{r}
19 \\
\times 21 \\
\hline
19 \\
38 \\
\hline
57
\end{array}
$$

Then we found out that we left out the zero in the second number.

Sandra: *How do you know there should have been a zero in the answer? And how did you realize that your first answer was wrong?*

Children: *There should be a zero in the second number because when you multiply with tens you put a zero in the ones place because you are not working with the ones. We realized that the answer should be much bigger than 57 because if you put 21 down 19 times it wouldn't add up to 57. It would be much bigger.*

Next we wrote down 19 21 times. Then we crossed off two 19's at a time, and put down 38. Then we crossed off two 38's at a time, and put down 76. Next we crossed off two 76's at a time, and we put down 152. It looked like this when we finished.

$$
\begin{array}{r}
152 \\
152 \\
+\ 95 \\
\hline
399
\end{array}
$$

Finally we put it like this and it was right.

$$
\begin{array}{r}
19 \\
\times\ 21 \\
\hline
19 \\
380 \\
\hline
399
\end{array}
$$

Sandra: *How did you decide to write it this way?*

Children: *We figured out the answer with addition and then we figured it out this way.*

If merely given a quiz on which they were asked to do the computation, the Red Group would most likely have gotten it correct. Yet in both their explanation and answers to Sandra's questions, the children consistently resorted to following the rules they had learned without being able to explain why. The other two groups were able to relate multiplication to addition and to verify their answers that way. The Blue Group seemed to be farthest along in making sense out of the partial products. When urged to explain where the 380 came from, they wrote that it was the result of multiplying 19×20. The Purple Group, however, could justify the final algorithm as reasonable only because it worked to produce the correct answer. What do these children understand about multiplication?

In the March 1983 issue of *School Science and Mathematics*, Thomas C. O'Brien and Shirley A. Casey reported the results of a study they conducted with fourth-, fifth-, and sixth-grade children. The children were asked to complete the following computations using paper and pencil:

1. $6 \times 3 = $ _____
2. $16 \times 3 = $ _____
3. $60 \times 1 = $ _____
4. $13 \times 16 = $ _____
5. $3 \times 60 = $ _____

Then the children were asked to write a story problem for 6×3.

The five computations yielded success rates of 82 percent in grade four, 75 percent in grade five, and 97 percent in grade six. The story problems, however, yielded different results. Of the fourth graders, only 25 percent wrote a story problem that was multiplicative in context. For the fifth graders, the figure was 15 percent, and for the sixth graders, it was 69 percent. More than half of the nonmultiplicative responses involved stories that described $6 + 3$, not 6×3, even though many of these stories ended with the statement, "$6 \times 3 = 18$." What do these children understand about multiplication?

A student who is able to perform paper-and-pencil computations for the operations shows procedural understanding, knowing "what to do" in a situation. This does not necessarily mean that the student understands the "why" of that procedure — why it works, why it makes sense, why it is useful to problem situations. Knowing "what to do and why" means understanding the arithmetic procedure in relation to its meaning and application.

The Red Group in Sandra's class demonstrated procedural understanding of the algorithm multiplying 19×21. They knew "what to do" to produce the correct algorithm and arrive at the correct answer. When asked to explain where the partial product of 380 came from, they resorted to the rule that dictates a zero on the second line in two-place multiplication: *two times 19 equals 38. (Remember, it's a rule to put a zero on the second line.)*

The Blue Group, however, was struggling to explain the meaning behind the same partial product, not just following a rule: *You multiply 19×20 to get 380.... The 20 is the 21 without the one because you times the one already.* Although their understanding was incomplete as shown in their written work, their reasoning indicated a "what to do and why" understanding beyond rules learned by rote.

Sandra tried a different experiment with her class the next year, again in December. This was a class of fifth graders. She gave them an individual assignment to complete: Work this problem, and when you think you have the correct answer, explain why you think your answer is reasonable.

Sandra had the children attempt this assignment before she did any formal instruction with them in multiplication. They had, however, been taught the multiplication algorithm the previous year. Nine of the students did the computation accurately, producing either of the two results shown below. Following are their actual explanations, with their misspellings, of why their answers were reasonable.

$$\begin{array}{r} 47 \\ \times 23 \\ \hline 141 \\ 940 \\ \hline 1,081 \end{array}$$

My answer was reasonable because I added 141 and 940.

I think my answer is reasonable because I worked it out carefully.

My answer is reasonable because it is right multiplying and adding.

My answer is reasonable because I checked it.

$$\begin{array}{r} 47 \\ \times 23 \\ \hline 141 \\ 94 \\ \hline 1,081 \end{array}$$

I think it's reasonable because I added the right numbers and timed the right numbers.

I think my answer is reasonable because I took my time and check it.

I think my answer is reasonable because if you estimated 47 it would become 50 and if you estimated 23 it would become 20. 20 × 50 = 1,000 and 1,000 is close to 1,081.

I think my answer is reasonable because twenty three is almost twenty, and forty seven is about fifty and fifty times twenty is 1,000. My answer is about 1,000.

The incorrect answers students gave varied, as did their explanations. For the following responses, see if you can identify the calculation errors that the students made.

$$\begin{array}{r} 47 \\ \times 23 \\ \hline 141 \\ 840 \\ \hline 981 \end{array}$$
My answer is reasonable because I know how to mutply this way.

$$\begin{array}{r} 47 \\ \times 23 \\ \hline 141 \\ 940 \\ \hline 1,161 \end{array}$$
My answer is reasonable because I know my times tabels and I was paying attention.

$$\begin{array}{r} 47 \\ \times 23 \\ \hline 141 \\ 94 \\ \hline 1,135 \end{array}$$
I think my answer is reasonable because I understud the problem.

$$\begin{array}{r} 47 \\ \times 23 \\ \hline 141 \\ 614 \\ \hline 755 \end{array}$$
My answer is OK because if you were to take the four and the two and times it you would get eight and the 755 and rounded it you would get 800.

$$\begin{array}{r} 47 \\ \times 23 \\ \hline 134 \\ 1480 \\ \hline 1,614 \end{array}$$
Its reasonbal becouse I did what Im saposto do.

$$\begin{array}{r} 47 \\ \times 23 \\ \hline 141 \\ 1210 \\ \hline 1,351 \end{array}$$
cause I worked it out four times

$$\begin{array}{r} 47 \\ \times 23 \\ \hline 141 \\ 8,140 \\ \hline 8,281 \end{array}$$
I think my answer is reasonable because I did the problem step by step and this is what I came out with 8,281.

$$\begin{array}{r} 47 \\ \times 23 \\ \hline 141 \\ \times 00 \\ \hline 1,083 \end{array}$$
My answer is reasonable because 141 × 23 is 1,083.

Most of the students, whether their answers were right or wrong, struggled with explanations in the context of the procedures, rather than in the meaning of the operation. Only three students tried to justify their answers by referring to the numerical quantities.

THE LIMITS OF LEARNING RULES

Learning rules and applying them are common to many children's experiences in mathematics. Children are taught to add the ones first and then the tens in two-place addition, to borrow in subtraction, to put a zero in the second line in multiplication, to start from the left when doing long division, to multiply across the numerators and denominators to find the product of two fractions, to divide the numerators and denominators of fractions by the same number to simplify them, to line up the decimal points before adding, to count up the decimal places to see where to place the decimal point in the answer to a decimal multiplication problem. A blatant example of teaching for "what to do" understanding is the two-line rhyme for division of fractions:

Yours is not to reason why;
Just invert and multiply.

Sometimes the rules for algorithms do not even make sense to follow, yet children are asked not to veer from the prescribed procedure. For example, it is common for second graders to learn to add two-place numbers. This is usually first presented with no required regrouping and in vertical form:

The procedure taught is standard — first you add the ones and then you add the tens. When a teacher notices a child adding the numbers in the tens place first, the teacher will most likely redirect the child to add the ones first instead. Why? It certainly makes no difference which you add first to arrive at the correct sum.

The teaching rationale, however, is that if children learn correctly in this simpler example, they will more easily transfer their learning to the next, and more complex, task of adding when regrouping is necessary. It seems as if the decision is made in the interest of supporting the children's learning. However, teaching "what to do" in this instance is mainly to make children's arithmetic pursuits easier a few pages further in the book.

What do children perceive from being taught this rule? Many merely learn to add the numbers on the right first, and then the numbers on the left, without thinking that first they are adding "ones" and then "tens." To some children, a page of such problems looks much like a page of one-digit addition placed vertically, except that some of the numbers have been shoved together.

There is a danger in this instructional approach, even for those children who learn rules well. Such instruction teaches a child that it is okay for something not to make sense, that it is not necessary to understand the sense in what you are expected to do. This message is counterproductive to having children approach mathematics with the goal of understanding concepts and skills.

Other second graders, however, notice that they can do the exercises either way and get the same answer, but they know that they are supposed to add the right-hand column first. If they ask why, what might the teacher say? (What would you say?) The answer most likely will be a this-is-the-way-we-do-it answer or this-will-make-your-life-easier-later answer. There is no other reason why.

Lacking in this instructional approach is support for the child who is trying to make sense out of the procedure. The most obvious message to children is that arithmetic requires that you follow rules. It would be a bleak and joyless arithmetic picture for second graders if they imagined all the rules they have to face in the school years that stretch ahead! Fortunately for us, most children don't take this future view of life; hopefully, those that do will be forgiving.

Teaching "what to do" in mathematics is widespread practice. Check your students' mathematics textbooks for instances of teaching by procedural approaches. Recall your own elementary and high school mathematics learning. Can you remember being taught long division, or how to find the area of a circle, or how to multiply algebraic expressions such as $(x + 3)(2x - 5)$ and not understanding why they worked? Think back on mathematics courses you have taken. Have you ever had the experience of passing a course, perhaps even with a good grade, yet feeling you did not really understand what you were taught?

There is nothing inherently or necessarily wrong in knowing rules and being able to apply them. It is important to realize, however, that teaching procedures and teaching procedures in relation to their meaning are two very different approaches to teaching arithmetic. When children do not have the broader understanding, they may lack the flexibility to deal with situations that may differ even slightly from the particular situations learned.

The ideas in this book are firmly rooted in the belief that teaching for understanding is essential. Children must see their learning task as one of making sense of whatever they're studying. It is an irresponsible choice to teach children how to do a procedure without teaching them how to reason. Students should not be expected to do things by rote or be made to say things they do not honestly understand.

When children subtract in an example such as this:
$$\begin{array}{r} 31 \\ -16 \\ \hline \end{array}$$

it is not uncommon for them to arrive at the incorrect answer of 25. They have "learned" to subtract, but when confronted with a problem that requires regrouping, children will frequently just take the smaller from the larger — a procedure they have been practicing in appropriate situations. They are following a rule they've learned but are applying it to the wrong situation.

The following estimation question appeared on the 1982 National Assessment of Educational Progress (NAEP):

Estimate the answer to 3.04×5.3

a. 1.6

b. 16

c. 160

d. 1600

e. I don't know

The question was given on the test taken by both 13-year-olds and 17-year-olds. The item tested the ability to estimate that a bit more than 3 multiplied by a bit more than 5 is about 16. The answer of 16 is the only possible choice that makes mathematical sense. The following shows the percentages of each answer chosen in the two age groups.

	Age 13	Age 17
a. 1.6	28%	21%
b. 16	21%	39%
c. 160	18%	17%
d. 1600	23%	11%
e. I don't know	9%	12%

However, on items that required the students to perform computations with decimals, both 13-year-olds and 17-year-olds were able to do so with 80 percent to 90 percent success. The fact that so many of our graduating high school students demonstrate such a disparity between following a rule in one situation and using their reasoning ability in another is discouraging.

TEACHING "WHAT TO DO" VERSUS TEACHING "WHAT TO DO AND WHY"

Why is the practice of teaching the procedures of mathematics detached from meaning and applications of these procedures so pervasive in schools? There are a host of reasons that support the emphasis on teaching procedures. These reasons have to be understood before any widespread change in this practice will occur.

1. Learning "what to do" is usually easier than learning "what to do and why." Actually, learning "what to do" is sometimes much easier. Take the example of learning how to divide fractions. The standard algorithm is to turn the fraction on the right-hand side upside down and then multiply across the tops and bottoms. This rule is simpler to learn (and to teach) than the principle that division is the inverse of multiplication — or that dividing by a number is the same as multiplying by its multiplicative inverse, which in the case of dividing by a fraction means multiplying by its reciprocal. If the goal of the mathematics instruction is to prepare students to produce a page of correct answers, teaching the appropriate procedures will meet this goal more quickly and easily.

2. The textbooks emphasize the learning of procedures. The basic goal of textbooks and workbooks is to teach students to write correct answers, rather than to think and understand. This may sound harsh. After all, no textbook publishers or authors say or even suggest that they do not care if students think as long as they get the answers on the pages correct. Teachers' guides urge teachers to teach for the underlying understanding and often provide additional suggestions for doing so. But the reality is there, implicitly or explicitly: Children will show their understanding by being able to complete the work on the pages. Writing correct answers is the primary goal of teaching "what to do"; thinking, understanding, and seeing relationships is the primary goal of teaching "what to do and why."

3. The pressure of tests looms. Standardized tests are another reality. Teachers are accountable for students' performance, and, in some communities, test scores are published in the local newspapers. For the most part, these tests evaluate students' proficiency with mathematical procedures. The procedures themselves are more quickly and efficiently learned by focusing specifically on how to do them. The fact that students continue to do poorly on test items that require more than rote learning does not seem to be a compelling enough reason to change the current emphasis on procedural mathematics.

4. It is difficult to assess if students understand the "why" of arithmetic. It is not possible to tell what a student is thinking merely from the paper-and-pencil work they submit. Think back to the work of the Red Group in the fourth-grade class. They successfully performed the algorithm for multiplication but could explain what they had done only by resorting to rules they had learned. Judging their computational work alone would not reveal this important information.

5. Some teachers do not understand the difference between teaching procedures and teaching reasoning in arithmetic. Many teachers do not feel competent or comfortable with mathematics. Although proficient with the computational algorithms, they themselves were probably taught these algorithms without learning the underlying reasoning behind them. It has been shown that teachers generally teach as they were taught. Besides, teachers cannot teach what they do not truly understand. These circumstances seriously hinder the effort to offer children a thinking mathematics curriculum.

Other reasons could be cited as well. Parental pressure often affects what teachers teach. Changing a habit is in itself difficult, especially without consistent support. Also, students make demands. Many teachers have had the experience of explaining the meaning behind a procedure, only to have the students listen, wait patiently, and finally say, "If you'll just show me how to do it, I'll do it."

In contrast, what are the reasons for teaching arithmetic in the context of meaning and application, of teaching the "why" as well as the "what to do" in mathematics? These reasons, too, are important to consider.

1. When you understand why, your understanding and skills can be applied more easily to new tasks. For example, teaching how to add, subtract, multiply, and divide decimals from the procedural approach focuses primarily on the various rules for what to do with the decimal points in each of the operations. When you add and subtract, you line up the decimal points; when you multiply, you count up the decimal places to figure where the decimal point goes in the answer; when you divide, you move decimal points when they appear in the divisor but not when they don't appear. Should you forget the rule for one particular operation, a rule from another has no bearing.

If, however, you learn why the rules for each of the operations make sense — if you learn to reason with decimals as well as to compute with them — then you will understand which answers are sensible in any situation. The example from the NAEP test illustrates the limitations of students' learning procedures without reasoning. When learning procedurally, you not only have to memorize rules, but you also have to memorize which problems the rules work for, and often you have to memorize different rules for each type of problem.

More important than the ability to follow rules, children must develop the kind of understanding that allows them to apply their learning to the new and different situations they will be sure to meet. This requires they understand why as well as knowing how. It is not an either/or situation; both are necessary. Knowing only the rules for figuring percents is not sufficient for choosing the best savings or money market accounts, the type of mortgage that makes most sense, or the best way to finance a new car. These decisions require understanding and judgments that extend beyond algorithmic thinking.

2. Learning the meaning in arithmetic procedures makes them easier to remember. When you understand the reasons behind rules, you are not keeping a large number of unrelated rules in your memory. A common error when adding fractions is for students to add the numerators and denominators; for example: $1/2 + 1/3 = 2/5$. Students who do this are merely following a rule and, unfortunately, a rule that is totally inappropriate in this instance. Much of mathematics requires looking for the sense in the situation, not merely following a rule. It does not make sense to start with 1/2, add to it, and wind up with an answer, 2/5, that is less than the amount you started with. Yet many students do not notice this inconsistency or even think about looking for it.

Another estimation question on the NAEP test produced distressing results:

Estimate the answer to 12/13 + 7/8.

  a. 1

  b. 2

  c. 19

  d. 21

For the 13-year-olds, approximately equal numbers of students chose each of the answers, with 24 percent making the correct choice. For the 17-year-olds, 37 percent made the correct choice. (What was the thinking behind each of the incorrect choices? Why would so many of our students answer incorrectly?)

Objectives for arithmetic instruction are usually organized into bite-sized pieces. This structure is often seen as making curriculum goals more manageable. However, beware of such objectives. Teaching children in bite-sized pieces does not necessarily help them learn anything other than bite-sized skills. Some children do make connections between the individual pieces. However, children who have difficulty usually have to repeat their experience with the pieces, as if a second go-around, or a third, will produce eventual success. Such instruction has never worked and never will work.

Breaking the learning of mathematics into tiny pieces is like giving children a heap of graham cracker crumbs and wondering why they have no concept of the whole graham cracker. It's an attempt to simplify learning that may seem to be in the interest of children. But it is, in fact, counterproductive and in conflict with what is known about how children do learn. It is wrong to think that children cannot deal with meaning and complexity.

3. Learning to reason is a goal effective in itself and leads to the continued support of learning. All of us (hopefully) have experienced the joy of accomplishment that comes from figuring something out in order to produce a satisfying result. When children are taught to make sense out of mathematics, they receive support for seeing connections between ideas. Their connections can lead them to further learning in ways that do not occur when learning is approached as a series of unconnected events.

In his essay, "Nature Closely Observed" (*Daedalus*, Spring 1983), David Hawkins describes the distinction ancient Greeks made in their language between what they called "arithmetic" and what they called "logistic." He writes:

> Arithmetic was the investigation of the world of numbers; logistic was a set of rules, to be memorized, for doing rote sums, differences, products, quotients. Arithmetic was a kind of science, always fresh and open to endless investigation. Logistic was a dull art, needed for bookkeeping and other such practices, which you could learn by rote. If you understood something of arithmetic, you could easily master the rules of logistic; if you forgot those rules, you could reinvent them. What we mainly try to teach in all those early years of schooling is logistic, not arithmetic. We drag, not lead, and the efficiency of learning is scandalously low.

The true measure of the failure of teaching only the "what to do" is the feeling of mathematical incompetence and negativity toward mathematics experienced by so many otherwise highly educated people. This rejection of mathematics, sadly so common, is a clear indication that something is very wrong. It is not possible to appreciate something you do not truly understand, and the charge to teachers is a crucial one — to teach mathematics so that children are encouraged to make sense out of all they learn to do.

HAVING STUDENTS INVENT ALGORITHMS

How can children be taught arithmetic so that they will learn both what to do and why? How can children learn procedures for solving arithmetic problems? What should be the place of the standard algorithms?

The advantage of algorithms is that they provide reliable ways to compute and, therefore, simplify potentially difficult calculations. It's important for children to understand that algorithms are procedures that have been invented by people to carry out calculations that are done repeatedly. It's important for them to learn how algorithms are based in the structure and logic of our number system. Also, it's important for children to understand that one particular algorithm may be no better or more efficient than another, and that many methods, including ones they invent themselves, are equally valid. There is no need for all students to do arithmetic calculations in the same way any more than it is essential for all children to develop identical handwritings or writing styles.

A major risk of instruction that emphasizes the teaching of algorithms is the risk of interfering with children's learning to make sense of numbers. When learning algorithms, children focus on learning sequences of steps to carry out procedures, rather than on thinking and reasoning to make sense of numerical situations. Teachers know that it's common for children, when using standard algorithms, to make calculation errors and not even notice when they reach absurd solutions.

Constance Kamii's research with young children supports these findings. In "Achievement Tests in Primary Mathematics: Perpetuating Lower-Order Thinking" (*Arithmetic Teacher*, May 1991), Kamii and her coauthor, Barbara Lewis, report data gathered from comparing second graders in two schools. One of the schools offered a constructivist primary mathematics program in which teachers had children invent their own procedures for solving computation and story problems. The other school provided traditional instruction in which children were taught algorithms and given opportunities to apply them in exercises and story problems.

Kamii and Lewis compared achievement test results and collected interview data on 87 children in four second-grade classes. They analyzed the children's understanding of place value, double-column addition, story problems, and mental arithmetic and estimation. The achievement test scores from both schools were similar, with the children who received traditional instruction scoring slightly higher. For example, on the achievement-test cluster called Problem Solving, children solved routine word problems; out of a possible raw score of 15, the two groups scored 12.62 and 12.76.

However, during interviews, when children were asked to explain their thinking, to solve nonroutine problems, and to figure mentally — tasks that called for higher-order thinking — the children who had not been taught algorithms did significantly better. When asked to mentally calculate $98 + 43$ and 3×31, 17 percent of the children from the traditional classes answered each correctly; 48 percent of the children from the constructivist classes answered the first correctly and 60 percent answered the second correctly. When asked to figure how many cars were needed to take 49 children to the zoo when 5 children could fit in each car, 29 percent of the children in traditional classes answered correctly, while 61 percent of the children in constructivist classes answered correctly.

The implication of this research for the classroom is that the emphasis of arithmetic instruction should be on having students invent their own ways to compute, rather than learning and practicing procedures introduced by the teacher or textbook. Children should not only be given the challenge of figuring out their own methods for calculating but also be required to explain the reasoning for their invented procedures. In this alternative approach, time must be provided for students to present their methods to the class. Describing their methods helps students cement their thinking, while also giving students the opportunity to learn from each other.

Dee Uyeda's third graders in Mill Valley, California, learned about division through a problem-solving approach. Working in pairs and small groups, the children were asked to find solutions to division problems and to explain how they reasoned. Problems with remainders were introduced along with problems without remainders.

For example, children were asked to figure out how to share 17 cubes among four children, describe their method, and then use the cubes to test their solution. Several of the children added to get the answer. Verity, for example, wrote: *Each kid gets 4 cubes and 1 goes to the classroom. I figerd it out by 4 plus 4 is 8 and 8 plus 8 = 16.*

Joel used what he knew about multiplication. He wrote: *First I just gave one of the cubes to the good will. Then I devided 16 cubes. Because I know that 4 × 4 = 16 so 4 kids each get 4 cubes.*

Jenee drew 17 cubes in a vertical line and then counted to divide them into four parts. She wrote: *They each get 4 cubes and there will be one left over.*

Rebecca wrote: *I'm going to draw pictures of 17 cubes and four baskets. I put one cube at a time in the basket. Each basket gets four cubes if you want it to be even. Since you have sixteen cubes in all the baskets, the extra cube can go to someone.*

Elliot wrote: *I'm going to do it in 2's. I will count 8 2's and have 1 left. Each child would get 4 cubes.*

Lisa decided to use a calculator. Her paper shows how she coped with her limited understanding of decimals. She wrote: *We each get 4. And put one in the box. How I did it: On the calculater, I pressed 17 ÷ 4 = that didn't work. Then I pressed 17 ÷ 2 = 8.5. .5 is a half. Two halfs is a whole. That is 8 + 9. Half of 8 is 4. And there is one left over.*

Some of the division problems given to the children involved money. Children were asked to share $5.00 among four children. This problem was solved correctly by all groups. Michelle, Michael, Timothy, and Alana's solution was typical. They wrote: *Each person gets $1.25. We think this because if each person got a dollar there would be one dollar left. And there are four quarters in a dollar. So everybody gets a $1.25.*

As groups finished their work, they were given the problem of sharing $.50 among four children. Children found this problem more challenging. The numbers were more difficult for them and they had to decide what to do with the remainder. For their solution, the same group wrote: *We think each person gets 12¢ and there would be 2¢ left over that they could not split up, but they could buy bubble gum with the two cents and split the gum. We think this because we have to share the last two cents.*

Whenever possible, classroom situations were used to pose problems. For example, the children counted and found there were 163 pencils in the class supply. They were given the problem of figuring out how many pencils each child would receive if they were divided equally among them. Laura, Teddy, and Grace drew 27 circles, one for each student, and use tally marks to distribute the 163 pencils. They wrote: *Everybody would get 6 and there would be 1 left over. We figured this out by drawing 27 circles. Grace put talley marks in them while Teddy and Laura counted. We proved it by adding 27 6 times and adding one.*

Kendra, Bryce, and Marina wrote: *We think that each child will get 6 pencils and there will be 1 left over. We think this because we made a circle for each kid and gave them each five pencils. We added it up. It came to 135 so we took 135 from 163 and there were 28 left. There are 27 kids in the class so each kid gets one more and there is one left.*

After children solved problems, they presented their results and methods to the class and discussed the different methods used. After discussing each problem, the children were shown the standard notation for representing division: $17 \div 4$ and $4 \overline{)17}$, for example. With more experience, the children began to use the standard symbols in their own writing.

When Cathy Humphreys taught percents to her seventh and eighth graders in San Jose, California, she did not teach them how to solve the three standard types of percent problems. As described in *A Collection of Math Lessons Grades 6–8*, by Marilyn Burns and Cathy Humphreys (pages 137–182), Cathy organized the unit on percents around a series of problem-solving situations that called for applying percents. Students worked in small groups and presented their answers and methods to the class. For all problems, Cathy kept the emphasis on students' making sense of the situation and justifying the methods they used for their calculations. One such problem was the following:

> A school has 500 students. If a school bus holds 75 students, is there enough
> room on one bus for all the school's left-handed students?

Cathy gave the class the information that from 12 percent to 12 1/2 percent of Americans are left-handed. After collecting information to compare their class data with the national statistic, students worked in pairs to solve the problem. They produced a variety of solutions.

Martin and Tony, for example, wrote: *There will be 60 left-handed students on the bus. Out of 100 12% would be 12 people. Since 500 is 5× more than 100 you times 12 × 5 = 60.*

Marshal and Kiet wrote: *Yes, there are enough seats to hold all of the left-handed people because 10% of 500 is 50 people, 2% of 500 is 10 people, so 50 plus 10 is 60 people, and each bus holds 75 people.*

Liz and Audrey wrote: *To get the answer we multiplied 500 students by 12% and got 60 people and the bus can hold 75 people so there is enough room.*

Khalil and Gina took a completely different approach. They wrote: *We think you can because 75 is 15% of 500. We only have to put 12% on of the left handed people.*

Not all students' methods were appropriate. Jon and Phi, for example, divided 500 by 12 and wrote: *After we did the problem we got 41.66 and it kept on going on so we rounded it off to 42 students. We then subtracted 75 into 42 and got 33. After we got 33 seats we knew all the left handed people could get on the bus.*

Raymond, Paula, and Stephanie also used division, but they divided 12 by 500. They wrote: *Yes, 12 ÷ 500 = 0.024 so out of 500 students 24 of them are left handed so the bus can hold all the left handed people.* Even though their reasoning was erroneous, the students who used division arrived at the correct conclusion. Correct answers can hide a lack of understanding — a reason for being sure to have students explain their thinking.

This lesson occurred near the beginning of the unit, and Cathy knew to expect this sort of confusion. As stated in the *Mathematics Model Curriculum Guide* published by the California State Department of Education (1987, 14):

> We must recognize that partially grasped ideas and periods of confusion are
> a natural part of the process of developing understanding.

Cathy led a class discussion during which students presented their methods and the class discussed them. She kept the focus of the discussion on making sense of the procedures presented.

From many experiences during the unit with problems such as this one, students began to formulate their own understanding of how to work with percents. Teachers often fear that if they don't teach the standard procedures for percent problems, students won't learn to solve these types of problems. The reverse may be a greater worry, however. Teaching the standard procedures for percent problems can result in students' not being prepared to reason with percents to solve problems.

The change from teaching time-honored algorithms to having children invent their own methods requires a major shift for many teachers. It requires, foremost, that teachers value and trust children's ability and inventiveness in making sense of numerical situations, rather than on their diligence in following procedures. It requires a total commitment to making thinking and reasoning the cornerstone of mathematics instruction. Also, it requires teachers to be curious about children's ideas, to take delight in their thinking, and to encourage their inventiveness.

QUESTIONS TEACHERS ASK

Teachers working toward making such a change in their mathematics instruction have raised many questions. Following are the ones most often asked.

Should I ever teach the standard algorithms?
Just as students present their ideas for calculating, teachers can also present the standard algorithms, explain why they make sense, and offer them as another way to calculate. For older students, teachers may want to refer them to textbook presentations of algorithms and ask them to explain why the methods work.

It's important, however, that standard algorithms be presented with a light touch, not as better ways, or the "real" ways. The standard algorithms should not be mandatory procedures that students must use when calculating. The goal of instruction should be for students to find ways that are appropriate and make sense to them. In this way, arithmetic is taught through a problem-solving approach.

Also, know that your explanations of standard algorithms may not make sense to all students. Similarly, when students present their methods for calculating, it's unlikely that all the others in the class will understand them. It's difficult to follow others' reasoning. Encourage students to seek the meaning in others' ideas, continue to have students explain why their ideas make sense, and keep true to the principle that students are to do only what makes sense to them and to persist until it does.

What about learning the basic facts?
The instructional approach of having students invent their own algorithms does not eliminate the need for students to learn the basic facts. Being able to compute by any method, whether figuring an accurate answer, estimating, or justifying the reasonableness of a calculator answer, requires facility with addition and multiplication facts. Ideally, students

will learn these facts from repeated use in problem-solving situations. However, additional practice may be needed for students to commit basic facts to memory.

Several guidelines are important, however. It's not wise to focus on learning basic facts at the same time children are initially studying an operation. A premature focus gives weight to rote memorization, rather than keeping the emphasis on developing understanding of a new idea. The danger to avoid is having children believe that giving quick, right answers is really what is most important when learning arithmetic.

Also, when learning facts, children should build on what they already know and focus on strategies for computing. For example, the doubles in addition, such as 5 + 5 and 8 + 8, are easier for children to remember. It's helpful for children to see how combinations, such as 5 + 6 and 7 + 8, relate to the doubles.

What about using timed tests to help children learn their basic facts?

Teachers who use timed tests believe that the tests help children learn basic facts. This makes no instructional sense. Children who perform well under time pressure display their skills. Children who have difficulty with skills, or who work more slowly, run the risk of reinforcing wrong learning under pressure. In addition, children can become fearful and negative toward their math learning.

Also, timed tests do not measure children's understanding. Teachers concerned with the results of timed tests necessarily maintain a vigorous and steady program of drill and practice. The danger in this pedagogical focus is that an instructional emphasis on memorizing does not guarantee the needed attention to understanding. It doesn't ensure that students will be able to use the facts in problem-solving situations. Furthermore, it conveys to children that memorizing is the way to mathematical power, rather than learning to think and reason to figure out answers.

Children's own methods are often cumbersome and inefficient. Doesn't it make more sense to help them learn the standard ways for computing?

The goal for arithmetic instruction must not be efficiency but the development of children's numerical capability and confidence. If efficiency were the goal of arithmetic instruction, then teaching any method other than using a calculator would be risky, less effective, and, therefore, foolish. Math instruction should seek to help children learn to think, reason, and make sense of numbers.

What kind of arithmetic drill and practice is appropriate?

Children benefit from many and varied opportunities to apply their computation and numerical reasoning skills. An instructional approach based on developing children's thinking and reasoning should address broader goals for arithmetic competency than mere computational facility. Children should be required to analyze problem situations, decide on the operations needed, choose appropriate numbers, perform needed calculations, and evaluate results. Arithmetic practice that focuses on isolated numerical exercises does not prepare students to apply their skills to unique and diverse problems.

One challenge of teaching mathematics is to emphasize in arithmetic instruction and practice the same approaches used in other areas of the mathematics curriculum so that children explore, justify, represent, solve, discuss, use, investigate, describe, develop, and predict. These actions are the heart of doing mathematics and should be incorporated into arithmetic drill and practice.

RELATING ARITHMETIC TO REAL LIFE

Most daily math problems that adults face require reasoning that goes beyond mere computation. In real-life problems, all the needed information is rarely provided in one tidy package; often the data has to be collected, frequently from a variety of sources. There's rarely only one possible method or strategy for real-life problems; usually there are several viable ways to solve them. Often, there's no one solution that is the "right" or "best" one; life has no answer book.

One example of a real-life arithmetic problem arises annually at Thanksgiving time — the preparation of the traditional turkey. For the cook, the responsibility is a real and important one, calling for roasting a turkey that will be deliciously succulent, large enough to feed all the guests with enough leftovers for the following days, and ready to serve at the time planned for dinner.

One problem for the cook to solve is: What time should I get up in the morning to start the preparations so the turkey will be ready on time? Although this may not seem to be an arithmetic problem, it is. Of course, other kinds of decisions need to be made in this endeavor, but the tasks also require the application of arithmetic skills.

First of all, what information do you have? You would like dinner to be served at 5 p.m.; the turkey you have purchased weighs 17 pounds, 8 ounces; according to the cookbook, it takes 15 to 18 minutes a pound for the turkey to roast, the longer time for a turkey that has been stuffed. You know you plan to stuff the turkey. How much time do you estimate the turkey will need to be in the oven? How close do you need to be in this estimate?

Of course, you need to take the turkey out of the oven long enough before 5 p.m. to make the gravy and let the turkey cool before it is carved. And, of course, it will take time in the morning to make the stuffing and truss the bird, something that every cookbook cautions never to do the night before. Perhaps you have purchased packaged bread cubes for stuffing instead of planning to use leftover bread. This can save time but also may require another arithmetic decision. Each package provides enough to stuff a 12-pound bird. What do you do? Use one package and stretch it? Use two packages and cook the extra in a casserole? Use a package and a half and wrestle with some more arithmetic to adjust the recipe accordingly? How much time will all this take? And once you have made all your estimates, you then have to decide what time you really do need to get up in the morning to make it all happen on schedule.

When solving problems such as these in real life, you call on all the resources you have — knowledge, previous experience, intuition. You need to analyze, predict, make decisions, evaluate. And there are always factors of variability — how your oven behaves, how long this particular turkey will actually take to cook, how close your estimate is to the time it will take you to truss the bird.

Students would benefit from problems that reflect the spirit and intent of the Thanksgiving turkey problem. An example: How much would it cost to raise a medium-size dog to the age of 11? The problem requires several phases to get to its solution:

1. Decide what information is needed and where to collect it. What are the costs that most likely will be encountered? What others are possible? How can you find out how much food, veterinarian care, licenses, etc., will cost?

2. Choose the numerical information to use. Which of the amounts are reasonable to use? How can you predict possible changes in these costs over the 11 years? (Uncertainty and variability are always elements of problems in real life.)

3. Do the necessary calculations.

4. Use judgment to interpret the results and make decisions about a possible solution.

A problem of this sort is wonderfully suited for small groups of students. Working together gives children the opportunity to draw on the resources of other students, expand their individual views, and have the support needed for solving a complex problem. After completing the first phase, groups can compare decisions they made about what information is needed and decide if they have included all that is important. Similarly, they can later compare the information they collected and their final solutions.

There is no correct or absolutely verifiable answer to a problem such as this. However, a family that is deciding if they would like to add a dog to their household would benefit from having some sense of the potential cost. Exact accuracy is not possible, or necessary. Who can predict if your dog is going to gnaw on a leg of the dining room table or do some other damage for which repairs have to be made? How can you predict how often the family will take a vacation and will have to board the dog? What about unpredictable medical needs? There is value for students in tackling such problems for which solutions will always be somewhat uncertain, and it will be important for them to defend the reasonableness of their solutions.

Other such problems may come directly from class or school situations. How much will it cost to have a class party? How many cars will be needed for a class field trip? What needs to be done to plan a school dance? What is a fair way to organize the scheduling of the computer room for the school? How can we divide our class into two fair teams for a track and field event?

Other examples of problems include: How many Friday the 13ths can occur in one year? What is a fair allowance for a student in your grade level? How can we figure out how many buttons are on all our clothes or how many pockets we have altogether? How can we find out how many dogs live in our town? According to the newspaper shopping information, which is the most economical supermarket to buy groceries for a family of four?

In order to function in our complex and changing society, people need to be able to solve a wide variety of problems. Preparing children to become effective problem solvers requires broadening the typical classroom applications of arithmetic. The challenge is to provide motivating problems that spark children's natural curiosity and allow them to learn and use skills in situations that simulate the way arithmetic is really used in life.

HOW CAN ARITHMETIC UNDERSTANDING BE DEVELOPED?

Well-rounded instruction in arithmetic should be organized so that it:
- introduces arithmetic concepts to students in real-world contexts
- develops number sense and understanding of relationships between the operations
- integrates arithmetic with the other strands of the mathematics curriculum

- builds on children's own ways of thinking and language for describing their thinking
- relies heavily on estimating and mental computation
- encourages children to invent their own ways to do arithmetic calculation

The rest of Part III offers suggestions for teaching arithmetic organized into nine sections: Beginning Number Concepts, Place Value, Addition and Subtraction, Multiplication, Division, Extending Multiplication and Division, Fractions, Decimals, and Percents. The teaching ideas in each section present whole class lessons, independent activities, and ways to assess students' understanding. They are designed to serve as models for classroom instruction that builds children's understanding, confidence, and competence in arithmetic.

INTRODUCTION

Mathematics instruction in the primary grades should make numbers an integral part of children's classroom experiences. Children need many opportunities to identify quantities, see relationships between numbers, and learn about the operations of addition and subtraction. When developing beginning concepts of number, children benefit from exploring concrete materials and relating numbers to problem situations. They also benefit from talking about their ideas and hearing how other children think. The learning activities should be varied in their contexts and involve the children directly in thinking, reasoning, and solving problems.

WHOLE CLASS LESSONS

Using Classroom Situations

Everyday classroom situations provide many opportunities for solving math problems. Relating math to classroom routines helps children apply mathematics in a real setting and helps them see the usefulness of mathematics.

For example, daily attendance taking can suggest a math problem. Once you ascertain how many children are absent, ask the children to figure how many are present.

When the children need partners for an activity or are lining up in pairs, have them figure out if everyone in the class will have a partner or if there will be an extra person. Also, ask them to figure how many pairs there will be.

If some children have returned their field trip permission slips, have the children figure out how many more slips need to be returned.

If children need recording booklets for a project, have them make them by folding 12-by-18-inch newsprint in half and making a cover from construction paper. Ask the children first to figure out how many sheets they need so they'll have twelve pages to write on. (Decide first if children are to write on right-hand pages only or on both sides of the paper.)

Have the children figure out how many pairs of scissors are needed if each child shares a pair with a partner.

Show the children a can of juice, a box of crackers, a bag of apples, or some other item with which they are familiar. Ask them to guess how much it costs. After each guess, give a clue by telling the children whether the item costs more or less than the amount that was guessed.

If each pair of children needs one die for a math activity, have them figure out how many dice are needed in all.

In all situations, don't settle just for answers. Have children explain their reasoning.

Number Games

Games are fun and provide a relaxed setting in which children can think about number relationships. The following games give children experience with comparing, addition, and subtraction, and also provide informal experience with ideas of statistics and probability.

How Many Reds?

This is a two-person card game. Introduce the game by having two children play while the rest of the class watches. Tell the children that they need 20 playing cards, Ace through 10 of a red suit and a black suit. They also need a recording sheet. Show them how to fold a piece of newsprint into 10 areas, as shown:

Have two children model how to play. One child mixes the cards by placing them face down and stirring them, then deals them out, 10 to each person. They each count the number of reds they have, and one child records in one space on their paper. Take this opportunity to introduce or reinforce the standard way to record addition: 4 + 6, for example.

Now the other child mixes and deals the cards. Again, they count the number of red cards they have, and the other child records on their paper. When you feel comfortable that the class understands how to play, distribute cards and have all the children play in pairs.

Although it is obvious to adults that the total of red cards in both children's hands is always 10, this may not be obvious to the children. From playing this game, they have the chance to become familiar with the addends of 10 in a game context.

For a statistical extension, make a class graph of the addends children recorded. By having the children speculate about why some pairs of addends come up more often than others, the activity incorporates thinking about probability as well.

Empty the Bowl

For this activity, you need 20 cubes or tiles in a small bowl and one die. Explain to the children that you are going to roll the die and that the number that comes up tells how many cubes to remove from the bowl. Ask them how many rolls they think it will take to empty the bowl. Allow all children who have ideas to share them with the class.

Demonstrate the game. Choose a child to come to the board and record the numbers as they're rolled. Have different children take turns rolling the die and reporting the number of cubes you are to remove. (You don't have to go out exactly; that is, if there are 2 cubes left in the bowl, and a 3 is rolled, it's okay to remove the cubes so the bowl is empty.) Once the bowl is empty, you may want to ask the children to figure the sum of the rolls recorded on the board.

Leave the information about the rolls on the board, and play the game again several more times until you're sure the children understand the activity. Then ask the children some questions to probe their thinking about the game so far. Although all children won't be able to answer these questions, raising the issues sets the stage for the kind of thinking you would like them to do. Also, their responses give you information about what individual children understand.

> What do you think is the most number of rolls it could possibly take to empty the bowl?
> Why couldn't the bowl be emptied in just one roll?
> Why couldn't it be emptied in two rolls?
> What do you think is the fewest number of rolls you need to empty the bowl?

On the board, list the numbers from 1 to 20, and put tally marks to indicate how many rolls it took you to empty the bowl in each of the demonstration games. Tell the children that now they are to play five games in pairs and keep track of the numbers that come up each time, as you did on the board. After five games, they are to come up and tell you how many rolls it took for each game so you can mark the class graph. Recording on a class graph gives the children experience with collecting statistical data.

For children who finish their five games quickly, have them play some more and contribute additional information to the class graph. After all the children's data has been recorded, again discuss the questions you posed previously. Push the class to make a prediction about the fewest number of rolls they think generally would be needed to empty the bowl. Opinions may differ, and that's okay. Children can test their hypotheses on the *Empty the Bowl* menu task.

Introducing Addition and Subtraction with Word Problems

When children are learning about the operations of addition and subtraction, it's helpful for them to see the connection between these processes and the world around them. Story problems accustom children to looking at groups of people or objects, help them see the actions of joining and separating, and give them experience figuring out sums and differences. Have children act out stories that involve addition and subtraction, either by pretending or using concrete materials to represent situations.

Acting Out Addition and Subtraction Stories

Tell stories in which the children pretend to be animals, people, or things. The following are examples:

____, ____, ____, and ____ are clowns at the circus. ____, ____, and ____ are more clowns who also come to perform at the circus. How many clowns are in the circus?

____, ____, and ____ are birds sitting in a tree. ____ and ____ flew away. How many birds are left in the tree?

____ put four books on the reading table. ____ put two more books on the table. How many books are on the table altogether?

____, ____, ____, and ____ are standing near the door. ____ and ____ sat down. How many are still standing near the door?

Once the children are comfortable acting out stories, model how to record stories symbolically. Write the addition and subtraction sentences so the children can see how symbols are used to represent the situations you present. When children understand how to connect stories and symbols, have them write arithmetic sentences to describe other stories.

Addition and Subtraction Stories with Cubes

Tell stories and have the children use interlocking cubes, such as Snap, Multilink, or Unifix cubes, to represent the people, objects, or animals in the stories. Have the children work on construction paper or tag or prepare counting boards on which you have drawn trees, oceans, corrals, etc., to correspond to the stories you tell. The following are examples:

There were four ladybugs and three ants in the grass. How many were there altogether?

We gave our rat six kibbles. He ate four of them. How many kibbles were left?

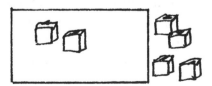

There were four horses in the pasture. Two more horses wandered into the pasture. How many horses were there in all?

Seven cars were in the supermarket parking lot. Two people came out of the store and drove away. How many cars are left?

Beyond Word Problems

While routine word problems can serve to introduce children to the language and symbolization of addition and subtraction, other kinds of number problems require children to organize and stretch their thinking. Nonroutine problems contribute to building children's number sense and strengthening their ability to deal with new situations. The following suggests one problem-solving experience that supports children's learning about numbers.

The Necklace Lesson

This lesson involves the children with pattern, estimation, addition, graphing, and comparison of volume. To prepare for the lesson, mix red food coloring with alcohol, and dye enough macaroni to fill a pint jar. Fill another jar with macaroni that hasn't been dyed. Cut lengths of string long enough for necklaces, and dip one end of each in glue to make it easier for children to string the macaroni.

Make a necklace for the children using the following pattern: one red, one white, two reds, one white, three reds, one white, and so on, ending with six red and one white. Explain the pattern as you make the necklace. Show how to tie the ends of the string.

Tell the children they each are to make a necklace following the same pattern. Before they get started, discuss the following questions:

Do you think I've brought enough macaroni?

Do you need more red or more white macaroni for your necklace? Why do you think that?

When you've all made your necklaces, will we have more red macaroni left over, more white, or about the same of each?

How would you describe the pattern you'll be using?

After the children have made their necklaces, ask the same questions again. Have the children compare the amounts of the remaining macaroni.

On another day, tell the children that they'll have the chance to make another necklace using the same macaroni pattern, but with a color other than red. Have them record on a class graph to indicate whether they would like to use yellow, blue, green, orange, or purple. The children can either sign their names or post colored squares on which they've written their names.

```
What color macaroni?
Yellow  □ □ □□ □
Blue    □ □ □
Green   □ □ □ □□□□□
Orange  □ □
Purple  □□ □□□□□□□□□□ □
```

Process the graph, discussing which color was chosen most, which was chosen least, how many children chose each color, etc. Then talk about how much of each color macaroni the class will need. Use the jar of red macaroni as a reference. The children's responses will reveal whether they can relate information from a graph to the practical problem of deciding on quantities of macaroni to dye.

Finally, dye the macaroni, using food coloring and alcohol, showing the children how to mix colors to get green, orange, and purple. Tell them they'll be able to make their necklaces the next day when the dyed macaroni has dried. Also tell them that in the meantime, they are to figure out how many white and how many colored macaroni they each need. You may want to prepare a sheet on which they can record their solutions and thinking. The next day, have children make their new necklaces.

How many whites? How many _____? Show your work.

Using Children's Books

Children's books can be valuable resources for math lessons. They capture children's imagination and interest and are effective vehicles for stimulating children's mathematical thinking and reasoning. The following suggestions model the kinds of activities that can be initiated from simple counting books. The five books mentioned in this section are a very few of the many children's books that help to develop young children's beginning number concepts. Two Math Solutions Publications books that present teaching lessons using children's literature are *Math and Literature, Book One (K–3),* by Marilyn Burns, and *Math and Literature, Book Two (K–3),* by Stephanie Sheffield.

The Rooster's Journey

Rooster's Off to See the World, by Eric Carle, tells the story of a rooster who decided one day that he wanted to travel. Strikingly illustrated with colorful collages, the book describes how the rooster was joined by two cats, three frogs, four turtles, and five fish. A problem arose, however, when night fell and the animals realized that no plans had been made for food or shelter. They all became hungry, cold, and afraid and decided to return home.

Read the book and then present the children with the problem of figuring out how many animals altogether set out to see the world. Tell the children they need to show how they figure out the answer and explain their reasoning. Children who have difficulty writing can dictate their explanations.

One Gorilla and More

One Gorilla, by Atsuko Morozumi, received the New York Times Best Illustrated Children's Book Award. This counting book begins, "Here is a list of things I love." The list includes one gorilla, two butterflies, three budgerigars, four squirrels, and on up, to ten cats. The gorilla appears on each page and children take delight in the illustrations.

This book suggests an extended version of the problem presented for *Rooster's Off to See the World.* Ask the children to figure out how many things the author loved, show their work, and explain their reasoning. For children who find the numbers too difficult, suggest the alternative problem of figuring out how many things he loved that could fly. This simplifies the problem to adding 2 + 3 + 9, the numbers of butterflies, budgerigars, and birds.

Other children's books also suggest this same problem: *1 Hunter,* by Pat Hutchins, and *The Midnight Farm,* by Reeve Lindbergh, for example. There are others as well. Although the mathematical thinking required for all these books is similar, the change in context makes each a new problem for the children. Giving these problems to children over time gives you the opportunity to assess their progress.

Making Books with Dots

Donald Crews begins *Ten Black Dots* with a question: "What can you do with ten black dots?" He answers the question by incorporating black dots into colorful illustrations of everyday objects, beginning with one dot and continuing up to ten dots. Simple rhymes accompany the graphics. The book begins:

> One black dot can make a sun
> or a moon when day is done.
> Two dots can make the eyes of a fox
> or the eyes of keys that open locks.

After reading the book several times, ask the children what they might do with one, two, three, and so on, up to ten black dots. After all have had the opportunity to make their suggestions, have them begin making their own Ten Black Dots books. Plan for children to complete a page or two a day. Black adhesive dots, 3/4-inch in diameter, are available at office supply stores and easy for children to use. Newsprint with an unlined top portion for illustrations and a lined bottom portion for their writing works well.

When children have completed and shared their books, have them figure out how many dots they each used. As for all problems, ask the children to show their work and explain their reasoning. To help them begin their explanations, write on the board: We each needed ___ dots. I got my answer by _____. More able children may be interested in figuring how many dots were used by the entire class.

INDEPENDENT ACTIVITIES (MENU)

Build a Stack

You need: interlocking cubes

This activity is suitable for a small group of six to eight children. The children need interlocking cubes. Give a variety of directions that use more and less, and have the children build the stacks. For example:

"Build a stack that has one more than four."
"Build a stack that has two more than six."
"Build a stack that has one less than seven."

An easier version: "Build a stack of four. Now build a stack that has one more than four. How many did you use?"

More of a challenge: "What number do you think is one less than five? Let's build a stack and see."

Grow and Shrink

You need: cubes
a cube numbered from 1 to 6 (or 0 to 5)

The children take turns rolling a numbered cube. You and the children (who are able) call out the number rolled. Each child builds the number rolled on his or her working space paper.

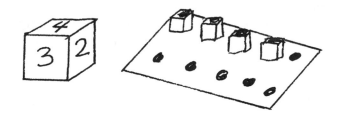

Yarn Shapes

You need: yarn
tiles

Each child cuts a piece of yarn as long as his or her arm and then uses the yarn to make a shape, to cover it with tiles, or to count. They make and cover other shapes. Ask the children to see what they can discover about shapes that hold more tiles and those that hold fewer tiles.

Spill and Compare

You need: Two-Color Counters

Children take a given number of counters, spill them, and record which color comes up more or if there is an equal number of each. They keep track by making tallies on a chart as shown:

More red	Same	More yellow

Have children play the game with different numbers of counters and notice which numbers never come up with both colors the same.

Trace and Compare

You need: tiles

Have children trace around one of their shoes. Then have them predict which would take more tiles — to cover their foot shape or to place tiles on the outline like a fence. They then measure with the tiles to find out.

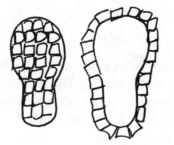

They repeat by tracing other shapes: a book, their hand, a chalkboard eraser, etc.

Snap It

You need: interlocking cubes

Children each make a train of interlocking cubes using the same number. On the signal "Snap," they break their train into two parts and hold them behind their backs. They take turns showing the cubes in one hand and then in the other while the other children say the combination.

Extension: When they are able, each child shows the cubes in one hand and the others predict how many are in the other hand. The child then shows the other cubes for the children to check. Also, have children record addition sentences to describe how they broke apart their trains.

$$\begin{array}{r} 1 \\ +5 \\ \hline 6 \end{array} \quad \begin{array}{r} 3 \\ +3 \\ \hline 6 \end{array} \quad \begin{array}{r} 2 \\ +4 \\ \hline 6 \end{array}$$

Grab Bag Subtraction

You need: a partner
cubes or tiles
a paper bag

Children work in pairs. Select a number for the children to work with. One child fills the paper bag with the appropriate number of cubes or tiles. The other reaches in and takes out some, showing how many have been removed. Both predict how many they think are left. Then they check their predictions, and each records the equation.

Extension: Have the children use a 5–10 die or spinner to generate the number of cubes or tiles to put in the bag.

Empty the Bowl

You need: a partner
　　　　　a bowl with 20 cubes
　　　　　one die

Choose a test number and see if you will empty the bowl in that many rolls.
For each game, one person rolls the die and the other records the numbers that
come up. For each roll of the die, remove the number of cubes shown. After
rolling the die the number of times of your test number, record "Yes" or "No"
to indicate whether the bowl was emptied.

ASSESSING UNDERSTANDING OF BEGINNING NUMBER CONCEPTS

Observing Children

Observing children in class discussions and when they are working on independent activities provides information about their understanding of number concepts. Children's verbal
responses to questions and reactions to others' ideas reveal their levels of interest and
understanding. Also, children's written work can be an indication of their thinking, especially when they've explained their reasoning processes.

It's important to look not only at whether children's answers to problems are right or
wrong, but how they arrived at their solutions. Was the answer appropriate or reasonable?
Did they have a strategy for finding a solution or were they guessing? What does their
work reveal about their understanding of different size numbers?

To continue to learn about children's thinking, continually probe by asking questions
such as the following:

　　　How did you figure that out?
　　　Are you sure?
　　　Can you explain why you're sure?
　　　What made you think of that?
　　　Can you think of another way to figure it out?

For example, seeing how children approach the problems from books such as *One Gorilla*
tells you about their comfort with numbers and their ability to calculate. Looking at their
solutions to the number of macaroni needed in *The Necklace Lesson* can tell you about their
ability and comfort with larger numbers. Observing their strategies as they play *Grow and
Shrink* can reveal their understanding about relationships between numbers.

Individual Assessments

The following assessment is adapted from *Mathematics Their Way,* by Mary Baratta-Lorton, Addison-Wesley Publishing Co., Inc.

TEACHER	CHILD	INTERPRETATION
"Count five blocks into my hand."	Child is able to do so.	Appropriate level. Shows ability to count with 1-to-1 correspondence.
	Child is unable to do so.	Inappropriate level. Try it with three blocks. If this is not possible, do not go on.
"How many blocks do I have in my hand?"	Child says "five" without counting.	Appropriate level. Child conserves for five. Ask next question.
	Child must recount.	Inappropriate level. Child doesn't conserve. Try with three blocks.
Hide some blocks in one hand and show the others. Ask: "How many am I hiding?"	Child answers instantly, correctly, and confidently.	Appropriate level. Check several other combinations, and then assess for six. As long as the level is appropriate, continue assessing up to ten.
	Child guesses wrong, or cannot guess, or does not know instantly with confidence.	Try several other combinations to make sure level is inappropriate. If so, try again with three blocks.

The assessment gives a general idea about children's understanding of number relationships. Also, children's responses indicate their confidence with number combinations.

INTRODUCTION

*O*ur place value system, which allows us to represent any number with just 10 digits, is not simple for children to understand. Children need to learn to make groups of 10 items and then count those groups as if they were single items. They must learn that digits have different values, depending on their position in numbers. The difference between 36 and 63, for example, though obvious to adults, is not always easy for young children to understand.

When learning about place value, children benefit from grouping concrete materials into tens and hundreds and linking their experience to standard numerical symbols. Children also benefit from involvement with problem situations that call for estimating large numbers of things. This section suggests whole class lessons and independent activities in which children estimate and count large quantities of objects, look for patterns in the numbers on a 0–99 chart, learn several games, and explore geometric shapes. While the activities focus on the idea of place value, they also provide experience with probability, measurement, patterns, and logic.

WHOLE CLASS LESSONS

Counting Large Quantities

Engage the class in a variety of situations in which they estimate and count large numbers of objects. Plan lessons in which children figure out the following:
- how many buttons or pockets there are on all their clothing
- how many feet or thumbs or fingers there are in class altogether
- how many feet there would be if the adults living in all the children's houses came to the class at the same time
- how many cubes there would be altogether if each child put a handful in a box
- how many letters there are altogether in all the children's first or last names
- how many books are in the class library

Spacing such explorations throughout the year makes it possible to assess changes that occur over time in children's thinking about large numbers. It's important to remember that teaching children the usefulness and logic of grouping objects into tens to make sense of large quantities should not be a lesson objective. It's a long-range goal that must not be attached to one day's activity. Children need many experiences over time to learn to connect the idea of counting by tens (which many can do by rote) to our place value system of representing quantities symbolically.

While children are learning, it's important they feel that their own methods for counting large numbers of objects are also valid. The pedagogical challenge is to make the connection between grouping by tens and our number system but to do so with a light touch. The goal is for children to have the chance to consider the connection, understand it, see its usefulness, and eventually use their experience to construct an understanding of our place value system for themselves.

The following describes how two such explorations might be conducted in a classroom.

How Many Fingers?

Pose the problem of figuring out how many fingers there are on the children's hands altogether. Ask students for their ideas about ways to solve the problem. Also, ask children for estimates of what the answer might be.

Tell the class that when solving a problem, it sometimes helps to try a similar but smaller problem. Ask seven or eight children to come to the front of the room and hold up their hands. Ask the class for different ways to count their fingers. Typically, children will suggest counting by twos, fives, tens, and, perhaps, by ones. As each way is suggested, have the class count aloud in unison.

Then ask how many children would be needed for there to be 100 fingers altogether. For some children, this will be obvious; others may be uncertain or have no idea at all. If 10 children are suggested, have that many come to the front; otherwise use whatever number is offered. Go through the process of counting by twos, fives, and tens, and even ones, if the children want, to see how many fingers there are.

Ask: Are there enough children in class to have 200 fingers? More than 200 fingers? More than 300? Keep the discussion going, bringing up children to count and verify, as long as the class is interested. Record the final answer on the board. You may want to write this in several different ways; for example, two hundred and seventy, 27 tens, 100 + 100 + 70, 270.

How Many Pockets?

Ask the students how many pockets they think are on all the clothing they're wearing that day. Have them discuss this among themselves in pairs or small groups. Then have volunteers give estimates and have them explain why they think their estimates make sense.

Give the children interlocking cubes, such as Multilink, Snap, or Unifix cubes, and ask them to put one cube in each of their pockets. Collect the extra cubes, and then have the children remove the cubes from their pockets, snap them into trains, count how many they each have, and compare with the others in their group.

To figure out how many pockets there are in all, ask the pairs or groups to 10 cubes and bring the trains to the front of the room. Have the class count by tens. Then have children bring up their extra cubes and use them to trains of 10. Again, have them count aloud by tens. Then have them count u. Record the final answer on the board to connect their counting to the numerical rep. tion; for example, 6 tens and 8 ones = 68.

Tell the children they'll repeat the activity for the next few days to see if the number of pockets changes. Keep the activity going for as many days as the children are interested.

Note: Be aware that in a lesson such as this one, you are imposing on the children the structure of organizing by tens. It may seem that grouping by tens is the most efficient way to count the cubes, but left to their own choices, children may prefer to group objects in other ways, by twos or fives, for example. The method of grouping by tens is convenient because of its relation to our place value system; however, do not expect this reason to be compelling or even make sense to all the students.

When doing other explorations, such as figuring the number of buttons or books, vary the materials. Use beans, for example, to represent buttons, and group them into tens in small cups. Use tally marks to record the number of feet in the room and, after counting by twos, draw circles to group them into tens.

Class discussions are useful for giving children opportunities to hear each other's ideas and also for helping you assess their understanding. Raise questions such as the following for children to discuss:

> If you group the cubes (or whatever) by twos or fives or tens, will you get the same number when you count how many there are altogether? Always? Explain your thinking.

> Some people say it's easy to count by tens. Why do you think they say that?

> Which takes fewer numbers — to count to 100 by fives or by tens? Why? How else can you count to 100?

Using Money

Children's interest in money makes it a useful model for place value. The following game takes advantage of children's familiarity with money. Before introducing the game, however, review for the children the relationships of the denominations to each other.

Race for $1.00

For each group of four, prepare a baggie with about 60 pennies, 40 dimes, and 4 pretend dollar bills. Do not distribute them until you've explained the rules and played a game with one of the students.

To play, children take turns rolling the dice. They add the numbers that come up and take that many pennies. Then they pass the dice to the next person. If children have enough pennies to exchange for a dime, they may do so only when the dice are in their possession. The winner is the first person to get a dollar.

Play the game with a child to model the rules. Then provide the materials for each group and have them begin to play. Circulate to make sure they are playing correctly. Notice if children take shortcuts; that is, when they roll a sum larger than 10, such as 12, some may take 1 dime and 2 pennies rather than count 12 pennies. Others in the group may question this and ask if it's allowed. Respond that shortcuts are allowed only if everyone in the group understands what is being done and agrees.

A Logic Game

The game of *Digit Place* appears on page 110 in the Logic section. The game focuses children on the importance of the digits' positions in numbers, while also challenging them to think logically. In the simpler version described below, the game is played with two digits instead of three.

Digit Place

To introduce the game, have the children gather near the chalkboard. Tell them that they'll learn a game in which they are to guess the two-digit number you are thinking about. Check to see if the children know what is meant by "two-digit number." Ask for examples, and then ask if anyone can explain what "digit" means. Also, be sure to point out that although numbers such as 55 and 99 are two-digit numbers, they aren't allowed in this game; the digits have to be different.

Play a practice game. Tell the class your number is 17. Show them how you would give clues for several pretend guesses. Tell them that each clue reveals how many of their digits are correct and how many of those are in the correct place. Then play a real game with the class, having children guess while you record the clues. Each time you give clues, ask the children what they know for sure. This

Guess	Digit	Place
74	1	0
16	1	1
84	0	0

encourages them to reflect on what the clues mean before they charge ahead with new guesses.

Play a game or two each day for several days to help the children learn the rules.

Looking for Patterns

Writing numbers on a 10-by-10 grid arranges them in an orderly way, making it possible for children to see patterns and relationships in our counting system. This activity focuses children on patterns in the numbers from 0 to 99.

Patterns on the 0–99 Chart

You need a 10-by-10 grid that is large enough for all the children to see. On the chart, write the numerals from 0 to 25.

Then ask children questions such as the following:

What number would come next?

Where do you think 40 will land? 50? 53? 63?

(Point to a square.) What number do you think belongs here?

Continue until you've filled in the chart completely.

Direct the children to study the chart quietly for a few moments and look for patterns. Then have them share what they noticed.

Typically, children will see patterns in the rows and columns. For example, the first column has all numbers that end in 0; all the numbers in the bottom row start with 9. Children don't often look for diagonal patterns. You can prompt this by saying: I see a pattern in the numbers that have both digits the same.

Talk about other patterns, such as odd and even numbers, numbers with 6 in the ones place, and numbers for which the two digits add to 10. As you talk about these ideas, write them on the board.

    Odd numbers
    Even numbers
    Numbers with both digits the same
    Numbers with a 6 in them
    Numbers whose digits add to 10

Distribute recording sheets with 0–99 charts on them. Have pairs choose one of the number descriptions you've recorded and color in the numbers. Together, they should write a description about the patterns of the numbers they've colored.

INDEPENDENT ACTIVITIES (MENU)

These activities use the idea of place value in a variety of situations that give children experience with several strands of the curriculum. Some of the activities require that children make an estimate. It's important to talk with the children about estimating to make sure they don't think estimates must be exact. Let the children know that the purpose of estimating is to give them the chance to think about numbers, better understand what they mean, and make guesses that they can then check.

Race for $1.00

You need: a partner
           baggie with dimes, pennies, and dollars
           two dice

Players take turns rolling the dice and taking that many pennies. The game continues until one player collects 10 dimes and exchanges them for $1.00. Record how much each player has at the end of the game.

Digit Place

You need: a partner

One player chooses a two-digit number. (The digits must be different.) The other player tries to guess the number. For each guess, the first player tells how many digits in the guess are correct and how many of the correct digits are in the correct place. (If only one digit is correct, do not tell which it is; just say that one is correct.)

A chart helps:

Guess	Digit	Place
27	0	0
13	1	1

Play again so that the other player can guess.

Stars

You need: a partner

a way to time 1 minute

Predict how many stars you think you can draw in 1 minute. Record your prediction.

Make stars while your partner times 1 minute.

Count. Record your answer. Describe how you counted.

Fill the Cube

You need: one Unifix cube

popcorn

lentils

Predict how many kernels of popcorn you think will fill the cube. Record your prediction.

Fill the cube.

Count. Record your answer and describe how you counted.

Repeat with lentils. Use your popcorn count to make your estimate of lentils.

Five Tower Game

You need: a partner
interlocking cubes
two dice

Roll the dice and take that many cubes. Snap them into a tower. Take turns doing this until you each have five towers.

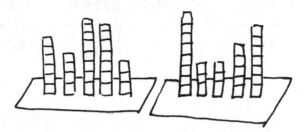

Each of you now figures out how many cubes you have.

Compare your counts. See if one of you has more than the other or if you both have the same number of cubes. Report your findings.

Number Puzzle

You need: a 10-by-10 grid (duplicate 1/2-Inch Squares — see blackline masters
— and trim into 10-by-10 grid)
scissors
envelope

Write the numbers from 0 to 99 on your grid.

Cutting only on the lines, cut the chart into seven interesting pieces. Write your name on the back of each piece.

Test your puzzle by fitting the pieces back together.

Put your puzzle pieces into an envelope. Write your name on the envelope, and place it in the puzzle box for others to try.

Choose someone else's puzzle to put together. When you solve it, sign your name on the back of the envelope. Return the puzzle to the puzzle box.

Pinch a 10

You need: kidney beans

Take a pinch of kidney beans and count. Did your pinch have fewer than 10, more than 10, or exactly 10? Make a chart as shown and record with a tally mark. Do this 10 times.

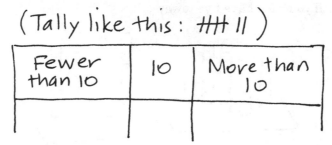

(Tally like this: ℍ‖)

Fewer than 10	10	More than 10

Write a statement about your results.
Repeat and see if you get better at pinching tens. Or pinch popcorn.

Make a Shape

You need: a partner
crayon or marker
Color Tiles

On a plain sheet of paper, draw a shape that both of you think can be covered with 32 tiles.
Test with Color Tiles. Use 10 of one color, then use 10 of another color, and so on, until your shape is covered.
Record the number of tiles you used.
Try this activity a second time, drawing a new shape that you think can also be covered with 32 tiles. Again, cover, count, and record.

Coloring 0–99 Patterns

You need: a partner
              0–99 charts (see blackline masters)
              six direction strips (in envelope)

Pick one pattern direction strip from the envelope. Together, read the directions and decide which numbers to color. Each of you should color your own sheet.
     Write a description of the pattern of the numbers you colored.
     Pick another strip and repeat on another 0–99 chart.
       Note: The following are the directions for the six strips:
     Color all the numbers with both digits the same.
     Color all the numbers with digits that add to 8.
     Color all the numbers with first digits that are larger than the second digits.
     Color all the numbers with a 4 in them.
     Color all the even numbers.
     Color all the numbers with digits that add to 10.

ASSESSING UNDERSTANDING OF PLACE VALUE

Observing Children

When children are working on the independent tasks, circulate and observe them. Also, whole class discussions can help reveal what children understand.

With *Race for $1.00,* notice how children organize their pennies and dimes. See if they exchange when possible and if they take shortcuts, such as taking one dime and two pennies when they roll a sum of 12. Interrupt them to ask who is winning and see how they compare their two quantities.

With *Stars, Fill the Cube,* and *Five Tower Game,* see which children group the objects into tens, and which group by twos and fives or persist in counting by 1s. Ask children how many groups they would have if they grouped by tens. Don't insist that children group by tens; there's no point in children doing something mechanically without understanding. Encourage them, talk about grouping by tens, but respect their need to do what makes sense to them.

In *Fill the Cube,* ask children how they could use the information from their popcorn count to predict how many lentils the cube will hold.

When children count the beans in *Pinch a 10,* notice how they count — by ones, twos, or some other way.

Notice how children fit together the pieces from each other's puzzles from *Number Puzzle.* Ask questions such as the following: What clues do you look for? How will you know when the puzzle is together correctly? What's easy and what's hard about the puzzle?

Individual Assessments

Choose from the following suggestions to find out what children understand:

1. Give children 24 or so counters and ask them to put them into groups of 10. When they've done this, ask three questions:

    a. How many groups do you have?

    b. How many extras?

    c. How many counters are there altogether?

Children who cannot tell without counting them one by one are not making use of grouping by tens and need more experience.

2. The following assessment appears in Part 1 of *Mathematics: Assessing Understanding,* a three-part videotape series I produced for Cuisenaire (see the bibliography).

    a. Show the child 16 counters and ask him or her to make a drawing of them.

    b. Then ask the child to write 16 with numbers on the same sheet of paper.

    c. Circle the 6 in 16 and ask the child to indicate in the drawing what 6 means. (Children usually correctly circle 6 counters.)

    d. Then ask what "this part" means, circling the 1 in 16. (Some children correctly circle 10 counters; others erroneously circle 1 counter, indicating that they need more experience.)

    e. Then ask what "the whole thing" means, circling the 16. (Most children will circle all 16 counters.)

    f. For children who only circled 1 counter in part d, ask why "these" (the 9 remaining counters) were not circled.

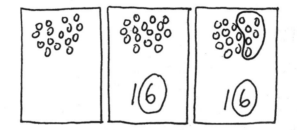

3. Check to see if children can count by tens to 100. To 150 or higher.

4. Give children two or three small cards with a different numeral on each. Ask them to arrange the numerals to make the largest number possible. Ask for the smallest.

5. Dictate several numbers for children to write.

6. Show the child several numbers to read aloud.

Addition and Subtraction

INTRODUCTION

*T*his section focuses on having children use and compare two-digit numbers. The activities model ways to involve children with addition and subtraction of two-digit numbers in the context of problem-solving activities. The activities draw on ideas from various strands of the math curriculum: number, probability and statistics, geometry, and measurement. In this way, while children are developing their understanding of number, they have opportunities to broaden their view of mathematics and see relationships among the different areas of the math curriculum.

In all activities, the emphases are on having children invent their own methods for adding and subtracting and having them explain their strategies, both orally and in writing. As a regular part of their work, children are expected to justify their answers and explain why they make sense. The standard algorithm is not taught; rather, children are encouraged to find ways to represent their own procedures symbolically.

This approach differs from typical textbook instruction. Rather than a steady diet of worksheet practice, this approach suggests a steady diet of problem-solving explorations. Although the children's methods may not be as efficient as the standard algorithms, the pedagogical choice is to risk sacrificing efficiency for the sake of understanding. The credo for the children is: Do only what makes sense to you, and persist until it does.

WHOLE CLASS LESSONS

A Statistical Investigation

Statistical investigations offer rich opportunities for children to develop their number sense. In this lesson, the lengths of the children's names are organized into two class graphs. The children interpret the data and compare the number of letters needed for their first and last names.

The Name Graphs

Ask each child to write his or her first name on a 3-by-3-inch Post-it.™ List the numerals from 1 to 10 on the board, and have the children, one at a time, come to the board and post their names next to the numeral that indicates the number of letters. In this way, the Post-its™ are organized into a graph.

Discuss the graph with the children. This is a good opportunity to introduce the ideas of range and mode. On the graph shown, the range is from 3 to 8. The mode is 5 because there are more names with 5 letters than with any other number of letters. You might want to talk about the idea of average by asking the children how long they think a "typical" name is.

Have the children estimate how many letters they think are in all their names together. Talk about how they might determine the total from the information on the graph. Have students work in groups to solve the problem and then share their answers and strategies.

To confirm the total concretely, and also give children experience with the idea of our place value structure, have each child make a train using as many interlocking cubes as letters in his or her name. Ask groups to organize their cubes into trains of 10 and bring the 10s to the front of the room. Then call for the extra cubes, making additional trains of 10. Count the 10s and extras to arrive at the total.

Then give each student another Post-it.™ Have them write their last names, and organize these into another graph. Ask the students to look at both graphs and describe how the shapes of the data compare. Ask if they can tell from looking at the graphs if there are more letters in their first or last names altogether. Have volunteers offer their opinions and explain their reasoning.

At a later time, as an independent task, have students use the information on the graph to figure how many letters there are in their last names altogether and find the difference between the totals of letters in their first and last names.

Measurement Activities

In these activities, children's measurements provide both a purpose for adding and subtracting and the numerical data to use. Although children will be working with different numbers, and therefore arriving at different answers, they are thinking about the same problem situations.

How Much Ribbon?

This investigation involves students in figuring out how much ribbon or yarn they need to wrap a package. For this activity, you need a box for each pair or small group. Larger boxes, such as boxes for shoes, sweaters, blouses, kitchen mixing bowls, and large pitchers or vases, require children to combine larger numbers. Smaller boxes, such as those for candy, ties, and other smaller gifts, produce problems with smaller numbers.

You also need yarn or ribbon for this activity. Cut a length for each pair or group of children that measures about 1 yard. Also, have several rolls of yarn or ribbon available from which children can cut additional lengths as needed.

Begin by showing the children a box and asking them to estimate how much yarn or ribbon they think they need just for making a bow. Then give each pair or group a yard-long length and have them tie a bow around a pencil. Tell them that it's up to their group to decide on the size of the bow and the length of the ends. After they make a bow and trim its ends, they measure the length of the yarn they used. When all have completed this, have them show their bows and report their lengths. Record this information on the board.

Then give each pair or group a box. Tell them that their job is to figure out how many inches of ribbon or yarn they would need to wrap their box, including the bow. (They can use their own measurement for the bow, or any other one that is reasonable according to the class list of bow measurements.) Write the following directions on the board:
1. Talk about a plan to solve the problem.
2. Decide on the length of yarn you need.
3. Write about how you got your answer.
4. Measure and cut yarn to test.

When all groups have completed the problem, have them present their results and procedures to the class. Presentations such as these help children learn about other ways to solve problems and work with numbers. After several presentations have been made, before subsequent groups present their findings, have the rest of the class look at their boxes and use the information they already have to predict a reasonable range for the solution.

How Big Is Your Hand?

This activity involves the children with measuring area. Have the children trace one of their hands, fingers together, on centimeter squared paper and figure its area. Talk with the children about the approximate nature of their answers and about dealing with the bits and pieces of squares. Have the children explain in writing how they did their calculations.

Typically, some children will avoid the incomplete squares. In cases such as these, have children pair up and share how they each solved the problem. Then give students a chance to revise or refine their work.

Also, talk with the children about how they think their measurements would compare if they traced their hands with their fingers apart. Have those who are interested try this experiment.

At a later time, as an independent task, have children figure the area of a kindergarten child's hand and an adult's hand and compare with their own measurements.

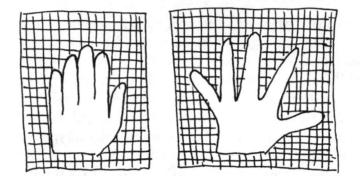

Probability Activities

Games of chance are always appealing to children. The two suggested here are sure favorites. Both are two-person games that involve children in mental addition and encourage them to think strategically. The first game gives practice with sums under 20; the second requires adding to 100. After the games are taught to the whole class, children can play them independently.

Roll 15

To play this game, each pair of children needs four cubes, two numbered 0 to 5, and two numbered 5 to 10. The object of the game is to get a score as close to 15 as possible.

Choose two students to demonstrate the game. The first player chooses any cube to roll, then rolls a second cube, and finds the sum of the two numbers rolled. (If the two numbers rolled are 3 and 4, the sum is 7 so far.) The player may now choose to stop or to roll a third cube. This third number is then added to the previous sum. (If the number rolled is a 9, the sum is now 16.) It's all right to go over 15. After the third roll, if the sum is still less than 15, the player may choose to roll the fourth cube. Then the second player rolls the cubes one at a time in the same way. Have the class decide which player's score is closer to 15.

Have the class play the game in pairs. Ask them to record each time they roll, keeping track of which cubes they roll, the numbers that come up, and the sums they have. Have them play five rounds.

Use the following questions for a class discussion: How many times did you usually roll before stopping? Which cube did you use first? Second? How many times did you go over 15? What might you roll to produce a result of exactly 15?

Have the children play five more rounds.

The Game of Pig

This game appears on page 71 in the Probability section. Demonstrate the game by playing with a volunteer. Emphasize to the children that they are to keep the running totals mentally for each round, then record them, and add them to their previous totals. Also emphasize that children are to check each other's addition.

After a demonstration game, give each pair of children two dice and have them play the game. Give the children time over the next several days to play. Also, you might give them the homework assignment of teaching the game to someone at home.

When all the children are familiar with the game and have had the opportunity to play it several times, have a class discussion about their methods for adding mentally, their strategies for deciding when to roll and when to stop, and what they noticed about the sums that came up. Use the following questions: How did you decide when to keep rolling and when to stop and keep your score? How often did a 1 come up? How often did doubles come up? Suppose you had a score of 15 and rolled a sum of 9, what would your new total be? How did you figure that in your head? Suppose your score was 19 and you rolled 11, what would your score be now? (Give all children who have strategies the chance to share them.) What advice would you give to a new player?

INDEPENDENT ACTIVITIES (MENU)

Children benefit from many activities to add and subtract numbers throughout the year. Three of the activities that follow are extensions of the whole class lessons — *Last Names, Too Short,* and *Comparing Hands.* The others offer other problem situations that give children experience with adding and subtracting.

Last Names

You need: a partner
the class graphs of first and last names

Figure out how many letters there are altogether in the last names in the class. Compare this with the total for letters in everyone's first names. Find the difference. Explain how you did this.

Too Short

You need: a measuring stick, tape, or ruler

five gift boxes of varying sizes — for shoes, sweaters, ties, etc.

a 3-yard roll of ribbon

Suppose you needed to wrap each of the five boxes and only had one 3-yard roll of ribbon. If you wanted to waste as little ribbon as possible, which would you choose to wrap with the ribbon you have? How much more ribbon would you need to buy?

Explain your reasoning and defend your answer with numerical data.

Comparing Hands

You need: your hand traced on centimeter squared paper

the hand of a kindergarten student traced on centimeter squared paper

Find the area of the hand of a kindergarten child. Find the difference between the area of your hand and the area of the kindergarten child's hand. Explain how you figured this out.

Record the difference on the class chart.

Homework: Trace one of your parent's hands on centimeter squared paper. Figure its area and compare with yours. Is your hand half grown yet? Explain your reasoning.

How Old Is Ramona the Pest?

You need: a partner

Ramona the Pest

In the book, *Ramona the Pest,* Ramona is in kindergarten, which makes her about five years old. According to the copyright date, the book was written in 1968. How old is Ramona now?

Estimate and Measure

You need: a partner

interlocking cubes

Measure the length of at least five different things. For each, do the following:

1. Make an estimate and record.
2. Measure.
3. Count and record.
4. Figure how far off your estimate was. Record.

Estimate and Measure			
Object	Est.	Meas.	How far off?

In 1 Minute

You need: a partner

a way to time 1 minute

While your partner times 1 minute, write the letters of the alphabet. (If you get to "z" before time is up, start over with "a.")

Repeat, this time writing numerals, starting with "1" and continuing until time is called.

Switch so your partner writes letters and numerals while you keep time.

Each of you counts the number of letters and numerals you wrote. See if you wrote more letters or more numerals, and figure how many more. Record your results.

Compare results with your partner.

Extension: Predict how many letters and numerals you think you would write in half a minute. Time each other to test your estimates. Compare your results with your 1-minute data. Write about what you notice.

Billy Goes Shopping

You need: dimes and pennies

Billy wants to buy some new school supplies. He has nine dimes to spend. He needs to save 25¢ for the bus. Look at the price list and choose some things for Billy to buy. (He can buy different things or more than one of the same thing.)

List the items you choose, along with the cost of each. Find the total. Use the dimes and pennies to figure out the change.

Find at least three ways Billy can spend his money. Remember, he needs 25¢ for the bus.

Price List
Erasers 10¢
Rulers 29¢
Pencils 25¢
Pens 39¢
Book covers 20¢

Covering Covers

You need: Color Tiles
two books

Choose two different books from the class or school library. Estimate which cover has the greater area. Measure each book cover with tiles and record. Figure out how many more tiles are needed for the larger cover and explain how you arrived at your answer.

Repeat for two other pairs of books.

Fill the Cube

(**Note:** This activity is similar to *Fill the Cube* on page 178 in the Place Value section. In this version, the children figure the difference between the two counts.)

You need: a Unifix cube
popcorn
lentils

Find out how many kernels of popcorn fill the cube. Record.

Predict how many lentils you think will fill the cube. Record your prediction and explain why you think it makes sense. Test your prediction.

Now figure out how many more lentils than popcorn it took to fill the cube. Explain how you figured it out.

Cross Out Singles

You need: a partner or small group
one die or a 0–9 spinner

This is a game for two or more players. Follow these rules:

1. Each player makes a recording sheet, as shown, for a game of three rounds.

2. To begin the game, one player rolls the die or spins the spinner.

3. All players write the number in a square on their first chart. Once a number is recorded, it cannot be changed.

4. Another player now rolls or spins to generate a number for everyone to record in another square. Take turns rolling or spinning until players have filled all nine squares on their charts.

5. Players then find the sums of the rows, columns, and diagonal, and record them in the respective circles.

6. Players examine their sums. Any sum that appears in only one circle must be crossed out.

7. The total of the sums that are *not* crossed out is the player's score for that round. For example:

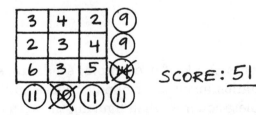

SCORE: 51

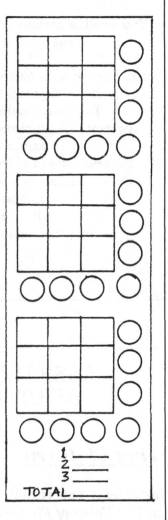

8. Play two more rounds. Then compare totals.

Extensions:
1. Find ways that produce a zero score.
2. Using the numbers 1 to 9 once each, what is the highest score you can get?
3. Discuss strategies for how to place numbers.

101 and Out

You need: a partner or small group
  one die or a 0–9 spinner

This is a game for two or more players. Follow these rules:
  1. Each player makes a recording sheet as shown.
  2. Take turns rolling the die or spinning the spinner to generate six numbers.
  3. On each turn, all players write the number in either the tens column or ones column of their recording sheet. Once a number is recorded, it cannot be changed.
  4. After six numbers, fill in any blank spaces in the ones column with zeros and add.
  5. The player closest to 100 without going over wins.

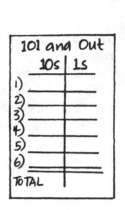

ASSESSING UNDERSTANDING OF ADDITION AND SUBTRACTION

Observing Children

Class discussions can reveal how students think. For example, students' strategies for adding in *The Game of Pig* reveal information about their number sense and ability to add mentally. How they deal with the incomplete squares when figuring the area of their hands gives information about their understanding of fractional parts. How they decide whether there were more letters in their first or last names provides information about their number sense and ability to interpret statistical data. Although some of this information may not relate specifically to comparing quantities or the processes of addition and subtraction, it contributes to your understanding of each child's mathematical thinking.

When children are working on the independent tasks, circulate, observe, and, at times, question children about their thinking and reasoning. The following are suggestions for your observations: What methods do children use for the calculations in the various tasks? Are the methods children use for one task similar to their methods in other tasks? Are there children who deal effectively with small numbers but are lost with large numbers? Which children rely on their mental calculations and which use other methods? How do the children use calculators?

Individual Assessments

To find out about children's understanding of addition and subtraction and their abilities to compute, give them problems to solve similar to those they have been working on in class. Be sure to ask children to describe their thinking processes and explain why their answers make sense.

Such assessments are the same as learning tasks. However, looking at a class set of such papers gives you information about the abilities of the class in general and the progress of specific students. The following are some suggestions:

1. Give children problems to solve that use information from two or three of their results from *Estimate and Measure*. For example: *Lindsay and Laura measured Lindsay. Their estimate was 86. Their measurement was 69. How far off was their measurement?*

2. Give them the copyright date on one of their library books. Ask them to figure out how long ago the book was written.

3. Ask them to write a paper titled "What Is Addition?" or "What Is Subtraction?"

4. Ask that they write an addition (or subtraction) story that follows two rules:

    a. It must end in a question.

    b. The question must be one that's possible to answer by adding (or subtracting).

Have them solve their story problem in as many ways as they can.

Multiplication

INTRODUCTION

Traditionally, instruction in multiplication has focused on two objectives: learning the multiplication facts and developing computational facility. After memorizing the times tables, children learn to multiply with paper and pencil, first practicing with one-digit multipliers and progressing to two-digit and three-digit multipliers. Word problems are usually the vehicle for giving students practice with applying multiplication in problem situations.

The ideas in this section provide a shift toward a broader view of multiplication and a more active approach to learning. The activities introduce multiplication from several perspectives: geometric, numerical, and through real-world contexts. To integrate multiplication with the rest of mathematics, the activities include ideas from the strands of number, geometry, statistics, and patterns and functions.

The standard mathematical representation for multiplication is introduced in the context of the activities, helping children connect the abstract representations to their own experiences. Also, rather than teaching the standard computational algorithm for multiplying, the activities give students the challenge of creating their own procedures for computing.

WHOLE CLASS LESSONS

Multiplication in Real-World Contexts

Having children investigate groups of objects in a real-world context helps them link the idea of multiplication to the world around them. It also helps them avoid the pitfall of seeing mathematics as totally abstract and unrelated to their lives. Too often, math exists for children only on the pages of textbooks and worksheets. They need opportunities to see mathematics as integral to their daily experiences.

The Chopstick Problem

Use this problem to initiate the exploration of multiplication in contexts. First, make sure children know that when people use chopsticks to eat, two are required. Then pose a problem for class discussion: How many chopsticks are needed for four people? Hear from all children who want to respond, asking them to explain how they arrived at their answers.

Then pose another problem: How many chopsticks are needed for everyone in the class? Ask the children to discuss and solve this problem in small groups. Then have individuals report their answers, again asking them to explain their reasoning. Record on the chalkboard the methods they report, modeling for the children how to use mathematical notation to represent their ideas. Keep the emphasis on children's different approaches for solving the problem.

Things That Come in Groups

Collect the materials needed for this activity: a 12-by-18-inch sheet of newsprint for each small group of children and 11 sheets of 9-by-12-inch drawing paper. Post one 9-by-12-inch sheet of paper and title it: Things That Come in 2s.

Have the class brainstorm things other than chopsticks that come in twos. List their suggestions. It's common for children to think of examples from their bodies — eyes, ears, hands, feet, thumbs, etc. If they are limited by a particular category, such as their bodies, offer a few suggestions to broaden their thinking — wheels on a bicycle, wings on a bird, slices of bread in a sandwich.

Give the class the problem of making lists for other numbers. Have the children work in small groups and think of objects that come in threes, fours, fives, and so on, up to twelves. Give each group a sheet of 12-by-18-inch newsprint on which to organize their lists.

Post the additional sheets of 9-by-12-inch paper and label them for the numbers from 3 to 12. Have groups take turns reading an item from their charts. After a group reads an item, the others guess the list on which it belongs. Should uncertainty or a dispute arise about items, such as "sides on a stop sign," "wings on a butterfly," etc., start a separate "research" list and resolve the questions at a later time. Continue having groups report until all their findings have been offered. Keep the lists posted for the remainder of the unit to provide a resource of subjects for problem solving.

Also, encourage the children to continue thinking about other items to add to the lists. You may choose to give children the homework assignment of asking their parents to help think of additional items.

Multiplication as Repeated Addition

Because children learn in different ways, it's helpful to include a diversity of approaches in lessons. The following game suggests a way to introduce children to multiplication as repeated addition, with the additional benefit of providing a visual representation of multiplication. In this game, the children interact with the idea of multiplication pictorially (by drawing circles and stars), symbolically (by writing the multiplication sentences), and verbally (by reading the sentences).

Circles and Stars

Collect the materials you need for the game: one die for each pair of children, a sheet of unlined paper (such as duplicating paper) for each child, a pair of scissors for each child or pair of children, two or three staplers.

Tell the children that you're going to teach them how to play a game called *Circles and Stars* that they will then play in pairs. To model how to play, invite a child to be your partner and join you at the chalkboard.

Begin by rolling a die and reporting to the class the number that comes up. Draw that many circles on the board, pointing out to the class that you're drawing the circles large enough to be able to draw stars inside. Then have the child who is your partner roll the die and draw the appropriate number of circles. Roll the die again, report the number to the class, and draw that many stars in each of your circles. Have your partner roll the die and draw the correct number of stars. Ask the class to figure out how many stars each of you drew. Write the correct number of stars underneath each drawing. Play another round to be sure the children understand, and then ask the volunteer to be seated.

Tell the class that a complete game takes seven rounds. Demonstrate how to fold a piece of paper into fourths, cut it apart, and staple it into a booklet. Write *Circles and Stars* and your name on the front. Have the children count as you show that seven pages remain for playing. Tell the children that although they can see who wins each round by comparing how many stars each player drew, the winner of the game is the person who has more stars altogether in the booklet. After seven rounds, children are to figure out the total and record it on the cover.

Have the children make their booklets and play the game. Those who finish more quickly can make a second booklet and play again.

When all the children have played at least one complete game, show them how to record a multiplication sentence on each page. First draw on the board a sample page of three circles with two stars in each and underneath write: 3 × 2. Explain to the children that this is a way to write "three sets of two" or "three groups of two" with math symbols. Tell them that you can also read the sentence as "three times two" and it means the same thing. Show how adding "= 6" tells how many stars there are in all. Write on the board the three ways to read "3 × 2 = 6":

$$3 \times 2 = 6$$

3 sets of 2 equals 6
3 groups of 2 equals 6
3 times 2 equals 6

Then ask the children to work with their partners and agree on the math sentence to write on each page of their booklets. Tell them that as they write the math sentences, they should read them aloud to each other in two different ways. Also tell them that when they complete recording in a booklet, they should save it for later analysis and data collection.

After all the children have played at least one game, have them work in small groups and compare the number of stars on each page of their booklets. Ask them to look for the different numbers of stars that came up, which numbers of stars on a page came up frequently, and the different ways they got them. Have children present their findings in a class discussion. On a later independent task, they will more formally analyze the possible numbers and ways to get them.

For homework, have children teach someone at home how to play *Circles and Stars*.

A Geometric Model for Multiplication

Investigating rectangular arrays introduces children to a geometric model for multiplication. The students investigate rectangular arrays as they research how to package candy. The "candies" are 1-inch square tiles that are packed one layer deep in rectangular boxes. Children use the tiles to identify various dimensions of boxes for different numbers of candies.

Candy Boxes

Collect the materials you need for this activity: Color Tiles (at least 12 per child), 1/2-inch squared paper, scissors, tape or glue.

Distribute tiles so that each pair of children has 24. Explain that the tiles are pretend candies that come in rectangular or square boxes and are always packed in just one layer. Tell the children that a sampler box has 4 candies in it. Ask each child to take 4 tiles and see how the candies might be arranged to fit into a box.

Typically in a class, students produce the two possible options. Draw them on the chalkboard. If only one is found, however, show the other and have the children build it with the tiles. If children suggest an L-shaped arrangement, remind them that the boxes must be rectangular or square. This is a good opportunity to point out that squares are really special rectangles because each of their sides is the same length.

Write the dimensions 2×2 and 1×4 inside each rectangle you drew.

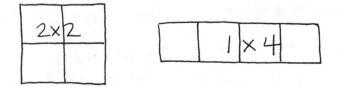

Read them aloud as "two by two" and "one by four" and explain to the children that the numbers tell how many tiles there are on adjoining sides. Then, using 1/2-inch squared paper, cut out the two different arrays and record the dimensions on each.

Next, pose the research problem: Each pair of students is the design research team of the candy company. The president of the company has asked for a report about the different boxes possible for 6, 12, and 24 candies. Give the children three directions.

1. For each number, use the tiles to find all possible rectangles.

2. Cut out each rectangular shape as you find it, using 1/2-inch squared paper.

3. Write a memo to the president explaining what you've learned about boxes for each quantity and what shape box you recommend. Include your cutout boxes with your memo.

Have children report their findings and recommendations in a class discussion.

INDEPENDENT ACTIVITIES (MENU)

The independent activities provide children with a variety of experiences with multiplication. Three of the activities — *Patterns in Multiples, More Circles and Stars,* and *Candy Box Research* — extend the whole class lessons. Two versions of *Candy Box Research* are included; the first version is simpler for children to do.

The other activities — *Billy Wins a Shopping Spree, Calculator Patterns, Multiplication Stories, Times Tables Plaids, How Long? How Many?, How Many Were Eaten?,* and *The Factor Game* — provide additional ways for children to learn about multiplication.

Patterns in Multiples

You need: "Things That Come in Groups" charts
           0–99 chart (see blackline masters)

Choose an item from one of the "Things That Come in Groups" charts. List at least 12 multiples and write multiplication sentences.

Color in the multiples on a 0–99 chart. Then continue the pattern to the end of the chart.

Write about the patterns you see in the numbers on your list and on the 0–99 chart.

Repeat for an item from a different list.

More Circles and Stars

You need: a partner
         one die
         scissors
         stapler

Make a booklet and play *Circles and Stars* as you did before.

After you've played, make tally marks on the class chart to show the number of stars you drew on each round.

Note: The class chart lists the numbers from 1 to 36.

Candy Box Research (Version 1)

You need: a partner
Color Tiles
1/2-inch squared paper (see blackline masters)
scissors
tape
bag with numbers

Pick a number from the bag.

Using Color Tiles, build all the rectangular boxes possible for that number of candies. Cut out each from the squared paper and label its dimensions. Tape on the class chart. Repeat for another number from the bag.

Note: The bag has slips of paper numbered from 1 to 36, excluding 4, 6, 12, and 24. The class chart is a large horizontal chart with spaces marked for the numbers from 1 to 36. The students already investigated rectangular arrays for the numbers 4, 6, 12, and 24; post the rectangles for each of these numbers.

Candy Box Research (Version 2)

You need: a partner or small group
Color Tiles
1/2-inch squared paper (see blackline masters)
several large sheets of newsprint
scissors
tape

Use Color Tiles to build the rectangular boxes possible for all the numbers from 1 to 36. Cut out each from the squared paper and label its dimensions. Tape the rectangles on newsprint ruled into sections for each number.

When you've completed your chart, write answers to the following questions:

1. For which numbers are there rectangles that have sides with two squares on them? Write the numbers from smallest to largest.

2. For which numbers are there rectangles that have sides with three squares on them? Write the numbers from smallest to largest.

3. Do the same for numbers with rectangles that have four squares on a side.

4. Do the same for numbers with rectangles that have five squares on a side.

5. Which numbers have rectangles that are squares?

6. How many squares are in the next larger square you can make?

7. What is the smallest number with exactly two different rectangles? Three different rectangles? Four?

8. Which numbers have only one rectangle? List them from smallest to largest.

Billy Wins a Shopping Spree

You need: a partner

Billy won a $25 shopping spree at the Science Museum Store. He could choose items from the price list shown. Decide what Billy could buy. Record your choices.

PRICE LIST

$3	$4	$5
1. Origami paper	1. Kaleidoscope	1. Koosh ball
2. Crystal and gem magnets	2. Large magnifying bug box	2. Glow-in-the-dark solar system stickers
3. Furry stuffed seal pups	3. Sunprint kit	3. Inflatable world globe
4. Prism	4. Inflatable shark	4. Wooden dinosaur model kit

Make a receipt that shows how many items of each price Billy bought. Show the total he spent and the credit he has left, if any.

Extension: Find the combinations of differently priced objects that Billy could buy and spend $25 exactly. Note that buying five Koosh balls is the same price combination as buying three Koosh balls and two dinosaur model kits because in each case, Billy bought five items at $5 each.

Calculator Patterns

You need: a calculator

Choose a number from 2 to 12. Press the "+" key. Press the "=" key. (You should see the same number you first entered.) Keep pressing the "=" key. Each time you press, list the number displayed. Continue until there are at least 12 numbers on your list. Write about the patterns you notice.

Multiplication Stories

Write a multiplication story that follows two rules:
    1. It must end in a question.
    2. The question must be one that's possible to answer by multiplying.
Solve your story problem in as many ways as you can.
Exchange papers and solve each other's problems.

Times Tables Plaids

You need: multiplication chart

Choose a number from 2 to 12. List the multiples of the number up to 144. (You may use a calculator and the method described in *Calculator Patterns*.)

On a multiplication chart, color all the multiples on your list. Check with other students to compare your pattern with patterns generated from the multiples of other numbers. Write about the similarities and differences among the patterns.

How Long? How Many?

You need: a partner
Cuisenaire Rods
one die
centimeter squared paper (see blackline masters)

Two versions of the game are described below. Try both versions.

Version 1
Each player uses a different 10-by-10 grid of centimeter squared paper. Take turns. On your turn, roll the die twice. The first roll tells "how long" a rod to use. The second roll tells "how many" rods to take.

Arrange the rods into a rectangle. Trace it on your grid and write the appropriate multiplication sentence inside.

The game is over when one of you can't place your rectangle because there's no room on the grid. Then figure out how many of your squares are covered and how many are uncovered. Check each other's answers.

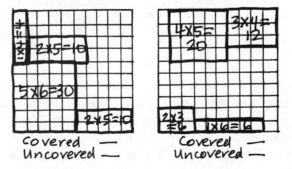

Version 2
Both of you use one notebook-sized piece of centimeter squared paper. The goal is to cover as much of the paper as possible. As in the first version, take turns rolling the die and taking the appropriate rods. Together, decide how to form them into a rectangle and where to trace it on the paper. Continue until you can't place the rectangle for the numbers you rolled. Figure out how many of your squares are covered and how many are uncovered.

How Many Were Eaten?

You need: a candy box with seven cubes inside

There are seven candies left in the box. Figure out how many were eaten. Show your work and explain your reasoning.

Note: Have several different size candy boxes, each with seven cubes inside, from which students can choose. Some may be interested in solving the problem for more than one candy box.

The Factor Game

Note: This game appears in *Factors and Multiples*, a book in the Middle Grades Mathematics Project series (Addison-Wesley).

You need: a partner
markers in two different colors
a sheet of paper with the numbers 1 to 30

```
The Factor Game
 1   2   3   4   5
 6   7   8   9  10
11  12  13  14  15
16  17  18  19  20
21  22  23  24  25
26  27  28  29  30
```

Each player uses a different color marker. One player selects a number and circles it with his or her marker. The other player finds all the proper factors of the number, circling each with his or her marker (of a different color). The process alternates between the two players until there are no factors left for the remaining numbers. Players add the numbers they circled. The winner is the player with the larger score.

Caution: Selecting a number with no factors left is an illegal move. If you make an illegal move, you get to add the number to your score. But ... you lose your next turn to select a number.

ASSESSING UNDERSTANDING OF MULTIPLICATION

Observing Children

When children are working on the independent tasks, circulate, observe, and, at times, question them about their thinking and reasoning. When children play *Circles and Stars,* for example, some figure out how many stars there are on a page by counting each star. Others count by twos, or add, or know the multiplication fact. Asking children to explain how they figured the number of stars on one or more pages can give insights into their thinking. In *Candy Box Research,* ask children how they know when they've found all the possible rectangles for a particular number. In *Billy Wins a Shopping Spree,* notice how children do the calculations when they decide what Billy can buy or how much he spent.

The children's stories for *Multiplication Stories* reveal whether children can relate contextual situations to the idea of multiplication. Their solutions from *How Many Were Eaten?* help you see if they can interpret multiplication geometrically.

Talk with children about the patterns they are noticing in *Candy Box Research, Patterns in Multiples, Calculator Patterns,* and *Times Tables Plaids.* After they have the opportunity to play *How Long? How Many?,* have children explain their strategies for filling as much as possible of the centimeter squared paper.

Individual Assessments

Rather than testing the children on the times tables or having them do arithmetic calculations, give assessments that help reveal their thinking. The following are several suggestions.

1. Before beginning instruction, ask students to write what they know about multiplication. Have them do this again at the end of the instructional unit. Return both papers to the students and ask them to reflect on their learning.

2. Give the children a multiplication fact; 6×5 or 7×6, for example. Ask them to explain how to figure out the answer. If students say they already know the answer, ask how they would tell a younger child how to figure it out.

3. Give children a word problem to solve and ask them to find the answer in as many ways as possible and explain why their solutions make sense.

Division

INTRODUCTION

*T*here are two different types of division. One is sharing or partitioning, which involves dividing a collection of objects into a given number of equal parts. Sharing twelve candies among three friends is a division situation of this type. The second type is grouping, splitting a collection of objects into groups of a known size. Figuring how many 15-cent pencils can be purchased with $1.00 is an example of division by grouping.

   Children should become familiar with both types of division. Their formal instruction with division should begin with problem situations for them to solve. The situations can then be related to the standard symbolic representations. Also, children's understanding of division becomes more powerful when they begin to see the connection between sharing and grouping and between division and the other operations.

WHOLE CLASS LESSONS

Introducing Division Through Problem Situations

Presenting children with problem situations helps develop their familiarity with the language and process of division. Be sure to present problems for each type of division. Have children work with partners or in small groups so that they have opportunities to talk about their thinking. For all problems, when children present answers, have them explain their reasoning orally and in writing. Link the situations and solutions to mathematical symbols so that children learn the standard notation. The following are samples of problems to present to students throughout the year.

Division Sharing Problems

Tell the children the following story: While walking to school one day, four children found a $5.00 bill. When they arrived at school, they told their teacher, and she asked them to tell the principal. The principal thanked the children and told them she would try to find out who lost the money. A week later, the principal called the children back to her office, and told them no one had claimed the money and that it was theirs to keep. However, they first had to figure how to share it equally among the four of them.

Have the children work together to solve the problem. Ask them to record their solution and explain their reasoning. It may help to write the following prompt on the board for the children to follow:

Each person gets ____. We think this because ____.

For groups who finish first, ask them to solve a similar problem. Choose one with a remainder. For example, if four children found 50¢ on the way to school, how much would each get if they had to share it equally?

Have children share their solutions. Show them how to record the stories and solutions mathematically:

$$50¢ \div 4 = 12¢ \ R \ 2¢$$

$$4\overline{)50¢} \quad 12¢ \ R \ 2¢$$

On other days, continue with stories about the four children who find things on the way to school. They can find a bag of marbles with 54 marbles, a train of 17 interlocking cubes, a bag with 22 apples, and so on.

Also, give problems with other divisors. For example, suppose someone gives the class a gift of 100 pencils. If they are divided among all the students, how many pencils will each student get?

If eight children were at a birthday party, and there were a box of cookies with three packets of ten cookies each, how many cookies could each child get?

The Doorbell Rang

The Doorbell Rang, written by Pat Hutchins, provides children the opportunity to think about several division problems. The book begins with two children who are about to have a snack. There is a plate of a dozen cookies. Have the class figure how many cookies each child could eat.

Just as the children are about to divide the cookies between them, however, the doorbell rings. Two more children enter. Have the class figure how many cookies they each could then have.

Then, just before the four children begin to eat their cookies, the doorbell rings again, and two more children enter. Have the class figure how many cookies each child could then have.

The six children are about to eat their cookies. But the doorbell rings once more. This time, six more children arrive. There are now twelve children and twelve cookies.

The doorbell rings again and the children sit frozen. When the door opens, it is grandma with a plate of freshly baked cookies!

Read the story a second time, this time recording on the board the mathematical sentences for each problem.

$$12 \div 2 = 6$$
$$12 \div 4 = 3$$
$$12 \div 6 = 2$$
$$12 \div 12 = 1$$

$$2\overline{)12}^{6} \qquad 4\overline{)12}^{3}$$

$$6\overline{)12}^{2} \qquad 12\overline{)12}^{1}$$

Have children practice retelling the story, referring to the mathematical sentences for cues. In this way, they see mathematical symbols related to the action of a story.

Division Grouping Problems

Tell the children the following story: There were two cartons in the refrigerator with a dozen eggs in each, plus three extra eggs in the holders in the refrigerator door. Mom liked to eat an omelette each day and used two eggs in each omelette. How many days could she make omelettes before she had to buy more eggs?

As with the other problems, have the children work in pairs or small groups, figure the answer, and explain their reasoning. Represent the story and solution with the correct mathematical symbols:

$$27 \div 2 = 13\ R\ 1$$
$$2\overline{)27}^{13\ R\ 1}$$

Present other grouping division problems. Keep the emphasis on the children's thinking. Have them share their reasoning processes and explain why their methods and answers make sense. As children present their solutions, represent the problems and their solutions mathematically on the board so that children see the mathematical symbols related to a variety of problem situations. The following are examples:

• Bring a loaf of sliced bread to class. Choose a loaf that is packaged in a clear wrap so children can count the slices. Ask them to figure how many sandwiches can be made from the loaf.

• Tell the class that for a math activity, each student needs 8 tiles. A box has 200 tiles. Have them figure out if everyone in the class can participate in the activity at one time.

• Talk with the children about the way paper is packaged. Tell them that a ream contains 500 sheets. Present this problem: If each student needs 20 sheets of paper to make a recording book, how many books can be made from a ream of paper?

• Tell the children about a person with an apple tree who had a giveaway celebration to get rid of 50 extra apples. She offered 3 apples to each person who asked. How many people could get free apples?

When solving problems, children often use a combination of operations. For example, consider the following problem: A woman decided to knit socks for holiday presents for her family. She was able to knit one sock a week. One year, she began knitting on January 1, and knit steadily until December 15. She then stopped to wrap each pair of socks. How many presents did she wrap?

Some children will solve the problem by counting to 50 by twos and keep track of how many 2s they count. Record this on the board by writing 2, 4, 6, 8, ..., 50, and also by recording the multiplication and division sentences that relate:

$$25 \times 2 = 50$$
$$50 \div 2 = 25 \qquad 2\overline{)50}^{\,25}$$

Other children solve the problem by a combination of multiplying, adding, and subtracting: For 10 people, she would use 20 socks. For 10 more, another 20. That's 40 socks altogether. So she has 10 socks left. That's enough for 5 more people. So add 10 + 10 + 5 and she has socks for 25 people. Record these ideas with several mathematical sentences:

$$10 \times 2 = 20$$
$$20 + 20 = 40$$
$$50 - 40 = 10$$
$$10 \div 2 = 5$$
$$10 + 10 + 5 = 25$$

Some children approach the problem differently: Each person needs two socks, and half of 50 is 25. That means 25 people get presents. Record this as follows:

$$\frac{1}{2} \text{ of } 50 = 25$$

It's important that children understand that a situation such as this one presents a division problem. However, it's also valuable for students to know that there are a variety of ways to find the answer. Although children may use different operations when calculating, they are finding the answer to a division problem in a legitimate way.

Don't shy away from problems with large numbers or with remainders. The wider the variety of problems, the more support children have for developing number sense, and the more mathematically flexible they will become.

A note about calculators: Calculators should be readily available to children. Even if children use a calculator to find or verify an answer, have them explain why the answer makes sense. In problems with remainders, calculators are valuable for introducing children to decimals. Using a calculator to solve the problem of sharing 17 cubes among four children, for example, gives the answer of 4.25. This may be the first introduction to decimals for some children. Talk about 4.25 being a number that is greater than 4 but less than 5.

Investigations with Raisins

Read about this investigation on page 129 in the Number section. The lesson involves the children with estimating, statistical reasoning, and whole number operations, and presents the sharing problem of dividing raisins equally.

Relating Division to Multiplication

Seeing the relationship between division and multiplication helps deepen children's understanding. In the section on multiplication, several activities were suggested in which students learned about multiplication through exploring "candy boxes" that were rectangular arrays. If students engaged in those activities, the following extension can relate their experience to division.

Candy Box Sales Guides

Present the following problem: Customers reported to the candy company that they sometimes had problems sharing the candy at home. The candies don't split into pieces. So when a family with five people buys a box with six candies, there is one extra candy. This sometimes causes squabbles. Not only is it a family problem, it is a company problem, because the people might not want to buy the candy anymore.

The problem for the students to solve is to prepare a guide for salespeople in the candy stores. When customers want to buy candy, the salesperson first asks how many people are in their family. Then they check in the guide for suggestions about an appropriate quantity of candies to buy. In this way, they provide advice for a squabble-free purchase.

Have children design such a guide. Since it's unreasonable to provide suggestions for every possible size family, have the class graph how many people live in their houses. Use that information to decide which size families are most typical.

As an extension, have children find which size box is a good recommendation that would work for most families — for families of two, three, four, five, and six, for example.

A Division Game

The following game of chance gives children experience with sharing quantities into equal groups and relating the action to the appropriate mathematical representation.

Leftovers

Children play in pairs. Each pair needs one die, one piece of paper for recording, six 3-by-3-inch squares of construction paper, and 15 Color Tiles or other counters.

The first player rolls the die, puts out that number of 3-by-3-inch paper squares, divides the 15 tiles equally on the squares, and keeps any tiles that remain. The second player records a mathematical sentence to describe what occurred, as shown on the next page.

The children then change roles. The second player removes the tiles from the squares (there may be fewer than 15 if the first player had a remainder and therefore kept the extra tiles), rolls the die, puts out the correct number of 3-by-3-inch squares, and divides the tiles among them. The first player records.

The game continues until no tiles are left to divide. The players count the tiles they each have. On a class chart, they record their sentences with remainders of zero. (Ask children to record only those sentences that haven't already been recorded on the chart.)

```
Leftovers  Bonny
           Monty
start with 15 tiles.

M 1.  15 ÷ 4 = 3 R 3
B 2.  12 ÷ 2 = 6 R 0
M 3.  12 ÷ 3 = 4 R 0
B 4.  12 ÷ 5 = 2 R 2
M 5.  10 ÷ 4 = 2 R 2
B 6.   8 ÷ 3 = 2 R 2
M 7.   6 ÷ 5 = 1 R 1
B 8.   5 ÷ 6 = 0 R 5

       M  6 points
       B  9 points
```

```
Class Chart
Sentences with R = 0
12 ÷ 2 = 6
12 ÷ 3 = 4
```

INDEPENDENT ACTIVITIES (MENU)

The independent activities give children additional experiences with division. Three of the activities — *Leftovers with 20, More Candy Box Research,* and *The Doorbell Rings Again* — extend whole class lessons. The other activities — *Division Stories, Chocolate Bars,* and *The Kings and Elephants Problem* — give children further opportunities to learn about division.

Leftovers with 20

You need: a partner
one die
20 Color Tiles
six 3-by-3-inch squares of construction paper

Play the game as before, following these rules:
1. The first player rolls the die, takes that number of 3-by-3-inch squares, and divides the tiles among them. If there are leftover tiles, the first player keeps them.
2. The second player writes the math sentence.
3. Switch roles. Continue until there aren't any tiles left.
When you're finished: On the class chart, record all sentences with R = 0. (Only record sentences that haven't already been recorded.)

Division Stories

Write a division story that follows two rules:
1. It must end in a question.
2. The question must be one that's possible to answer by dividing.

Solve your story problem in as many ways as you can.

Exchange papers and solve each other's problems.

More Candy Box Research

You need: Candy Box Sales Guides

List the numbers of candies that can be shared equally among two, three, four, five, and six people. Examine these lists and see what patterns you notice and which numbers appear on more than one list.

Suppose there were a box with 100 candies. On which lists would it fit? What about a box of 50 candies? 48? Do the same exploration for other numbers.

Chocolate Bars

You need: five "chocolate bars"

Some chocolate bars are scored to make them easy to break apart and share. Figure out how to share the five chocolate bars shown below equally among four people.

Explain how you did this. Write: Each person gets_____.

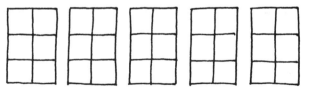

The Kings and Elephants Problem

You need: *17 Kings and 42 Elephants* by Margaret Mahy

This book tells the story of 17 kings and 42 elephants going on a journey through a jungle. Figure out how 17 kings could divide up the work of taking care of 42 elephants. Explain your reasoning.

Write other math problems that use the information in the story. For example: How many elephant feet were there altogether?

> ### *The Doorbell Rings Again*
>
> **You need:** *The Doorbell Rang* by Pat Hutchins
>
> Write another version of this story. You may change the number of cookies on the plate and also the number of children who arrive each time. Illustrate your story. Then read it to someone else.

ASSESSING UNDERSTANDING OF DIVISION

Observing Children

When children are working on the independent tasks, circulate, observe, and, at times, question them about their thinking and reasoning. When they are playing *Leftovers*, for example, ask children if they can predict whether there will be a remainder before they divide the tiles. The game gives children concrete experience with division problems that have a quotient of zero; make sure children understand when zero is an appropriate answer.

The children's stories for *Division Stories* reveal whether they can relate contextual situations to the idea of division. *More Candy Box Research* gives you information about children's comfort with numbers. If children are interested and able, discuss rules for divisibility with them.

Individual Assessments

The following written assignments suggest ways to find out about children's understanding of division.

1. Before beginning instruction, ask students to write what they know about division. Have them do this again at the end of the instructional unit. Return both papers to the students and ask them to reflect on their learning.

2. Give the children a division problem, $24 \div 3$ or $65 \div 5$, for example. Ask them to explain how to figure out the answer. If students say they already know the answer, ask how they would tell a younger child how to find out.

3. Ask the children to solve $21 \div 4$ in four different situations. For each, they are to report an answer, show how they arrived at it, and explain why the answer makes sense.

    a. Share 21 cookies among four children.

    b. Share 21 balloons among four children.

    c. Share $21.00 among four children.

    d. Do $21 \div 4$ on a calculator.

4. Assign a problem, such as one of those suggested for whole class lessons. Ask children to present a solution in writing and explain their reasoning.

Extending Multiplication and Division

INTRODUCTION

*I*n the upper elementary grades, students develop skills with which to estimate and calculate accurately when multiplying and dividing with large numbers. Students should be able to compute mentally as well as with paper and pencil and make estimates that allow them to judge the reasonableness of answers. When confronted with problem situations, they should know when it's necessary to be accurate and when an estimate will suffice.

Traditionally, instruction related to multiplying and dividing large numbers has focused primarily on computing accurate answers proficiently using paper-and-pencil algorithms. Unfortunately, the result of this focus has been that many students learn the algorithms for multiplication and long division without understanding why these algorithms make sense. Also, little emphasis has been given to calculating mentally.

In contrast, instruction should help students develop a repertoire of strategies for multiplying and dividing with large numbers both by figuring mentally and using paper and pencil. Learning different strategies requires that students understand several important ideas — how to multiply and divide by 10, powers of 10, and multiples of powers of 10; how to apply the distributive property to multiplication and division problems; and how multiplication and division relate to each other. When emphasis is placed on understanding and using these ideas, the role of paper and pencil expands beyond performing standard algorithms to using paper and pencil as a tool for keeping track of numerical reasoning and calculating in ways that relate to the specific numbers at hand. Standard algorithms may be part of instruction, but should be presented as one way to perform computations, not as the only or best way. Too often, for example, when faced with calculations like 463×100 or $360 \div 20$, students will reach for pencil and paper to apply the algorithm they learned rather than reason that for these problems, figuring mentally is more useful, appropriate, and efficient. Proficiency with multiplication and division should not be judged by students' ability to perform one particular algorithm but by their ability to calculate answers to multiplication and division calculations accurately and efficiently using approaches that are appropriate to specific problems.

WHOLE CLASS LESSONS

Multiplying by 10 and Powers of 10

Because of the structure of our base 10 number system, multiplying by 10 is made simple, calling merely for adding a zero. Six times 10, for example, is 60; 13 times 10 is 130; 247 times 10 is 2470; and so on. Learning this pattern allows students to multiply by 10 in their heads easily. It's important, however, that even when students know the pattern of adding a zero they can also verify answers in other ways. For example, they might reason that 13 times 10 is 130 because ten 10s are 100, three more 10s is 30 more, and 100 plus 30 is 130. Or they can verify that 25 times 10 is 250 by thinking that 25 times 2 is 50, doubling that for 25 times 4 gives 100, doubling again for 25 times 8 gives 200, and adding two more 25s makes 250 altogether. Using these and other strategies not only helps students develop computational flexibility but also helps them verify that applying the shortcut makes sense.

The pattern of multiplying by 10 extends to larger powers of 10. Multiplying by 100, for example, results in adding two zeros, so that 12 times 100 is 1200. (In this and similar problems, it seems to help students make sense of them if they read 1200 as "twelve hundred" rather than as "one thousand two hundred" or think of 37 times 100 as "thirty-seven hundred" rather than "three thousand seven hundred.") Again, although students know the pattern of adding two zeros, they should be expected to verify answers using other reasoning; for example, four times 100 is the same as four groups of 100 — 100 + 100 + 100 + 100.

It's a good idea to devote whole class discussions to solving just a few multiplication and division problems with 10 and powers of 10. Encourage students to think of multiple approaches and record their ideas on the chalkboard as they present them. Recording their reasoning models for students how to represent their thinking symbolically.

$$25 \times 2 = 50$$
$$50 + 50 = 100 \quad (25 \times 4)$$
$$100 + 100 = 200 \quad (25 \times 8)$$
$$200 + 50 = 250 \quad (25 \times 10)$$

$$10 \times 10 = 100$$
$$10 \times 10 = 100$$
$$5 \times 10 = 50$$
$$100 + 100 + 50 = 250$$

5 tens = 50
Count by 50 five times
50, 100, 150, 200, 250

Keep the emphasis of discussions on how students reason as well as on verifying correct answers. Start a class list of strategies. Talking about which strategies are better suited for specific problems is a way to have students think about the efficiency of certain methods. Keep in mind that the goal of this instruction is to develop students' ability to reason mentally accurately and efficiently. Follow your class discussions with small group work and individual assignments, asking students to solve a few problems in several different ways. Use the work students do in completing assignments as the basis for subsequent class discussions in which they tell how they used paper and pencil to keep track of and explain their numerical reasoning, making a bridge between reasoning mentally and using paper and pencil.

Using the Distributive Property

It's helpful to have frequent whole class discussions about strategies for mentally multiplying and dividing specific problems, presenting problems that traditionally have been relegated to paper-and-pencil solutions. Present the class with a problem, give students the chance to think individually for a bit, have them share their ideas with a partner or in a small group, and then ask volunteers to report their ideas.

When asked to calculate mentally the answer to 13 times 5, for example, one student may report that 10 times 5 is 50, three more 5s is 15, and 50 plus 15 is 65. Another student may reason that 6 times 5 is 30 and another 6 times 5 makes 60 altogether; this takes care of twelve 5s, and one more 5 makes 65. Or a student may think that 13 times 2 is 26, so 13 times 4 is twice that, or 52, and one 13 more makes 65. As described in the previous section about multiplying by 10 and powers of 10, record on the chalkboard as each student reports.

$$13 \times 5$$

$10 \times 5 = 50$	$6 \times 5 = 30$	$13 \times 2 = 26$
$3 \times 5 = 15$	$6 \times 5 = 30$	$13 \times 4 = 52$
$50 + 15 = 65$	$30 + 30 = 60$	$52 + 13 = 65$
	$60 + 5 = 65$	

Be sure to talk with the class about how recording is a useful tool for keeping track of and describing how you reason, not only for following a formerly learned procedure. In each of the above strategies, students do simpler multiplications, getting partial products, and then combine the results for a final answer. This is similar to what students will do when multiplying by 10 and powers of 10, but other numbers provide new challenges. At first, if students do not offer strategies like these, jump-start their thinking by encouraging students to begin with what they know. Or give them a suggestion about a place to start, such as multiplying 10 times 5, and have them talk in partners or small groups about how that might help. Or model one way as an example and then ask students to think of other approaches. Thinking about multiplying or dividing in this way is new for some students, and they need time to expand their computational repertoire to include ways other than using the procedures they may have learned and practiced.

Also, relating multiplication to rectangular arrays (see page 197) is a way to show why a particular way to reason numerically makes sense and offers a geometric interpretation of multiplication that can help students see how the areas of number and geometry can relate to each other. For example, a 5-by-13 array can be split into a 5-by-10 array and a 5-by-3 array, as shown below:

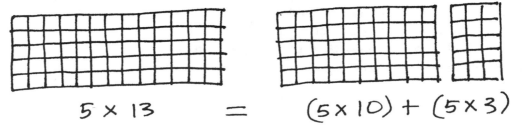

$$5 \times 13 \quad = \quad (5 \times 10) + (5 \times 3)$$

All of the strategies described for multiplying 13 by 5 make use of the distributive property of multiplication over addition. This means that instead of thinking of 13×5 as one multiplication, the problem is split into two or more problems. For example, by thinking of 13 as 10 plus 3, multiplying by 5 can be distributed over the two addends by doing 10×5 and 3×5.

Similarly for division, students can figure the answer to $150 \div 6$ by using the distributive property, this time distributing the division over addition. One way to do this is to think about 150 as $60 + 60 + 30$. Divide 60 by 6 to get 10 and then divide 60 by 6 for 10 more. This accounts for 120 of the 150, leaving $30 \div 6$ for 5 more. Adding two 10s and 5 gives 25, the answer to $150 \div 6$.

Making use of the distributive property helps students develop strategies for computing and, because applying the distributive property depends on the specific numbers involved, develops students' number sense as well. For example, when thinking about dividing 150 by 6, as explained above, choosing to think of 150 as $60 + 60 + 30$ helps make the problem more manageable. If the problem called for dividing 150 by 7, however, it might make more sense to think of 150 as $70 + 70 + 10$ or $140 + 10$. Making decisions like these focuses students on the particular characteristics of numbers and helps refine their number sense.

The distributive property is also the basis of why standard algorithms work, producing partial products for multiplication and the individual digits in quotients of long division problems. However, the focus of lessons should be on finding ways to make complicated computations simpler and more manageable, not on learning what the distributive property is. (I remember learning about the distributive property by being shown that $a(b + c) = ab + ac$, but never understanding why it was important or how it might be useful.) Keep the emphasis on the specifics of numerical calculations. It's fine to identify that what your students are doing is applying the distributive property, but don't make the distributive property the goal of instruction.

Relating Multiplication and Division

Jars, scoops, and various sizes of dry beans are easily accessible materials that are effective for engaging students with multiplication, division, and the relationship between them. The emphasis of lessons using these materials should be on having students solve problems for which they can use multiplication and explain how they reasoned. Lessons like these can be done from time to time during the year, varying the problems as well as the sizes of the jars, scoops, and beans. Following are several examples.

A Long Division Activity

This activity appears in *50 Problem-Solving Lessons*, a book compiling activities from ten years of Math Solutions Newsletters. Bonnie Tank developed this lesson to give fourth and fifth graders the opportunity to invent their own ways to divide, thus creating procedures that make sense to them. To prepare for the lesson, fill a jar with coffee scoops of beans and count them. Show the class the coffee scoop and the jar filled with beans, and ask the students to estimate the number of scoops they think it took to fill the jar. After revealing the number of scoops the jar holds, tell the class how many beans are in the jar and ask them to figure out how many beans will fill the scoop. Let the students solve the problem and have them describe their methods in writing. Then lead a class discussion about the different procedures they used. Finally, give groups of students a scoop of beans with which to verify their answers. Of course, the number of beans in different scoops will vary, giving the students the chance to talk about the problem as one for which an accurate answer doesn't make the most sense but for which an estimate will suffice or be even more appropriate.

To vary Bonnie's lesson, rather than asking the students to figure the number of beans that will fill a scoop, give each pair or group one scoopful of beans and have them use the information to figure out the number of scoops they think are in the jar. Because students' scoops will vary slightly, they may arrive at different answers. After discussing their solutions and methods, empty the jar and then refill it with scoops as the students count.

How Many Beans?

In *Developing Number Sense, Grades 3–6,* by Rusty Bresser and Caren Holtzman, the activity *How Many Beans?* is a different version of this lesson. Show the class an empty jar, a scoop, and a bag of beans. Ask the students to estimate about how many beans they think the jar will hold. After listening to their estimates, fill the scoop and pour the beans on one student's desk so she or he can count them. Talk with the class about how to use the number of beans in one scoop to figure out the total number of beans in the jar. After the students determine that multiplying the number of beans in one scoop by the number of scoops in the jar will produce a reasonable estimate, fill the jar with scoops of beans, stopping after several scoops to ask the students to calculate mentally the number of beans in the jar so far and discuss their methods. Continue adding scoops and having students calculate the number of beans until the jar is full. Repeat the activity with different-size beans and jars, sometimes giving the students writing assignments to explain how they figured.

A variation of this lesson is to give each pair or group of students a scoop of beans to count rather than having a student count just one scoop. The counts will vary, but all be close. Record the counts on the board and discuss with the class how to determine which number is the best estimate to use for how many beans a scoop holds. Doing this incorporates instruction about averaging into the lesson and can engage the students in using division to figure the mean.

Multiplication and Division Through Real-World Problems

Using situations that call for multiplying and dividing with large numbers as the basis for whole class discussions provides opportunities for students to explain their strategies and listen to strategies other students have used. As much as possible, choose contexts that relate to students' lives or are familiar to them. Also, ask students to make up their own multiplication and division problems to solve.

As described in *50 Problem-Solving Lessons,* David Ott created problems for his sixth graders to solve that involved data collection and measurement as well as multiplication and division. Here are three of them:

Replacing Floor Tiles. Figure out the number of floor tiles needed to tile the floor of our classroom. Then calculate the number of floor tiles needed for our wing and for all the

Dot Connecting

Suppose you draw 10 dots on a circle. If you draw lines connecting every dot to every other dot, how many lines will you draw?

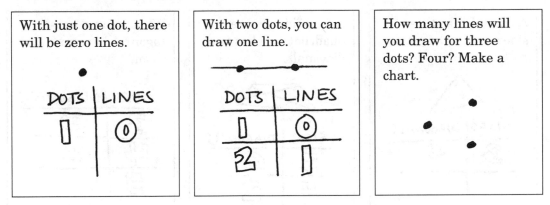

| With just one dot, there will be zero lines. | With two dots, you can draw one line. | How many lines will you draw for three dots? Four? Make a chart. |

Paper Tearing

Suppose you tear a piece of paper in half and give half to someone else. Then each of you tears your piece in half and passes half on to someone else. How many people will have a piece of paper after 10 rounds of tearing like this?

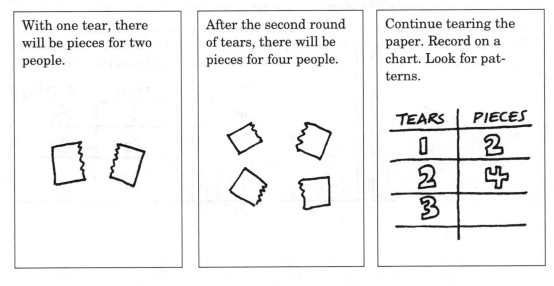

| With one tear, there will be pieces for two people. | After the second round of tears, there will be pieces for four people. | Continue tearing the paper. Record on a chart. Look for patterns. |

The Diagonal Problem

If you have a 12-sided polygon (a dodecagon), how many diagonals can you draw? Remember that diagonals connect the corners of shapes.

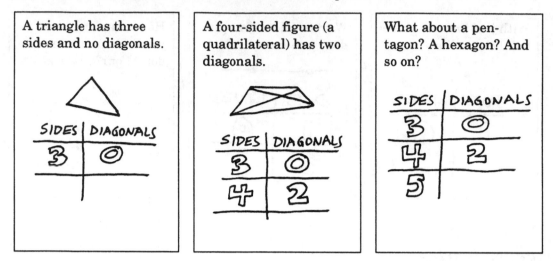

A triangle has three sides and no diagonals.	A four-sided figure (a quadrilateral) has two diagonals.

What about a pentagon? A hexagon? And so on?

SIDES	DIAGONALS
3	0
4	2
5	

Points Dividing a Line

If you put 20 points on a line segment, how many sections can you count?

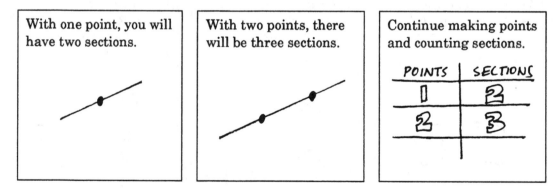

With one point, you will have two sections.	With two points, there will be three sections.

Continue making points and counting sections.

POINTS	SECTIONS
1	2
2	3

Use the following questions for a class discussion after students have played the game enough times to feel comfortable with the rules and the kinds of numerical reasoning expected:

1. What is the best number to use for a first move? Why?

2. What strategies did you use to decide which number was the best to use?

3. When a game is finished, the total of both players' scores, plus the last starting number that remains if it's more than zero, should add up to the original starting number of 100. Why is this so?

4. How would your strategies change if the starting number was 99?

5. How do you think the game would change if the divisors were limited to 1 through 15, or included 1 through 25? Try these versions to see which would be the best game.

As an extension, have students try the game with a different original number or by changing the possible divisors. Also, suggest that students use calculators to see whether this makes the game easier to play and, if so, how. Having students use calculators to play the game gives them the chance to think about the relationship between the whole number remainders used in this game, and decimal remainders represented on calculators. For example, dividing 100 by 8, 12, and 16 all produce a whole number remainder of 4; on a calculator, however $100 \div 8 = 12.5$, $100 \div 12 = 8.333[...]$, and $100 \div 16 = 6.25$.

INDEPENDENT ACTIVITIES (MENU)

Independent activities give students additional experience with multiplication and division of large numbers. After students have had experience with the independent activities, lead whole class discussions to have them present what they learned. *Hit the Target* and *Larger Leftovers* extend whole class lessons.

The Largest Product
You need: a die

Roll the die four times, recording the number that comes up each time. Use the four numbers to make a multiplication problem that produces the largest possible product. For example, if you roll 2, 5, 6, and 1, some problems you could make are 52×61, 51×62, and 612×5. Which is the largest product?

Repeat for at least five sets of numbers. Then investigate the following:

1. If you rolled the same number four times, for example four 2s, your choices are 22×22 or 222×2. Which gives the larger product? Does the same configuration of any number rolled four times give the larger product?

2. Repeat the activity trying to make the smallest product each time.

3. Repeat the activity rolling five times.

4. Do the activity with a 0–9 die or spinner so that you have more numbers to use.

Larger Leftovers

You need: a partner
two dice

This game is an adaptation of *Leftovers from 100*. As with the previous game, the goal is to get the highest score possible. Play the game using the following rules:

1. Agree on a starting number between 200 and 500.
2. The first player rolls the two dice and uses the numbers to make a two-digit divisor. For example, if the player rolls a 3 and a 5, the player can use 35 or 53 as the divisor. The player divides the starting number by the divisor and keeps the remainder as his or her score. The second player records the division sentence, marking the sentence with the first player's initial.
3. Both players subtract the remainder from the starting number to determine the next starting number.
4. Switch roles. The second player rolls the dice, forms a number, divides the new starting number by it, and keeps the remainder as his or her score. The first player records the division sentence. Both players then subtract the remainder to get the new starting number.
5. Continue switching roles and playing until either the starting number becomes zero or it's no longer possible for either player to score.
6. Total your remainders.

Remainders of Zero

You need: a die

Roll the die four times, recording the number that comes up each time. Use the four numbers to make division problems that have a remainder of zero. For example, if you roll 2, 5, 6, and 1, one problem that you could make is $156 \div 2$. See how many different problems you can find for the four numbers. If you are convinced that it isn't possible to make any problem with a remainder of zero, explain why you think this is so. Then investigate the following:

1. Repeat the activity trying to make problems with the largest remainder possible.
2. Repeat the activity rolling five times.
3. Do the activity with a 0–9 die or spinner so that you have more numbers to use.

Hit the Target

You need: a partner
a die

The goal of the game is to hit the target range in as few steps as possible. Play the game as on page 217 except use a die to determine the target range, as explained in step 1:

1. To choose a target range, roll the die three times (or four times to use larger numbers). Arrange the three or four numbers into the largest possible number; this is the lower end of your target range. (For example, if you roll 2, 6, and 3, then the number you make is 632.) Add 50 to your original number to determine the upper end of your range. (In the case of the example, the target range is 632–682.)

2. Player 1 chooses a number between 1 and 100 (14, for example).

3. Player 2 chooses another number to multiply the first number by, and player 1 verifies and records the result (14×50, for example).

4. If the product doesn't hit the target range, player 2 goes back to the original number and multiplies it by any another number. Player 1 verifies and records the result.

5. Players repeat step 4 until the product falls within the target range.

6. Players repeat the game, this time alternating roles.

Sample Game Scenario

Target Range:	632–682
Starting Number: 14	
$14 \times 50 = 700$	The number is too high.
$14 \times 40 = 560$	The number is too high.
$14 \times 45 = 630$	The number is closer but still too low.
$14 \times 46 = 644$	The number is within the target range.

Factor Fiddling

When multiplying two factors, suppose you double one. For example, change 5 $\times$ 3 to 5×6 (doubling the 3) or to 10×3 (doubling the 5 instead). What happens to the product? Try this for many other problems as well.

Then investigate what happens to the product of two factors when you fiddle with one or both of the factors in other ways:

1. Triple one factor.
2. Halve one factor.
3. Double one factor and halve the other factor.

Think of other ways to fiddle with factors and see what you discover.

ASSESSING UNDERSTANDING OF MULTIPLICATION AND DIVISION WITH LARGE NUMBERS

Observing Children

During class discussions and when students are involved with independent activities, circulate among them, observe what they are doing, and talk with them about their numerical reasoning. When students are engaged in small group or individual written assignments, ask them to explain what they have written.

Individual Assessments

1. Assign a multiplication or division problem and ask students to show at least three different ways to figure the answer and explain their reasoning.

2. Give students real-world problems along the lines of the examples suggested for whole class lessons. Ask students to present their solutions in writing and to explain their reasoning.

Fractions

INTRODUCTION

Children's introduction to fractions initially occurs outside of school. They hear adults use fractions in a variety of circumstances:

- I'll be back in three-quarters of an hour.
- I need two sheets of quarter-inch plywood.
- The recipe says to add two-thirds of a cup of water.
- The trim calls for two and a half yards of ribbon.
- There's a quarter moon tonight.
- The dishwasher is less than half full.

Also, children have learned to use the language of fractions to describe events in their own lives:

- You can have half of my cookie.
- Here, use half of my blocks.
- It's a quarter past one.
- I need half a dollar.

From their experiences, a number of ideas about fractions take shape informally in children's minds. However, children's understanding of fractions typically is incomplete and confused. For example, they often think of "half" as any part of a whole, rather than one of two equal parts, and they often refer to one half being larger than another. (It's common to hear children say: My half is bigger than yours.) They may be familiar with one-half, one-third, and one-fourth of a unit, but not with two-thirds or three-fourths. They may not have noticed relationships between fractions, that two-fourths of an hour is the same as one-half of an hour, for example, or that three-fourths of an inch is one-fourth less than one inch. Also, children's informal learning has most likely not been connected to the standard symbols of fractional notation.

Classroom instruction should build on children's previous experiences and help children clarify the ideas they've encountered. It should provide many opportunities throughout the year for children to make sense of fractions, use fractional language, and learn to represent fractions with the standard symbols. Children should deal with fractions concretely and in the context of real life before they focus on symbolic representations.

Some of the activities suggested in this section present fractions as parts of a whole, while others present fractions as parts of collections of objects. Various concrete materials are used so that the children do not link the concepts to the attributes of any particular material. (It may seem ludicrous to think children might generalize that fractions are "round"; but if their experiences with fractions deal only with fraction "pies," that misconception is not so improbable.)

The essential topics for instruction in fractions include naming fractions, comparing fractions, equivalence of fractions, and operations with fractions. It seems that fractions with numerators of 1 do not pose much of a problem for students. Yet when fractions such as 2/5, 3/4, and so on enter the picture, so does confusion. Also, children have difficulty deciding which of two fractions, 2/3 and 4/5, for example, or even 1/8 and 1/16, represents more, and why fractions such as 3/6 and 4/8 describe the same part of a unit. These types of difficulties indicate the need for further concept development with concrete materials and real-life situations.

When they teach older students who lack basic understanding of fractions, it's not uncommon for teachers to feel the pressures of time and the demands of the curriculum. In that situation, it's often a temptation to speed up instruction and to teach the rules for operating with fractions. Some teachers resort to telling students, for example, that multiplying the numerator and denominator by the same number gives an equivalent fraction, or that in order to divide you invert the fraction on the right and multiply across the tops and across the bottoms.

Giving students rules to help them develop facility with fractions will not help them understand the concepts. The risk is that when students forget a rule, they have no way to reason through a process. Try this test with your students: Give students a fraction problem they're "supposed" to understand, 1/2 + 1/3, for example. Ask them to show you what the problem means with any concrete material, or a drawing, or by relating it to some real-life situation. Watch the students' responses, and let their responses guide you when making instructional choices.

One last note: It's important to provide a variety of ways students can learn about fractions — with concrete materials, from a geometric perspective, with a numerical focus, and related to real-life situations. Let the students know that different people learn in different ways, and that they should pay attention to the kinds of activities that help them develop understanding. Encourage them to try activities with which they are less comfortable. Do not expect immediate results from any one activity. Students need time to absorb new ideas and integrate them with the understanding they already have.

WHOLE CLASS LESSONS

Introductory Lessons

Children need many opportunities to talk about fractional parts, see examples, work with concrete materials, and relate their experiences to the standard mathematical notation. Such experiences are best done over time, so that children can develop familiarity and understanding.

Introducing Fractions as Parts of Sets

The following are suggestions for introducing fractions and their symbols. These lessons can help children understand the structure of fractional notation.

Bring a six-pack of soft drinks to class. Remove one can from the pack and tell the children: If I drink this soft drink, I can write a fraction that shows what part of the six-pack I drank. On the board, write "1/6." Tell the children that this is read as one-sixth and means one of six parts. Then pose the following questions:

1. What do you think the 6 refers to?
2. What do you think the 1 stands for?
3. Why does this mathematical notation make sense?
4. What could I write to show the fractional part of the rest of the six-pack, the part I didn't drink?

Have students explain their thinking. Correct any erroneous notions. If this is the first time students have been introduced to this notation, remember they'll need time to understand and become comfortable with it.

Remove another can and ask the same sorts of questions. Continue, introducing 3/6, 4/6, 5/6, and 6/6. Be sure to point out that 6/6 equals one whole six-pack. Follow the same procedure for other sets of objects: a pack of five sticks of gum, a bunch of seven bananas, a box of crackers with three separately wrapped packages.

Also, have similar discussions about sets that contain different things. The following are examples:

• Ask a group of eight students to come to the front of the room. Ask: What fraction of the group are boys? Girls? Are wearing blue? Are wearing long sleeves?

• Show a box of colored birthday candles. Ask: What fraction of the candles in the box are pink? Blue? Green?

• Show a set of pencils, some sharpened and some unsharpened. Ask: What fraction of the set are sharpened? Unsharpened? Have good points? Have erasers?

• Stack about a dozen textbooks on a table. Ask: What fraction of the set are math books? Science books? Social studies books?

• Have nine students each take off one shoe. Set them on a table at the front of the room, or have students gather so all can see them. Ask: What fraction of the set are tennis shoes? Have laces? Don't have laces? Have bumpy soles?

• Bring to class a bag of apples, some red and some green. Ask: What fraction of the set are red? Green?

• Take a handful of Color Tiles, with some each of red, yellow, blue, and green. Ask: What fraction of the set are red? Yellow? Blue? Green?

Fractions with Two-Color Counters

Distribute 12 Two-Color Counters to each student. (Two-Color Counters are plastic disks that are red on one side and yellow on the other. Coins would also work or any counters marked with sides of two different colors.) Give students the directions and questions that follow. Have them discuss the questions in small groups and then present their answers to the entire class, explaining their reasoning for each.

1. Divide the 12 counters into three equal groups with all yellow sides showing. What fractional part of the whole set is represented by each group? How many counters are in 1/3?

2. Flip the counters in one group. What fractional part of the whole set is red? Yellow? How many are in 1/3? In 2/3?

3. Rearrange the counters into six equal groups with all yellow sides up. Flip the counters in one group. What fractional part of the whole set is red? Yellow? Flip another group. What fractional part of the whole set is red? Yellow? Flip another group. What fractional part of the whole set is red? Yellow? Continue until all groups have been flipped.

4. Arrange the counters so 1/4 of them have red sides showing. What fractional part of the whole set is yellow? Show another set with fewer than 12 counters that also has 1/4 of the set with red sides showing. See how many different solutions you can find.

5. Show a set of counters that has 2/6 of them with their yellow sides showing. Find as many different solutions as you can that use 12 or fewer counters. (Continue for other fractions: 2/8, 5/6, 3/5, etc.)

The Fraction Kit

This activity introduces students to fractions as parts of a whole. Organize students into pairs or small groups. Each student needs five 3-by-18-inch strips of construction paper in five different colors, a pair of scissors, and a number 10 envelope. (Four strips can be cut from a 12-by-18-inch sheet of construction paper.) Also, prepare fraction dice, cubes with the six faces labeled as follows: 1/2, 1/4, 1/8, 1/8, 1/16, 1/16; each pair or group needs one.

Give students directions to cut and label the strips. Ask students to take a strip of a particular color, fold it in half, and cut it into two pieces. Have them label each piece 1/2. (Review the rationale for the notation by explaining that the whole has been divided into two pieces of the same size, that each piece is one of the two pieces, and that the 1/2 notation means one of two equal pieces.)

Then choose a color for a second strip and have the students fold and cut it into four equal pieces. Talk about each piece being one of four, or one-fourth, and ask students to label each piece 1/4. Then have them fold, cut, and label a third strip into eighths and a fourth strip into sixteenths. Students leave the fifth strip whole, and label it 1, or 1/1.

Each student now has a fraction kit to use. Having students cut and label the pieces helps them relate the fractional notation to the concrete pieces and compare the sizes of fractional parts. They can see that 1/4, for example, is larger than 1/16, and they can measure to prove that two of the 1/8 pieces are equivalent to 1/4. Finally, have students label the backs of their pieces with their initials. Give them envelopes in which to keep their kits.

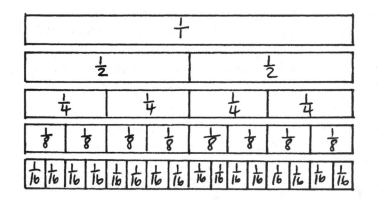

Following are activities for children to do in pairs or small groups.

Cover Up. This is a game for two or more players. Each player starts with a whole strip. The goal is to be the first to cover the whole strip completely with other pieces of the fraction kit. No overlapping pieces are allowed. Following are the rules for play.

1. Children take turns rolling the cube labeled with fractions.

2. The fraction face up on the cube tells what size piece to place on the whole strip.

3. When the game nears the end and a student needs only a small piece, such as 1/8 or 1/16, rolling 1/2 or 1/4 won't do. The student must roll exactly what is needed.

Uncover. This game gives children experience with equivalent fractions. Each student starts with the whole strip covered with the two 1/2 pieces. The goal is to be the first to uncover the strip completely. Following are the rules for play.

1. Children take turns rolling the cube.

2. A child has three options on each turn: to remove a piece (only if he or she has a piece the size indicated by the fraction face up on the cube), to exchange any of the pieces left for equivalent pieces, or to do nothing and to pass the cube to the next player. (A player may not remove a piece and trade on the same turn, but can do only one or the other.) It's important for children to check that each other trades correctly.

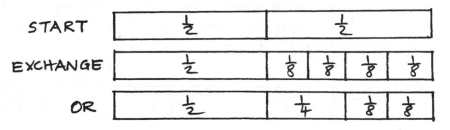

At this time, the only fractional symbols the fraction kit activities have used are 1/2, 1/4, 1/8, and 1/16. After students are familiar with both games, they can be introduced to fractions with numerators other than 1. They have probably already used the language of those fractions in their games: "I've got just three more sixteenths to take off," or "I can exchange this one-half piece for two fourths." The symbolism for these fractions needs to be connected to students' concrete experiences.

Recording Cover-Ups. Ask the students to cover their whole pieces with whatever smaller pieces they choose. Record several of their examples on the board. For example, if a child used three 1/4 pieces and two 1/8 pieces, record: 1/4 + 1/4 + 1/4 + 1/8 + 1/8 = 1. Then explain how to shorten the equation by counting the fourths and writing 3/4, and counting the eighths and writing 2/8: 3/4 + 2/8 = 1. Have children help you shorten several other of the recordings on the board. Then have them each cover their whole strip with at least five different combinations of pieces and record on a worksheet, with and without shortening their lists. Have students exchange and check each other's papers.

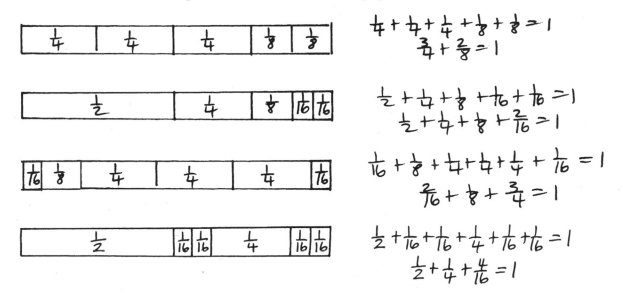

Fraction Sentences. Give the students incomplete fraction sentences and have them use their fraction kits to decide how to complete them. This is fairly standard fraction practice, but in this case it is related to the students' concrete experience with the fraction kits. In all cases, have students explain, orally and in writing, why their answers make sense.

Such exercises can have several forms:
- Give pairs of fractions and have students write >, <, or = to make a true sentence.
- Ask students to supply the missing number to make the fractions equivalent.
- Have students write other fractions that are equivalent to the one you give.
- Have students find a way to write one fraction to complete a sentence. They can use their fraction kits for this by covering the pieces with all pieces of the same size so the length can be represented with one fraction.

$$\frac{1}{2} + \frac{1}{4} + \frac{1}{8} = \frac{7}{8}$$

Using Graphs to Build Understanding of Fractions

Use data from class graphs for class discussions about fractions. Over time, such discussions help students develop and secure their understanding of fractional concepts. The graphing ideas that follow present variations on graphs about names. Check the list of graphs on page 76 in the Probability and Statistics section for other graphing ideas that you may find useful.

1. Is your last name longer, shorter, or the same length as your first name? (Ask: What fraction of the class has last names that are longer? Shorter? The same length?)

First and Last Names
Make a tally. (卌 II)

My last name is longer.	My names are the same.	My last name is shorter.

2. How many letters in your last name? (Ask: What fraction of the class has last names with more than five letters? More than seven? Fewer than six?)

Letters in Last Names
Color in a square.

2									
3									
4									
5									

3. How many syllables in your first name? (Ask: What fraction of the class has one syllable in their first name? Two? Three? More? What fraction of the class has fewer than three syllables in their first name?)

Syllables
How many syllables are in your first name? Write your name in the correct column.

1	2	3	4

4. Do you have a middle name? (Ask: What fraction of the class has a middle name? What fraction does not?)

Middle Names
Do you have a middle name? Make a tally. (卌 II)

Yes	
No	

5. Were you named after someone special? (Ask: What fraction of the class was named after someone special? What fraction was not?)

Were You Named After Someone Special?
Sign your name.

Yes	No

Exploring Fractions Through Sharing Problems

Students benefit from a variety of sharing problems that call for fractional solutions. They can use circles to share cookies, squares to share brownies, and rectangles to share apple crisp bars. Although the problems presented for each of the shapes can be the same, for some students, changing the shapes seems to change the problem and to present a new challenge. The following are models of sharing problems.

Sharing Cookies

In this investigation, children share different numbers of cookies among members of a group. It's important they know that each person should get the same amount. For younger children, you might introduce this task by presenting the following problem: If I gave each group of four children four cookies to share, how much would each person get? This will most likely be obvious to them, but it will give you the chance to discuss what is meant by "sharing equally." Then have children solve the problems of sharing one, two, three, five, and six cookies among four people.

> Share — cookies equally among 4 people. Paste each person's share in a box.
>
> How much did each person get?

Provide the children with paper circles to represent cookies (see blackline masters). Ask that they cut the circles, paste each person's share on a sheet of paper, and record how much each person got. Have groups present and explain their solutions.

Extend the investigation by changing the number of cookies they are sharing, by changing the size of the group to six or eight people, or by substituting rectangles for the round cookies.

Sharing Brownies

This activity uses grids made of four-by-four squares (see blackline masters). Using the context of brownies, students figure out different ways to divide the grids into halves, fourths, and eighths. Although these are the same fractional parts the students investigated when they constructed fraction kits, using grids gives them another way to build their understanding.

Begin with halves. On the chalkboard or a projected overhead transparency, draw several four-by-four grids. Ask students how to divide the grids in half so that two people would each get the same amount of brownie to eat. Students typically suggest the following three ways.

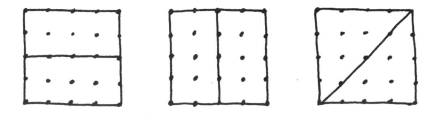

If students don't offer other ways, suggest that they think of ways that don't use one straight cut but that still produce two pieces the same size. Show an example.

Then have students work in pairs or small groups to find as many other ways as they can to divide the brownies into halves. Distribute worksheets of four-by-four grids (see blackline masters) on which they can record their work. In a class discussion, ask students to show their favorite solutions and explain how they know the two parts really are halves.

Repeat for fourths and again for eighths.

To extend the activity, use six-by-four grids (see blackline masters) and ask students to share these rectangular brownies among two, three, four, six, and eight people. This provides experience with halves, thirds, fourths, sixths, and eighths.

Comparing and Ordering Fractions

Learning to compare and order fractions is an important aspect of developing an understanding of fractions. Students must recognize that the size of the denominator affects the size of fractional parts of the same whole — the larger the denominator, the smaller the pieces. Students must also be able to determine when fractions are equivalent — that 2/4, for example, represents the same part of a whole as does 3/6, 4/8, and so on.

Put In Order

Write 12 fractions on 4-by-6-inch index cards, one per card, large enough for everyone to see. Prop one card on the chalkboard tray. Tell the students that their task is to place the rest of the fractions in order from smallest to largest. Then show the cards one at a time, each time asking a student to place it. Students should also explain their reasoning.

Put in Order is an appropriate follow-up to the fraction kit activities after students have made kits and have played *Cover Up* and *Uncover*. It's helpful for students to use their fraction kits when first encountering *Put in Order* to help them reason. The following set of fractions works well for a first lesson with this activity. Begin by propping on the chalkboard tray the card with 1/2 on it, giving students a familiar landmark fraction to use.

1/16, 1/8, 3/16, 1/4, 3/8, 1/2, 5/8, 3/4, 15/16, 1/1, 9/8, 3/2

Repeat the activity with different sets of fractions or using previous sets but presenting the fractions in different order. When making sets of cards, avoid including equivalent fractions so students don't try to order two fractions that have the same value.

1/8, 1/6, 1/4, 1/3, 1/2, 2/3, 3/4, 15/16, 8/8, 17/16, 7/6, 4/3
1/16, 1/12, 2/8, 3/8, 3/6, 3/4, 7/8, 11/12, 3/3, 17/16, 9/8, 5/4

After the class is familiar with the activity, have students work in pairs or small groups to create sets of fractions to present to the class. Have them first justify in writing the order of their fractions; after you check their reasoning, have them lead the activity with the rest of the class.

Who Ate More?

Build on the experience children have gained through thinking about fractional parts of circles in *Sharing Cookies* by having them compare shares of pizza. Vary the problems by changing the number of pieces cut and eaten. Either present the problems to the whole class, or first ask pairs or small groups to consider them before leading a class discussion.

• Joey and Roberta each had individual pizzas that were the same size. Joey cut his into four pieces and ate three of them. Roberta cut hers into six pieces and ate four of them. Who ate more pizza?

• Mario cut his pizza into eight pieces and ate two of them. Kim cut hers into four pieces and ate one of them. Who ate more pizza?

• William cut his pizza into eight pieces and ate five of them. Elissa cut hers into six pieces and ate four of them. Who ate more pizza?

• Sara cut her pizza into three pieces and ate one of them. Tomas cut his into eight pieces and ate two of them. Who ate more pizza?

Mental Calculation with Fractions

A great deal of emphasis traditionally has been put on paper-and-pencil algorithms for addition, subtraction, multiplication, and division of fractions. Too much focus is often put on "how to do the problem" rather than on "what makes sense." The following suggestions offer ways to have students calculate mentally with fractions. The emphasis shifts from paper-and-pencil computation with the goal of arriving at exact answers to mental calculation with the goal of arriving at estimates and being able to explain why they're reasonable.

Closest to 0, 1/2, or 1?

Give students fractions that are less than 1 — 3/8, 1/6, or 5/7, for example — and have them decide if the fraction is closest to 0, 1/2, or 1. Have students discuss in groups and then report back to the class, explaining their reasoning. You may want to give groups a collection of a dozen or so fractions to sort into three groups: closest to 0, closest to 1/2, and closest to 1. They should record their answers and write about the methods they use to sort their fractions.

Fractions in Contexts

Give students problems for which they are to find estimates mentally. Have students work in groups so they can talk about their ideas. As with all activities, have students defend their answers by explaining their methods.

Finding Fractional Parts. In order to do these problems, students should be able to figure mentally such fractional parts as 1/3 of 30, 1/2 of 24, and 1/4 of 32.

• A full tank of gas holds 14 gallons. The fuel gauge reads 1/4 full. About how many gallons are left? (If you get 20 miles per gallon, how much farther can you drive?)

- Jill's mother and aunt together have agreed to split equally 1/2 of the cost of a baseball glove with Jill. The glove costs $25.99. About how much does Jill need to contribute?
- A $7.98 shirt is on sale at 1/3 off. About how much will Tony save if he buys it?

Have students make up situations such as these for their classmates to solve.

Fraction Word Problems. Have students try the following problems. Be sure to keep the emphasis on reasonable answers and on the different methods they used.

- A bookshelf measures 2 1/2 feet. How many could you fit against a wall that measures 14 1/2 feet?
- If it takes 1 1/4 yards of fabric to make a cape and each of the six people on the cheering squad needs a cape, how much fabric should you buy?

Then have them try some of their textbook word problems, not to calculate exact answers, but to arrive at acceptable estimates and to be able to explain their reasoning.

Strategies for Operations

Encourage students to invent their own strategies for mentally estimating sums and differences. You may want to present a sample strategy to the class. For example, estimating whether fractions are close to 0, 1/2, or 1 can help in estimating sums. To estimate 12/13 + 4/9, 12/13 is close to 1 and 4/9 is close to 1/2, so the sum is about 1 1/2. But it's a little less, since the estimates were less than 1 and 1/2. Try some exercises with the whole class and then give small groups problems to discuss and estimate together.

In the same way, model techniques for estimating products and quotients. For example, to estimate the answer to 2 7/8 × 15 3/4, you can say that 2 7/8 is close to 3 and 15 3/4 is close to 16, and 3 × 16 is 48. So I know my answer is close to but less than 48.

INDEPENDENT ACTIVITIES (MENU)

Following are activities that engage students with fractions. Several activities suggest ways to use manipulative materials for investigating fractions. Have students work on the activities in pairs or small groups. Then have whole class discussions in which students present their findings, the different methods they used, and difficulties they encountered.

Fractions Close to 1/2

For each situation, decide whether the best estimate is more or less than 1/2. Record your conclusions and reasoning.

1. When pitching, Joe struck out 7 of 17 batters.
2. Sally made 8 baskets out of 11 free throws.
3. Bill made 5 field goals out of 9 attempts.
4. Maria couldn't collect at 4 of the 35 homes on her paper route.
5. Diane made 8 hits in 15 times at bat.

Make up three situations and exchange papers with a classmate.

Building Rectangles

You need: Color Tiles

squared paper (see blackline masters)

markers or crayons

Use tiles to build a rectangle that is 1/2 red, 1/4 yellow, and 1/4 green. Record and label it on squared paper. Find at least one other rectangle that also works. Build and record.

Now use the tiles to build each of the rectangles below. Build and record each in at least two ways.

1/3 green, 2/3 blue

1/6 red, 1/6 green, 1/3 blue, 1/3 yellow

1/2 red, 1/4 green, 1/8 yellow, 1/8 blue

1/5 red, 4/5 yellow

1/8 red, 3/8 yellow, 1/2 blue

These rectangles show two solutions for $\frac{3}{4}$ red, $\frac{1}{4}$ yellow.

Fraction Riddles

You need: Color Tiles

squared paper (see blackline masters)

markers or crayons

(A suggestion: First try the activity *Building Rectangles*.)

Riddle 1: A rectangle is 1/2 red, 1/5 green, 1/10 blue, and the rest yellow. How much of the rectangle is yellow? Draw the rectangle on squared paper and record the fraction that tells which part is yellow.

Riddle 2: A rectangle is 3/5 red. The rest is blue and yellow but not in equal amounts. What could the rectangle look like? Record.

Riddle 3: A rectangle is 1/2 red and 1/3 blue. Also, it has one green tile and one yellow tile. What could the rectangle look like? What fractional part is green? Yellow? Record.

Make up three riddles like these for others to solve.

Rod Relationships

You need: Cuisenaire Rods

The yellow rod is half as long as the orange rod. (Prove this to yourself with the rods.) This relationship can be written:

$$\tfrac{1}{2}\,o = y$$

Find all the other pairs of halves you can with the rods and build them. Record each.

Then do the same with thirds. For example, it takes three light green rods to make a train as long as the blue rod, so light green is 1/3 of blue. (Prove it with the rods.) Record like this:

$$\tfrac{1}{3}e = g$$

Find all the fractional relationships you can for halves, thirds, fourths, fifths, and so on, up to tenths. Explain why you think you've found them all.

Build the Yellow Hexagon

You need: Pattern Blocks

Find all the different ways you can build the yellow hexagon from different assortments of blocks. Count only different combinations of blocks. For example, if you use two blues and two greens, that combination counts as only one way even if the arrangements look different.)

These count as one way.

Use fractions to record the different ways you found. For example, the green triangle is 1/6 of the hexagon and the red trapezoid is 1/2 of the hexagon. Therefore, if you build the hexagon using one red and three greens, you can record as follows: 1/2 + 1/6 + 1/6 + 1/6 = 1. Also, you can shorten that by combining the three greens into one fraction: 1/2 + 3/6 = 1. Record each of the ways you built the yellow hexagon, recording each in different ways.

Wipeout

You need: a partner
Pattern Blocks
a cube with faces marked 1/2, 1/3, 1/3, 1/6, 1/6, 1/6

This is a two-person game. The goal is to be the first to discard your blocks. You each should start with the same number of hexagons, either one, two, or three. Follow these rules:

1. Take turns rolling the cube.

2. You have three options on each turn: to remove a block (only if it's the fractional part of the hexagon indicated by the fraction face up on the cube), to exchange any of your remaining blocks for equivalent blocks, or to do nothing and pass the cube to your partner. You may not remove a block and trade on the same turn; you can do only one or the other.

Be sure to pay attention to each other's trades to make sure they are done correctly.

ASSESSING UNDERSTANDING OF FRACTIONS

Observing Students

During class discussions and when students are working on the independent tasks, circulate, observe, and question them about their thinking and reasoning.

Individual Assessments

The following written assignments suggest ways to find out about children's understanding of fractions.

1. Before beginning instruction, ask students to write what they know about fractions. Have them do this again at the end of the instructional unit or even midway through. Return papers to the students and ask them to reflect on their learning.

2. Assign problems such as those suggested for whole class lessons. Ask students to present solutions in writing and explain their reasoning.

3. Ask the students to draw pictures to show the following fractional parts:

a. 2/5 of a set of circles are shaded

b. 4/5 of the squares are red

c. 3/4 of the triangles are blue

d. 1/3 of the balls are footballs

e. 4/9 of the fruit are apples

4. [The following suggestion is from Janet H. Caldwell's article, "Communicating about Fractions with Pattern Blocks," in the November 1995 issue of *Teaching Children Mathematics* (NCTM, Volume 2, Number 3).] Show students the following Pattern Block design made with three green triangles, six blue parallelograms, three red trapezoids, and one yellow hexagon.

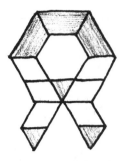

Ask students to respond in writing to the problem: What fraction of the design is blue?

5. On a national assessment, 13-year-olds were given the following item:

Estimate the answer to 12/13 + 7/8.

a. 1

b. 2

c. 19

d. 21

Only 24 percent of the students answered correctly, with approximately equal numbers of students choosing each of the wrong answers. (Can you explain to yourself what the thinking was behind each of the erroneous choices?) See how your students respond to this question.

Decimals

INTRODUCTION

*D*ecimals make it possible to use our place-value system of notation to write fractions, as long as they are expressed as tenths of a unit, hundredths, thousandths, and so on. The activities in this section assume that children have learned about fractions and have a base of understanding that can be expanded to incorporate the symbolism of decimals. They suggest ways to connect students' former experiences to the new notation.

When students are learning about decimals, it's helpful to distinguish between the way decimals are commonly read and what they mean. It's natural to read decimals such as 2.7 and .34, for example, as "two point seven" and "point 34." However, students should know that these decimals can also be read as "two and seven-tenths" and "thirty-four hundredths," and they should be able to relate decimal fractions to common fractions. Paying attention to this difference reinforces the fact that decimals are fractions written in different symbolic notation.

The lessons in this section suggest several ways to introduce students to decimal numerals and to help them discover how decimals relate to our number system. The emphasis is on helping students make sense of decimals in several different ways and building a foundation of understanding from which students later can learn about repeating decimals, scientific notation, and other related topics.

WHOLE CLASS LESSONS

Investigations with Calculators

The calculator is a useful tool for helping students learn about decimals. Following are several suggestions for using calculators to introduce decimals. Encourage students to make discoveries and to draw conclusions from their investigations.

Using Division Problems to Introduce Decimals

Give students a division problem such as the following: The library had extra copies of 50 books. The librarian decided to divide the books equally among the 12 classrooms in the school. How many books would each class get? Have students talk about this in small groups and then present their solutions to the class.

Then ask what answer they think they'd get if they did this problem on a calculator. Have them try it. They'll probably get an answer such as 4.1666666 or 4.1666667, depending on the particular calculator they use. Tell them that this number is called a decimal numeral and is the calculator's way to represent a number that is greater than four but less than five. Have the students try other divisions and compare the answers they figure themselves with the answers they get when they use a calculator. Have them report what they discover about decimal numerals.

Relating Fractional Remainders as Decimals

For another experience with division, give the children problems for which they can use fractions to express the remainders. For example, when sharing seven cookies between two children, there is one extra cookie. Most children solve the problem by suggesting that each child get an additional half, giving them each three and a half cookies. Give the students other such sharing problems that have remainders and ask them to represent the remainders as fractions. The following are examples.
- Share seven cookies among three children. How much does each child get?
- Divide nine apples between two people. How much does each person get?
- Share five brownies among four children. How much does each child get?
- Share seven brownies among four children. How much does each child get?
- Divide a whole pie among ten people. How much does each person get?

After you've discussed the answers to these problems with the children, return to the first problem of sharing seven cookies between two children. Ask the students what answer they think they would get if they did this problem on a calculator. Then have them do it. As in the previous activity, tell them that 3.5 is how the calculator represents a number that is greater than three but less than four, that it means the same as three and a half, and that it's called a decimal numeral. Have the students use calculators to solve the other problems. Then ask them to make up additional problems to solve mentally, finding fractional remainders, and then solving with a calculator. Have them record discoveries they make about decimals.

A Geometric Perspective on Decimals

Some students benefit from being able to visualize decimals. A 10-by-10 grid is useful for helping students see the relationship between decimals and common fractions and make sense out of operating with decimals. For these activities, students need 10-by-10 grids (see blackline masters) and markers or crayons.

Decimals on Grids

Introduce decimal notation by beginning with tenths. On the chalkboard or overhead, draw several 10-by-10 grids. Talk with the students about the grids — the number of rows, columns, and small squares. Although it may seem obvious to you that there are 10 rows and columns and 100 small squares, this may not be obvious to the students.

On one grid, shade three columns of squares. Ask: What fractional part of the grid have I shaded? Students may respond with 3/10 or 30/100. Record the fractions and have the students explain why those fractions make sense. If they only suggest one possibility, then record the other and have them discuss why this also makes sense. Then show the class how to record these fractions as decimals: .3 and .30. Talk about the differences between these two numerals.

Now do another example. Shade just three small squares and again ask: What fractional part of the grid have I shaded? As before, record the common fraction, 3/100, and the decimal fraction, .03. Choosing this example gives you the opportunity to discuss the importance of the placement of the digits.

Continue by shading other amounts. For example, shade two columns of ten squares and seven additional squares on the next column. Have students explain why 27/100 makes sense and show them how to write it as a decimal. Also point out that this could be written as 2/10 + 7/100. Ask students to discuss why this makes sense. Write both representations as decimals: ".27" and ".2 + .07."

When you feel they are ready, give students blank worksheets of 10-by-10 grids and have them make up their own problems. They should shade any amount they like and record. In these investigations, encourage students to be flexible and to look for all the different ways to record symbolically the portion of the grid they shade.

It's useful to relate the decimal notation you've presented to our system for recording money. Ask them to think of the 10-by-10 grid as $1.00; relate pennies to hundredths and dimes to tenths. Compare notations to see how they are alike and different. For example, on a grid, .14 can be described as one column and four extra squares or as 14 squares; similarly with money, $.14 can be one dime and four pennies or 14 pennies. However, while three columns on a grid can be represented as .3, three dimes isn't written as $.3, but as $.30. These are social conventions that students must learn.

The following are suggestions for extensions.

• Introduce how to write mixed numerals in the same way. For example, use three grids to show 2 3/10.

• Have students use the grids to compare decimal numerals. When they focus on the visual representations of decimals, they are less apt to mistakenly interpret that .52, for example, is more than .6. Also, coloring on grids helps reinforce that decimals such as .4 and .40 are equivalent.

Give students pairs of decimal numerals to compare, or several to put in order, such as .15, .2, .46, .3.

• Talk with students about how to use decimal numerals to represent common fractions that are not expressed as tenths or hundredths. Because of students' familiarity with money, begin with 1/4, 1/2, and 3/4.

• Introduce students to using rectangular arrays to multiply tenths by tenths. It may be necessary to review how arrays model multiplication of whole numbers.

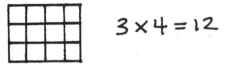

Below are two examples of using grids to multiply decimals. Examples such as these may help students see why multiplying tenths by tenths produces hundredths.

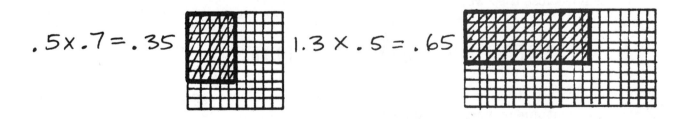

Mental Calculation with Decimals

A great deal of emphasis traditionally has been put on paper-and-pencil algorithms for addition, subtraction, multiplication, and division of decimals. The focus is often put on "how to do the problem" rather than on "what makes sense." The following suggestions offer ways to have students calculate mentally with decimals. The emphasis shifts from paper-and-pencil computation with the goal of exact answers to mental calculation with the goal of arriving at estimates and being able to explain why they're reasonable.

Closest to 0, .5, or 1?

Give students decimal numerals that are less than 1, .4, .15, or .7, for example, and have them decide if they are closest to 0, .5, or 1. Have students discuss these in groups and then report back to the class, explaining their reasoning. Include decimals with tenths, hundredths, and, if the students are able, thousandths.

Decimals in Contexts

Give students problems for which they are to find estimates mentally. Have students work in groups so they can talk about their ideas. As in all activities, have students defend their answers by explaining their methods.

- Jenny started jogging. Her dad clocked her distances by car. On Monday, she ran 1.5 miles; on Tuesday, she ran 2.1 miles. How many miles did she run in the two days?
- Raul bought three small bags of potato chips that cost $.69 each. How much did they cost altogether?
- Maria had $4.65 in nickels. How many nickels did she have?

Then have students try some of their textbook word problems, not to calculate exact answers, but to arrive at acceptable estimates and be able to explain their reasoning. Have them check their estimates with calculators.

Strategies for Operations

Encourage students to invent their own strategies for mentally calculating. You may want to present a sample strategy to the class for estimating products and quotients. For example, to estimate the answer to 3.24×4.9, you can say that 3.24 is close to 3 and 4.9 is close to 5, and 3×5 is 15. Then you can decide if the answer will be greater than or less than 15. Try some exercises with the whole class and then give small groups some problems to discuss and estimate together. After students make estimates, they can check with a calculator to see how close they were.

INDEPENDENT ACTIVITIES (MENU)

Following are activities in which students use decimals. They suggest additional ways for students to continue exploring decimal numerals.

Decimals in the Newspaper

You need: a newspaper

Look for articles in which decimals are used. Choose one to present to the class. In your presentation, explain the meaning of the decimals.

Multiplication Puzzlers

You need: a calculator

For each problem below, find the missing number by using your calculator and the problem-solving strategy of guessing and checking. Don't solve the problems by dividing, but instead see how many guesses each takes you. Record all of your guesses as shown.

For example, to solve $4 \times \underline{\hspace{1cm}} = 87$, you might start with 23 and then adjust. Below is a possible solution that shows how you are to record.

$$4 \times \underline{\hspace{1cm}} = 87$$

$$4 \times 23 = 92$$
$$4 \times 22 = 88$$
$$4 \times 21 = 84$$
$$4 \times 21.5 = 86$$
$$4 \times 21.6 = 86.4$$
$$4 \times 21.7 = 86.8$$
$$4 \times 21.8 = 87.2$$
$$4 \times 21.74 = 86.96$$
$$4 \times 21.75 = 87 \bigstar$$

It took 9 guesses.

Try the following:
$$5 \times \underline{\hspace{1cm}} = 96$$
$$6 \times \underline{\hspace{1cm}} = 106$$
$$4 \times \underline{\hspace{1cm}} = 63$$
$$8 \times \underline{\hspace{1cm}} = 98$$

Adding to One

You need: a calculator

Enter a number. Press the "+" key and then press the "=" key. (You should see the same number you entered.) However, if you continue to press the "=" key, each time the calculator will add the same number you entered over and over.

You task is to find numbers to enter so that by following this procedure of pressing the "+" key and then pressing the "=" key over and over, the display eventually shows a total of 1. For example, enter ".5" and then press the "+" key, followed by pressing the "=" key twice. The total is 1. You can record this: .5 + .5 = 1.

Find as many different ways as you can to repeat the same addends and get a total of 1. Record each.

The Place Value Game

You need: a partner or small group
a die or 0–9 spinner

The goal of this game is to make the largest number possible. Each player should draw a game board as shown:

— — — — · — —

Players take turns rolling the die or spinning the spinner. Each time a number comes up, every player writes it in one space on his or her game board. Once written, the number cannot be moved. The winner has the largest number and must be able to read it.

ASSESSING UNDERSTANDING OF DECIMALS

Observing Students

During class discussions and when students are working on the independent tasks, circulate, observe, and, at times, question them about their thinking and reasoning. Look and listen for evidence of students' understanding of decimals and their relation to fractions.

Individual Assessments

The following written assignments suggest ways to find out about students' understanding of decimals.

1. Before beginning instruction, ask students to write what they know about decimals. Have them do this again at the end of the instructional unit or even midway through. Return papers to the students and ask them to reflect on their learning.

2. Ask students to write about the ways our systems for decimals and money are alike and different. Ask them to include examples.

3. Assign problems such as those suggested for whole class lessons. Ask students to present solutions in writing and to explain their reasoning.

Percents

INTRODUCTION

Students have many experiences with percents before they study them formally in school. They know that a 50% sale means that prices are cut in half and that a 10% sale doesn't give as much saving. They understand what it means to earn a 90% grade on a test. They hear on TV that some tires get 40% more wear, that a tennis player gets 64% of her first serves in, that there is a 70% chance of rain tomorrow. Common to these sorts of experiences is that percents are presented in the context of situations that occur in students' daily lives.

The goal for instruction in percents should be to help students learn to use percents appropriately and effectively in problem situations. This means that, when given a situation that involves percents, students should be able to reason mathematically to arrive at an answer, to explain why that answer is reasonable, and to make a decision about the situation based on the answer.

The activities presented in this section are designed to build on what students already know and to help them extend their understanding of how to reason with percents. The ideas do not provide a comprehensive guide for teaching percents. Rather, they offer models of ways to introduce ideas about percents, suggest problem situations that engage students, and give alternative methods for assessing what students understand.

WHOLE CLASS LESSONS

Introducing Percents in Contexts

It makes sense for formal lessons on percents to build on what students already know. Instructional activities should expand students' knowledge from their daily life experiences into more general understanding. The following activity appears in *Problem Solving in Mathematics* by the Lane County Mathematics Project and is shown being taught in the *Mathematics for Middle School* videotapes (see bibliography).

Sense or Nonsense?

Students are to decide whether the statements are reasonable and why. You can discuss each of the statements in a whole class discussion or have small groups of students discuss and write about them and then present their explanations to the class. For another class activity or for homework, have students write additional statements like these and use them for further class discussions.

1. Mr. Bragg says he is right 100% of the time. Do you think Mr. Bragg is bragging? Why?
2. The Todd family ate out last Saturday. The bill was $36. Would a 50% tip be too much to leave? Why?
3. Joe loaned Jeff a dollar. He said the interest would be 75% a day. Is this a pretty good deal for Joe? Why?
4. Cindy spends 100% of her allowance on candy. Do you think this is sensible? Why?
5. The Never Miss basketball team made 10% of the baskets they tried. Do you think they should change their name? Why?
6. Sarah missed 10 problems on the science test. Do you think her percent is high enough for her to earn an A? Why?
7. Rosa has a paper route. She gets to keep 25% of whatever she collects. Do you think this is a good deal? Why?
8. The weather reporter said, "There's a 100% chance of rain for tomorrow." Is this a reasonable prediction for this month? Why?
9. Ms. Green was complaining, "Prices have gone up at least 200% this past year." Do you think she is exaggerating? Why?
10. A store advertised "Best sale ever, 10% discount on all items." Is this a good sale? Why?

The Harper's Index Problem

As a regular feature, *Harper's Magazine* includes Harper's Index, a listing of statistical information about a variety of world issues. An item in the October 1989 magazine read: "Percentage of supermarket prices that end in the digit 9 or 5: 80%."

Use this statement for a class investigation in which students collect and analyze data in order to test its validity. Ask students to bring to class supermarket receipts. In small groups, have students examine their receipts to see whether they support the statement. Ask groups to write a report about their investigation that includes the following:

1. Data (shown in a neat and organized manner)
2. Calculations (with an explanation about why the procedures they used make sense)
3. Conclusion (explained clearly and concisely)

Have groups present their findings. **Note:** Students in one class raised the issue that while fruit, vegetables, and meat might have prices per pound that end in 9 or 5, the cost on the receipt won't necessarily reflect this for different amounts purchased. Therefore, they did a second study of their data in which they eliminated items in this category. The discussion about this gave the students experience with the kinds of difficulties that arise in real-life statistical investigations.

A Geometric Perspective on Percents

This idea, also adapted from *Problem Solving in Mathematics* by the Lane County Mathematics Project, presents students with a spatial model for thinking about percents. The activity introduces students to the idea that percents are parts of 100 and gives them the opportunity to estimate areas and to express their estimates in terms of percents.

What Percent Is Shaded?

Make a transparency of the worksheet of nine 10-by-10 grids (see blackline masters) and cut them apart so each student has one grid. Also, prepare a sheet of shapes such as the ones shown below.

Before distributing any of the materials, do several sample problems with the class. Draw a square on the board and shade part of it. Ask the students to estimate about what percent of the square is shaded. Have them discuss this in small groups and then report their estimates and explain their reasoning. Do this for several shapes. Shade regions for which a range of responses is reasonable so that the emphasis is on students' reasoning, not on finding an exact answer that can be proved right or wrong.

Show students one of the transparent 10-by-10 grids. Ask them to discuss among themselves how to use the grid to estimate what percent of a square is shaded. It's important to introduce students to the idea that percent means "part of 100." Since there are 100 small squares on the grid, knowing how many small squares are shaded tells what percent of the grid has been shaded.

When you feel students understand the task, distribute a worksheet of shapes and the transparent grids. Ask them to estimate the percent of each square that is shaded and use their transparent grids to check their estimates. Have students do this individually and then compare their answers in small groups. Have a class discussion about any they couldn't resolve.

Have students make up shapes for others to try. Having them put their shapes on index cards is an easy way to create a class set of problems.

Using Graphs to Build Understanding of Percents

The questions that follow are ideas to be used for class graphs. The graphs suggested have been chosen so that students can compare the statistical result of their class samples with the percentages reported for the population at large. Use the graphs to initiate discussions about percents. For each, ask the following types of questions:

How many students indicated _____?

Is this more or less than 50%?

About what percent of our class reported _____?

How did you figure that percent?

The national statistic is _____. How does our class sample compare to this national statistic?

(The statistics presented have all been gathered from *American Averages* by Mike Feinsilber and William B. Mead, Dolphin Books.)

1. Do you bite your fingernails? (Between 25% and 36% of college students do.)
2. How many hours a day do you sleep? (63% of adults sleep between seven and eight hours a day.)
3. Do you get a regular allowance? (50% of 12- to 17-year-olds do.)
4. Do you view smoking as a sign of weakness? (75% of Americans do.)
5. Are you wearing athletic shoes or sneakers? (25% of shoes worn by Americans are athletic shoes or sneakers.)
6. Which do you generally take, a shower or a bath? (59% of teenage girls and 78% of teenage boys take showers rather than baths.)
7. What is your favorite animal? (9% of children report that the horse is their favorite animal.)
8. What animals live in your home? (33% of U.S. households have a dog; 12.5% have a cat; 10% have both.)
9. Do fish live in your household? (6.2% of households have fish.)
10. Have you ever taken piano lessons? (40% of American children take piano lessons at some time or another.)
11. How many TVs are there in your home? (50% of households have two or more TVs.)
12. Which soft drink would you order: Coke, Pepsi, Dr. Pepper, 7-Up, Other? (26% order Coke; 17% order Pepsi; the rest order something else when ordering a soft drink.)
13. Is there a child in your family under the age of six? (25% of American families have at least one child under the age of six.)

14. Is there a dishwasher in your home? (40.9% of homes have dishwashers.)
15. How are the dishes done in your home most often: by hand or by a dishwasher? (In 58% of American homes, dishes are done by hand.)
16. Are you right- or left-handed? (12% of Americans are left-handed.)

Mental Calculation with Percents

It's useful for students to learn to calculate mentally with percents and to find strategies for doing so that make sense to them. Initiate a discussion about this by asking the students: What is 50% of $100? Have volunteers respond, asking each to explain how he or she knows that $50 is the correct answer. It's important for students to know that you value their thinking, not just their right answers. Don't stop after just one student's explanation, but have others also explain their reasoning.

Then ask: What is 25% of $100? Again, have students give answers and explain their reasoning. Typically, fewer students are sure about 25%. If no one can explain, offer several ways for them to think about it: that 25% is half of 50%, so the answer is half of $50, that there are four $.25 in $1.00 and similarly there are four $25 in $100, that 25% is one-fourth of 100% and one-fourth of $100 is $25.

Continue the same sort of discussion for 10%, 5%, and 1%. Then write the following on the board:

    100% of $200 is _____.
    50% of $200 is _____.
    25% of $200 is _____.
    10% of $200 is _____.
    5% of $200 is _____.
    1% of $200 is _____.

Have students work in small groups to find the answers. Then have a class discussion in which they present their answers and reasoning.

Give the students other problems to solve by changing the $200 to another number: $500, $300, or $75, for example. Also, give the students problems such as the following:

  • Financing a loan costs approximately 11% a year. About what is the interest charge for a $400 loan?

  • A poll reported that 97.6% of a town's voters support the mayor. The voter population of the town is 12,500. About how many voters support the mayor?

  • If dinner in a restaurant costs $37.90, how much is a 15% tip?

INDEPENDENT ACTIVITIES (MENU)

Have students work on independent activities in pairs or small groups. Then have whole class discussions in which students present their findings, the different methods they used, and the difficulties they encountered.

Percents in the Newspaper

You need: a newspaper

Look for articles (not advertisements) in which percents are used. Choose one to present to the class. In your presentation, explain the meaning of the percents.

Figuring Tips in Restaurants

Read the following story.

Four people went to a restaurant for pizza. They ordered two medium pizzas: one pepperoni and one plain. They each ordered a coke. The waitress brought their cokes right away, which was good since they were all thirsty. The pizzas were ready soon afterward, and she brought them right over, with a stack of extra napkins for them to use. The bill was $18.90 without tax. Answer two questions:

1. What percent tip would you give?
2. How much money would you leave?

Explain your reasoning for each.

Write a restaurant story for others to solve.

Comparing Advertisements

You need: magazines or newspaper supplements that contain advertisements

Clip four advertisements that offer discounts for items and paste them on a sheet of paper. Include one that indicates the percent the customer will save, one that gives the sale price, and two of your choice. Decide which of the advertisements gives the customer the best deal. Record your decision, including an explanation of your reasoning.

Trade with other groups and decide on the best deal for the advertisements they clipped. Compare your decisions.

The Photocopy Problem

You need: six copies of a cartoon or drawing, including one full size, three reductions, and two enlargements

Figure what percent was used for each reduction and enlargement. Record your solutions and explain the procedures you used.

The Discount Coupon

You need: discount hamburger coupon

About what percent discount do you get with this coupon? Show your work and explain why your method and answer make sense.

Find one or two other coupons or advertisements that could be used for the same sort of investigation. Figure the percent discount for each of them.

Try the investigation for coupons other students have found.

Block Letters

You need: 10-by-10 grids (see blackline masters)

Make block letters on 10-by-10 grids, trying to make each one so it covers as close to 50% of the grid as possible.

The Warehouse Problem

Note: This problem appears in the book, *Thinking Mathematically*, by John Mason, Leone Burton, and Kaye Stacey (see bibliography).

For the following problem, explain your thinking and show all work that helps make your explanation clear.

A warehouse gives a 20% discount on all items, but you also must pay 6% in sales tax. Which would you prefer to have calculated first — the discount or the tax? Does it matter?

Percent Stories

Write a percent story problem that follows two rules:
1. It must end in a question.
2. The question must require that percents be used to answer it.

On a separate paper, solve your problem. Show your work and include an explanation of why your method makes sense.

Exchange papers and solve each other's problems.

ASSESSING UNDERSTANDING OF PERCENTS

Observing Students

During class discussions and when students are working on the independent tasks, circulate, observe, and, at times, question them about their thinking and reasoning. Look and listen for evidence of students' ability to calculate with percents and relate percents to contextual situations.

Individual Assessments

The following written assignments suggest ways to find out about students' understanding of percents.

1. Before beginning instruction, ask students to write what they know about percents. Have them do this again at the end of the instructional unit or even midway through. Return papers to the students and ask them to reflect on their learning.

2. Assign problems such as those suggested for whole class lessons. Ask students to present solutions in writing and to explain their reasoning.

PART IV

Mathematical Discussions

Introduction

*T*his section addresses the mathematics underlying some of the problems presented in this book. The problems included here were chosen for a variety of reasons — the topics involved, the problem-solving approaches used, the skills required, the connections offered to other ideas and activities, or the amount of mail we've received from teachers asking for help with them. Whatever the reason, all the problems selected are vehicles for delving more deeply into ideas that are important to K–8 mathematics.

Since you can't teach what you don't understand, this section offers those of you who have limited mathematics backgrounds a chance to learn more about some specific areas of mathematics and, in general, about thinking mathematically. And those of you with more mathematical experience will find either that the explanations confirm your own way of thinking or offer other approaches to solving some of the problems.

There are dangers in offering answers and explanations: answers often put an end to thinking, and other people's explanations can be hard to follow. However, there is even more danger in not understanding, especially as we work to help children become mathematically proficient. The purpose of these explanations is to model one way to think about the mathematics in the problems and, by so doing, make the mathematics more accessible. In the spirit that answers without understanding do not serve learning, the answers included are offered as checkpoints for your own learning.

To benefit from these explanations, merely reading them isn't enough. You have to think about the ideas and make sense of them for yourself. It may help to write or make sketches as you read to keep track of your reasoning or explore a new idea. You might read a paragraph or two and then go back and try to solve the problem on your own. Or you might work with a friend or small group on a particular challenge.

It's important to remember that we all learn in individual ways and on our own timetable. All of us have math problems we haven't yet solved and ideas we haven't yet learned. The goal is to stay involved as a learner of mathematics. Doing so will make us all better mathematics teachers.

Squaring Up (page 54)

I was mathematically flabbergasted the first time I encountered this problem. Following the directions of the Foot Area and Perimeter activity (see page 53), I traced my foot and figured its area by counting the whole centimeter squares and approximating areas of the partial squares. I also carefully cut a piece of string equal in length to the perimeter.

When I formed the perimeter string into a square, I thought this a much more efficient way to figure the area of my foot than dealing with all those bits and pieces of centimeter squares. But I was shocked when I found that the area of the square was so far off from the area I'd calculated earlier. Whoa, I thought, what did I do wrong? Why is the area of the square so much more than the area of my foot? I recalculated the areas of my foot outline and of the square. The difference was still substantial.

The best way to describe myself at this time is that I was experiencing *disequilibrium*. (Read pages 24–28 to learn about *disequilibrium*.) I was confused because I believed that two shapes with the same-length perimeter should have the same area but my measurements contradicted this belief.

It turned out that my belief was wrong. I learned this from immersing myself in other investigations. I did *The Perimeter Stays the Same*, on page 54. I experimented with my perimeter string, first shaping it into a pencil-shaped rectangle, long and skinny. It had hardly any space inside at all, so its area was much less than the area of the square and of my foot. But when I shaped the string into a rectangle with more footlike dimensions, the area was closer to the area of my foot. My understanding shifted. I no longer erroneously believed that shapes with the same-length perimeter had to have the same area. But don't just take my word for it. There's no substitute for firsthand experience, so try some investigations for yourself.

About the *Giant Foot* extension: the problem doesn't specify whether the giant foot should be twice the area of yours or a foot that's twice as long and twice as wide as yours. The wording is intentionally vague, providing another opportunity to think about area and perimeter in relationship to each other. Enlarging a foot so that it's twice as long and twice as wide as yours gives it an area that's much more than twice as large! Making it just twice as long doubles the area, but makes for a very long, thin foot. The challenge is to make a foot that is the correct shape with an area twice as large. It's a bit tricky. It may help to try to draw a square with twice the area of another and see how the lengths of the sides compare.

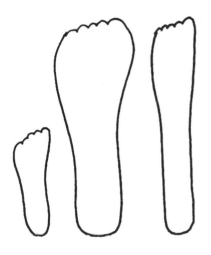

Box Measuring (page 55)

To solve this problem, I began by cutting 20-by-20-centimeter squares from centimeter squared paper, cutting squares from the corners, and then folding so that the cornerless squares formed boxes. If you haven't done this, I recommend doing so before reading further. I think it will help make my explanation clearer.

By following the directions and cutting the same-size square from each corner, cutting only on the lines so that the squares you're removing measure a whole number of centimeters on a side, you can make nine different-size boxes. Cutting a 1-by-1-centimeter square from each corner and folding what remains results in a very flat box that measures 18 centimeters by 18 centimeters by 1 centimeter. As pictured on page 55, cutting a 2-by-2-centimeter square from each corner results in a box not quite as flat. The larger the square you cut from each corner, the taller the resulting box.

You can cut squares from each corner up to 9 by 9 centimeters. (If you try cutting 10-by-10-centimeter squares, you wind up with four separate pieces and no box at all!) The nine boxes nest nicely, but merely looking at them isn't sufficient for comparing their volumes. (Students generally figure out from this activity that multiplying the three dimensions of a box gives its volume.)

The table below, which compares the volume of each box with the dimension of the square cut from each corner, shows that cutting a 3-by-3 square from each corner results in the box with the largest volume.

Side of corner square (cm)	Dimensions of box ($\ell \times w \times h$)	Volume of box (cm^3)
1	18 × 18 × 1	324
2	16 × 16 × 2	512
3	14 × 14 × 3	588
4	12 × 12 × 4	576
5	10 × 10 × 5	500
6	8 × 8 × 6	384
7	6 × 6 × 7	252
8	4 × 4 × 8	128
9	2 × 2 × 9	36

Suppose, however, that you weren't restricted to cutting squares that measure a whole number of centimeters on a side. (You didn't think this was the end of the problem, did you?) If you cut a 3.5-by-3.5-centimeter square from each corner, for example, the resulting box will be 3.5 centimeters tall and have a 13-by-13-centimeter base. Its volume is 591.5 cubic centimeters (13 × 13 × 3.5 = 591.5). This is larger than any of the boxes already cut. You might want to investigate what-size square to cut from each corner to get the box of maximum volume.

You might also compare the surface areas of the boxes. Removing squares from each corner reduces the surface area left to form a box, but a box with less surface area can have a greater volume!

Round Things (page 56)

I wish I had been introduced to this activity when I studied circles in elementary school. I remember learning that π was about 3.14, or 3 1/7. But I don't remember learning that it described a relationship that exists in all circles. If you divide the circumference of any circle by its diameter, the result is π, or about 3.14, or 3 1/7. Another way to say this is that π is the ratio of the circumference to the diameter of a circle. Any circle.

Because measurement is never exact, dividing the circumference by the diameter of the circular objects you chose to measure didn't produce identical results, but they should all be close to one another and to 3.14. If you got an answer that's way off, check your measurements.

Wrap-Around (page 56)

If you're stumped about how to proceed with this problem of making a measuring tape that when wrapped around a tree or pole or other circular object, tells you the diameter of that object, it might help if you first do the *Round Things* activity, also on page 56.

Here's an approach that makes sense to me. First, I made a table similar to the one suggested for *Round Things*, with data organized as shown below:

Diameter	Circumference
1	3.14
2	6.28
3	9.42
⋮	⋮

I then marked a tape in intervals of 3.14 inches, but labeled them to match the related diameters; that is, I labeled the 3.14-inch mark 1, the 6.28-inch mark 2, and so on. (I could have made it a metric measure by marking off intervals of 3.14 cm each.) Of course, since measurements are never exact, my tape produced only approximations, but they were close approximations.

Double the Circumference (page 57)

If this problem had been called *Double the Perimeter* and asked you to investigate a square instead of a circle, it would be easier to solve. You wouldn't need to find a square object to trace, but could draw any-size square. To make the investigation easy, you could decide that the area of the square you draw is one square unit. Then you wouldn't need string to measure its perimeter — its perimeter would be four units, one unit per side. Doubling the perimeter would be eight units, and a square with a perimeter of eight units would have two units per side. The area of the larger square is four times the smaller. Halving the original perimeter to two units would produce a square that measures one-half unit on a side with an area of one-fourth square unit. Trying this for other-size squares will show that doubling the perimeter consistently produces a square with an area that is four times as large and halving the perimeter consistently produces a square with an area that is one-fourth as large.

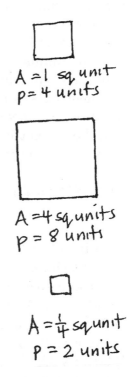

The examples you try may be convincing to you, but they're not enough for an acceptable proof. You also need a convincing argument. Algebra is a useful tool for proving that doubling the perimeter of a square always results in a square with an area that is four times as large. Suppose we call the side of the first square s. Its perimeter is $s + s + s + s$ or $4s$; its area is $s \times s$ or s^2. Doubling the perimeter to $8s$ results in a square with each of its four sides measuring $2s$. The area of this new square is $2s \times 2s$, or $4s^2$. And $4s^2$ is four times greater than s^2, no matter what s measures.

Try using algebra to prove that halving the perimeter produces a square with an area that is one-fourth as large.

What about circles? If you double the circumference of a circle, will the area of the new circle be four times as large? And if you halve it, will the area be one-fourth as large? Yes. As the activity suggests, you can experiment to see that this seems to be so. And you may notice as you investigate that doubling the circumference of a circle doubles its radius. The area of a circle with a radius r is $\pi \times r^2$, or πr^2. For a radius of three inches, the area is $\pi \times 3^2$, or $\pi \times 9$, which is about 28.26 square inches. Double the radius to six inches and the area is $\pi \times 6^2$, or $\pi \times 36$, which is about 113.04 square inches. And 113.04 is four times as large as 28.26.

The area of a circle with a doubled radius of $2r$ is $\pi \times (2r)^2$, which is $\pi \times (2r \times 2r)$, which is $\pi \times 4r^2$, or $4\pi r^2$. And $4\pi r^2$ is four times as large as πr^2. It's possible to use the same logic to verify that halving a circumference results in a circle with an area one-fourth as large.

A sticky part of this reasoning is to be convinced that doubling the circumference of a circle really does double its radius. The circumference of a circle is equal to π times the diameter. Since the diameter is the radius doubled, the circumference can be thought of as $2\pi r$. Doubling this circumference makes it $4\pi r$. This means that, for the larger circle, $4r$ is its diameter, so the radius is $2r$, which is twice the original radius of r.

If you find this explanation confusing, let this be a reminder about how difficult it can be to follow someone else's reasoning. You have to turn ideas around in your head to make sense of them in your own way. This reasoning works for me, and I've gotten clearer about it as I've worked to get it down in writing. It may help you to talk with a colleague about my thinking or to try writing down your own explanation.

The Area Stays the Same (page 57)

This activity is one of my favorites for several reasons. It's extremely versatile. I've had success with it in third through eighth grade. I like the fact that children create for themselves different-shape figures that all have the same area. I like using the shapes they make to introduce the terminology for polygons — *triangle, quadrilateral, pentagon, hexagon*, and so on. And comparing the perimeters of the figures they make themselves seems to offer convincing evidence to students that shapes with the same area can have different perimeters. *The Perimeter Stays the Same* (page 54) is a wonderful companion activity. (The Math By All Means unit *Area and Perimeter* uses these and other activities to help students learn about these ideas.)

Shake and Spill (page 69)

In this problem, you investigate what to expect when you shake and spill six two-color counters. Shaking and spilling six counters can result in seven outcomes:

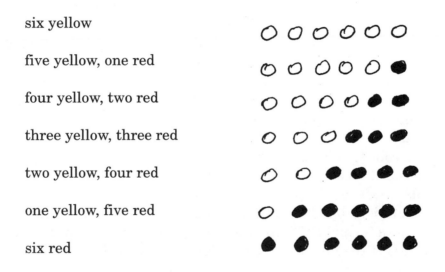

six yellow	○ ○ ○ ○ ○ ○
five yellow, one red	○ ○ ○ ○ ○ ●
four yellow, two red	○ ○ ○ ○ ● ●
three yellow, three red	○ ○ ○ ● ● ●
two yellow, four red	○ ○ ● ● ● ●
one yellow, five red	○ ● ● ● ● ●
six red	● ● ● ● ● ●

Shaking and spilling the six counters 25 times typically produces the evidence that these outcomes are not equally likely. Six yellow or six red come up much less frequently than do three yellow and three red, or four of one color and two of the other.

To understand why this is so, it may help to think about what happens when you shake and spill just one counter. For each counter there are two possibilities — red or yellow — and a 50-50 chance for either to come up. The two possibilities are equally likely. With six counters, however, and an equal chance for each counter to come up yellow or red, it's rare for all six to come up the same color on the same spill. It's more likely that some of the six counters will come up yellow and some will come up red.

Does this mean that there's a 50-50 chance that you'll get three yellow and three red when you shake and spill six counters? No, it's not that simple. If you're interested in learning about figuring the probabilities of three yellow and three red, all red, four yellow and two red, or any of the other possibilities, the discussion under *Shake and Spill Revisited* offers an explanation. But first read the explanation for *Two-Coin Toss*. It will help set the stage for your thinking.

Two-Coin Toss (page 69)

Two-Coin Toss is similar to doing *Shake and Spill* with only two counters. That's because coins and two-color counters both have two equally likely possibilities — heads and tails, or red and yellow. You can say that there's a 50-50 chance a coin will come up heads, or that the probability of a coin coming up heads is 1/2. The same is true for tails.

When tossing two coins, or two two-color counters, there are three possibilities:

two heads	two yellow
one head, one tail	one yellow, one red
two tails	two red

It may seem that each of these possibilities is equally likely, so that there's a 1/3 chance of getting two of the same or one of each. But that's not so, because there are two different ways that one head and one tail, or one yellow and one red, can come up. To understand this, think about tossing two different coins, a penny and a nickel, for example. For one head and one tail to come up, it either can be heads on the penny and tails on the nickel, or vice versa. If you were tossing two pennies, unless they had different dates and you noted them, it wouldn't be obvious that there are two ways for one head and one tail to come up.

So there are *four* equally likely outcomes when tossing two coins:

> two heads
> heads on coin 1, tails on coin 2
> tails on coin 1, heads on coin 2
> two tails

This means that there is a 1/4 chance that both coins will come up heads, a 1/4 chance that both will come up tails, and a 1/2 chance that one will come up heads and the other tails. (Note that the sum of the probabilities of all the equally likely possibilities for tossing two coins — 1/4 + 1/4 + 1/2 — adds to 1. The same holds true for tossing only one coin — 1/2 + 1/2 adds to 1. The sum of the probabilities of all the equally likely possibilities always adds to 1.)

These probabilities don't imply that if you toss two coins four times then both heads are sure to come up once, both tails once, and one of each twice. The probabilities are theoretical. They imply, but do not guarantee, that if you toss two coins many times, you can expect them to land with one head and one tail showing about twice as often as landing with two heads showing or two tails showing, and that two heads or two tails should come up about the same number of times.

Shake and Spill (page 69) Revisited

Let's go back to thinking about two-color counters. Shaking and spilling two counters is mathematically the same as tossing two coins — there are four equally likely outcomes. In order for this to make sense, it may help if you thought about labeling the two counters so you can tell one from the other, perhaps by writing a small 1 on both sides of one of them and a small 2 on both sides of the other. The four equally likely outcomes and the probability of each are:

> two yellow (1/4)
> yellow on counter 1, red on counter 2 (1/4)
> red on counter 1, yellow on counter 2 (1/4)
> two red (1/4)

Labeling helps you make an accurate count of what really is possible. Without labeling the counters 1 and 2, the two different ways that one of each color would come up would be indistinguishable, but it would still be a more likely possibility:

> two yellow (1/4)
> one yellow, one red (2/4, or 1/2)
> two red (1/4)

Now let's think about shaking and spilling three counters. Labeling them 1, 2, and 3 helps you list all of the equally likely possibilities:

> three yellow
> yellow on counters 1 and 2, red on counter 3
> yellow on counters 1 and 3, red on counter 2
> yellow on counters 2 and 3, red on counter 1
> yellow on counter 1, red on counters 2 and 3
> yellow on counter 2, red on counters 1 and 3
> yellow on counter 3, red on counters 1 and 2
> three red

There are eight equally likely possibilities, so each has a probability of 1/8. Ignoring the labels, I could combine the possibilities into four categories, and combine the probabilities:

> three yellow (1/8)
> two yellow, one red (3/8)
> one yellow, two red (3/8)
> three red (1/8)

Adding the probabilities — 1/8 + 3/8 + 3/8 + 1/8 — produces 1, ensuring that I've taken into account all the possible outcomes.

You can continue in this way to analyze what happens when shaking and spilling four two-color counters, then five, and finally six. Here's how I analyzed the situation for six two-color counters:

six yellow	(1/64)
five yellow, one red	(6/64)
four yellow, two red	(15/64)
three yellow, three red	(20/64)
two yellow, four red	(15/64)
one yellow, five red	(6/64)
six red	(1/64)

While it's more likely for three of each color to come up than any other possibility, the probability of getting three yellow and three red is 20/64, which is closer to a probability of 1/3 than it is to 1/2.

If you follow my reasoning, congratulations (to both of us)! If not, then you may need more time, more experience, the help of a friend, or another way to look at the situation. We all learn in our own ways and on our own timetables.

One more mathematical connection that may help. Instead of writing lists of the possibilities for shaking and spilling different numbers of counters, I could arrange the possibilities in a way that produces interesting patterns. For two counters, for example, I would arrange the possibilities like this:

YY YR RR
    RY

For three counters, I put those with two yellows and one red in one column, and those with two reds and one yellow in another:

YYY YYR YRR RRR
YRY RYR
RYY RRY

For four counters, I would arrange the possibilities like this:

YYYY YYYR YYRR YRRR RRRR
      YYRY YRYR RYRR
      YRYY YRRY RRYR
      RYYY RYRY RRRY
            RYYR
            RRYY

Now examine the number of entries in each column in relation to the probabilities for the possibilities. For two counters, the probabilities for each of the three columns are 1/4, 2/4, and 1/4. For three counters, the probabilities for the columns are 1/8, 3/8, 3/8, and 1/8. For four counters, since there are 16 possibilities altogether, the probabilities for the columns are 1/16, 4/16, 6/16, 4/16, and 1/16. (Try it for five counters and see how the pattern extends.)

Now look at Pascal's Triangle as shown on page 131:

$$
\begin{array}{ccccccccccc}
 & & & & & 1 & & & & & \\
 & & & & 1 & & 1 & & & & \\
 & & & 1 & & 2 & & 1 & & & \\
 & & 1 & & 3 & & 3 & & 1 & & \\
 & 1 & & 4 & & 6 & & 4 & & 1 & \\
1 & & 5 & & 10 & & 10 & & 5 & & 1
\end{array}
$$

The numbers in this pattern relate to the way I arranged the possibilities above and the numerators of their probabilities! For example, the numbers in the fourth row of Pascal's triangle are the numerators of the combined probabilities for shaking and spilling three counters — 1/8, 3/8, 3/8, 1/8. For five counters, the numbers are 1, 5, 10, 10, 5, and 1. And if you extend Pascal's Triangle, the next row has the numbers 1, 6, 15, 20, 15, 6, and 1 — the numerators of the probabilities for shaking and spilling six counters listed above. Connections like these help us see how mathematical ideas relate to one another. And while figuring the probabilities generates the numbers in Pascal's Triangle, you can also continue the pattern of numbers by adding any two adjacent numbers to get the number underneath. Try to figure out how extending Pascal's Triangle can help you think about what happens when you shake and spill more than six counters.

Got a Match? (page 70)

This problem invites you and a partner to spin two identical spinners, predict how often your results will match, and then test your prediction by spinning and recording the matches that come up in 24 spins. No specific spinner is suggested, but let's consider the problem with the 1-2-3 spinner shown on page 62. My method for thinking about this spinner can be applied to any other spinner.

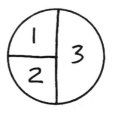

One complication with using the 1-2-3 spinner is that it's twice as likely that 3 will come up than either 1 or 2. In order to think about this problem, I need to figure out a way to compare equally likely outcomes. I can do this with the 1-2-3 spinner by imagining that it's divided into four quarters, with the number 3 in two of the quarters. To be clear, I'll label them 3a and 3b. This gives four equally likely outcomes from spinning — 1, 2, 3, and 3 — and is the same as having three outcomes with the 3 twice as likely.

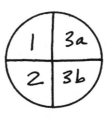

When I spin two spinners, I can get either a match or a nonmatch, and I need to investigate how often each of these options occurs. To do so, I'll make a list of all the possibilities. Here's how I reason.

If a 1 comes up on the first spinner, there are four equally likely possibilities for what will come up on the second spinner — 1, 2, 3a, or 3b. This means that a 1 on the first spinner produces either 1-1, 1-2, 1-3a, or 1-3b. This isn't so good for a match — only one out of four possibilities. The same holds true if a 2 comes up on the first spinner — 2-1, 2-2, 2-3a, or 2-3b — only one more possible match. This is not looking good for matches. Maybe the 3s will help.

If I spin 3a on the first spinner, then the four possibilities after spinning the second spinner are 3a-1, 3a-2, 3a-3a, 3a-3b. Ah, things are looking up. Since 3a and 3b are the same number, this produces two matches. And the same would be true if I spin 3b on the first spinner. There are two matches in the four possibilities — 3b-1, 3b-2, 3b-3a, 3b-3b.

I count up the total number of ways the two spinners could match (1-1, 2-2, 3a-3a, 3a-3b, 3b-3a, 3b-3b) — there are 6. Then I count up the total ways that the two spinners wouldn't match (1-2, 1-3a, 1-3b, 2-1, 2-3a, 2-3b, 3a-1, 3a-2, 3b-1, 3b-2) — there are 10. Of the 16 possible ways, there is a 6/16 chance of getting a match and a 10/16 chance of not getting a match.

The X-O Problem (page 71)

I found choosing a strategy for this problem perplexing. I first thought about the problem in a certain way, then decided I was wrong, and finally decided on the strategy that would be most effective. I offer my experience to reinforce the concept that erroneous ideas are often opportunities that lead us to correct thinking.

My first idea was this: There are three cards — one with X on both sides, one with O on both sides, and one with an X on one side and an O on the other. Okay, that means there are three Xs and three Os altogether. If I draw one card at random and look at what's marked on just one side, I "use up" one of the marks. So if I see an X, what's left are two Xs and three Os. And since there are more Os left, I'll predict that the other side of my card will be an O. I tested my strategy by playing 30 times, as directed in the activity, each time predicting the opposite of the mark that was showing. My prediction was correct less than half of the time. I played another 30 times; the results were about the same. I wasn't satisfied.

I mulled over the situation. I talked with friends. I mulled some more. I was stuck, frustrated, and took a break from thinking about the problem. When I came back to it, I decided to try a different approach, one that had been suggested by several other people. Instead of focusing on the numbers of Xs and Os, one friend suggested, consider that two of the cards have the same mark on both sides — both X or both O — and only one card has a different mark on each side. When you draw one of the cards at random, she told me, there's a 1/3 chance that you'll draw the card with an X on one side and an O on the other and a 2/3 chance that you'll draw a card with the same mark on both sides. A probability of 2/3 is twice as likely as a probability of 1/3, so predict the mark you see.

I was skeptical, although I could see the logic of her approach. I just couldn't see why it was better than my initial idea. But I decided to try it by predicting, each time I drew, that the same mark I saw would be on the other side, assuming that 2/3 of the time I would draw a card with either X on both sides or O on both sides.

Again, I played 30 times, as directed in the activity, each time predicting the same mark as the one showing. My prediction was correct 23 times, more than 2/3 of the draws. I played another 30 times; my prediction was correct 18 times, less than 2/3 but more than half. Now I was satisfied that if I predicted what I saw I'd do better in the long run. When I compiled my data with the data others collected in their trials, I was even more convinced. Not only did I have a theoretical prediction that made sense, the prediction was consistently supported by actual data. Case closed.

Some final notes. I thought more about why my initial idea was wrong. I decided that thinking about the Xs and Os as separate entities didn't make sense since they weren't independent of the cards on which they were drawn. My idea would make sense if there were six cards, three marked X and three marked O, but my idea didn't relate to the game in this problem.

Also, I've observed participants in classes choosing strategies different from either of the two I tried. Some decide to alternate predictions between X and O, not paying attention to what comes up first, but sticking to an X, O, X, O pattern. I saw one person toss a coin each time, predicting X on heads and O on tails. I've observed people predicting randomly, depending on a whim for each draw, feeling that it won't make any difference because it's a game of chance. In these cases, while there were occasional short runs of success, overall results were dismal. Remember, the larger the sample, the more reliable the data to substantiate a prediction or theory.

How Many Throws? And How Many Ways? (pages 72 and 73)

These two activities offer several ways to think about the probabilities that result from throwing two dice. From experiences they've had playing games with dice, many people learn that when throwing two dice, it's harder to get sums of 12 or 2 than sums of 6, 7, or 8. Also, some learn that in general it's harder to get a sum by rolling a double; for example, it's less likely to get a sum of 8 from throwing two 4s than it is from throwing 5 and 3, or 6 and 2. Experience is an excellent teacher for building our intuition about probabilities. Collecting and analyzing data about throwing two dice as suggested in these activities helped me fully understand the probability involved.

In *How Many Throws?*, one of the charts presented is an addition table for adding the numbers 1 through 6 to get 36 sums. The activity directs you to complete the chart by entering each sum as it comes up from throwing two dice and also to keep track of the number of throws it took to complete the entire chart. An important part of completing the chart is to use dice of different colors (red and white are suggested in the activity) or different sizes so that you can easily distinguish the dice and record sums correctly.

RED

	1	2	3	4	5	6
1	2	3	4	5	6	7
2	3	4	5	6	7	8
3	4	5	6	7	8	9
4	5	6	7	8	9	10
5	6	7	8	9	10	11
6	7	8	9	10	11	12

(WHITE)

Take the sum of 4, for example. You can get a sum of 4 by throwing 3 and 1 in two different ways — 3 on the first die and 1 on the second die, or 1 on the first die and 3 on the second die. Each of these possibilities is represented by a different location on the addition table. Also, you can get a sum of 4 by rolling 2 on both dice. There's only one way for this to happen — 2 on the first die and 2 on the second die – and therefore there's only one place on the chart to enter this sum. For the sum of 4, there are a total of three possible ways, with double 2s being half as likely as getting 3 and 1. Understanding this is the key to understanding the probabilities when throwing two dice.

When you complete the addition table, you've recorded all of the 36 equally likely outcomes possible when throwing two dice. Of these sums, you can count and see that the sum of 7 can be made in six different ways — more ways than any other sum, but not much more. The sums of 6 and 8 each come up in five different ways. The sums of 2 and 12 can each only come up one way — either double 1s or double 6s. This is why it's more likely to roll sums of 6, 7, or 8 than 2 or 12. Of course, when throwing dice to complete the chart, you may roll sums of 2 or 12 several times each, but according to probability theory, in a large sample of throws, 2 and 12 will each only come up about 1/36 of the time while the sum of 7 will come up 6/36 of the time.

The probabilities of the sums are:

P(2) = 1/36
P(3) = 2/36
P(4) = 3/36
P(5) = 4/36
P(6) = 5/36
P(7) = 6/36
P(8) = 5/36
P(9) = 4/36
P(10) = 3/36
P(11) = 2/36
P(12) = 1/36

While 7 is your best bet when throwing two dice, a probability of 6/36 means that you have only a 1/6 chance of throwing a sum of 7. These aren't very good odds, so take care when applying this knowledge.

The chart suggested for *How Many Ways?* is a different way of organizing the same information that appears on the addition table. Some people find it a clearer way to display what happens; others prefer the first way. One of the goals when studying mathematics is to learn to think flexibly, so it's a good exercise to try and make sense of both charts.

Possible Totals	2	3	4	5	6	7	8	9	10	11	12
	1,1	1,2 2,1	1,3 2,2 3,1	1,4 2,3 3,2 4,1	1,5 2,4 3,3 4,2 5,1	1,6 2,5 3,4 4,3 5,2 6,1	2,6 3,5 4,4 5,3 6,2	3,6 4,5 5,4 6,3	4,6 5,5 6,4	5,6 6,5	6,6
Total Ways	1	2	3	4	5	6	5	4	3	2	1

There are other ways of making sense and displaying the information about what happens when you throw two dice. For example, some people reason as follows: Suppose a 1 comes up on the first die. Then there are six possibilities for the second die — 1, 2, 3, 4, 5, and 6. This accounts for six possible sums when a 1 comes up on the first die — 2, 3, 4, 5, 6, and 7. If 2 comes up on the first die, again there are the same six possibilities for the second die — 1, 2, 3, 4, 5, and 6. The possible sums with 2 on the first die are 3, 4, 5, 6, 7, and 8. Continuing in this way will identify the 36 possible sums. Below is a way to diagram this way of thinking, often called a "tree diagram."

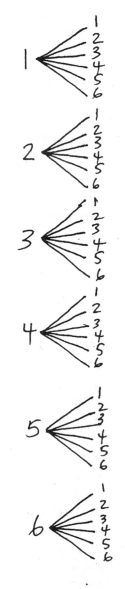

Tree diagram

Fair Game 1 (page 74)

This game of paper, scissors, rock as described is not fair! One way to analyze why is first to account for all of the equally likely possibilities and then see which player has an advantage.

There are three possibilities for what each person shows on a turn — paper, scissors, or rock. A player could show the same sign over and over again, but to analyze the game, you need to think of them as three equally likely random choices.

To analyze the possibilities, I made a list using p, s, and r to stand for paper, scissors, and rock. I also labeled three columns A, B, and C to represent the three players. I listed the following 27 equally likely possibilities:

A	B	C	
p	p	p	*
p	p	r	
p	p	s	
p	r	p	
p	r	r	
p	r	s	!
p	s	p	
p	s	r	!
p	s	s	
r	p	p	
r	p	r	
r	p	s	!
r	r	p	
r	r	r	*
r	r	s	
r	s	p	!
r	s	r	
r	s	s	
s	p	p	
s	p	r	!
s	p	s	
s	r	p	!
s	r	r	
s	r	s	
s	s	p	
s	s	r	
s	s	s	*

In these 27 possibilities, the same sign comes up only three times, a probability of 3/27. (I marked these with an asterisk.) Two players showing the same sign comes up 18 times, a probability of 18/27. All players showing different signs comes up six times, a probability of 6/27. (I marked these with an exclamation point.) To be sure that I counted correctly, I added the three probabilities — 3/27 + 18/27 + 6/27. The sum is 1, which indicates that I've accounted for all of the possibilities. To make the game fair, you either need to decide on new rules that give each person the same chance of winning, or keep the rules as they are and change the number of points each person gets when their option comes up.

Fair Game 2 (page 74)

Two versions of this dice game are suggested. In the first, player A scores a point if the sum is even and player B scores a point if the sum is odd. There are 11 possible sums when rolling two dice — 2, 3, 4, 5, 6, 7, 8, 9, 10, 11, and 12. Six of these sums are even; five are odd. But that's not enough information for deciding who has the advantage, because the sums aren't equally likely. You need to compare the combined probabilities for the even sums with the combined probabilities for the odd sums. For example, there is a 1/36 chance of rolling a 2, a 3/36 chance of rolling a 4, 5/36 for 6, 5/36 for 8, 3/36 for 10, and 1/36 for 12. Adding these results in a probability of 18/36 for rolling an even sum. That's the same as 1/2, leaving 1/2 for rolling an odd sum. (You can check by adding the probabilities for the odd sums.) So this is a fair game.

Thinking about the products requires collecting new information about dice. I did this by creating a multiplication table instead of the addition table suggested in *How Many Throws?* The multiplication table not only reveals the possible products — 1, 2, 3, 4, 5, 6, 8, 9, 10, 12, 15, 16, 18, 20, 24, 25, 30, 36 — but lets you count how often each occurs. (Remember, you have to account for all 36 possible ways the dice can come up.)

	1	2	3	4	5	6
1	1	2	3	4	5	6
2	2	4	6	8	10	12
3	3	6	9	12	15	18
4	4	8	12	16	20	24
5	5	10	15	20	25	30
6	6	12	18	24	30	36

But before listing and counting all the ways, I began to wonder if there was an easier way to think about the problem. (Mathematicians often — and gladly — spend more time seeking an "easier" way to solve a problem than it would take to do what's obvious but laborious.) I thought about what happens when you multiply even and odd numbers. If you multiply any number by an even number, the product will be even. That means that you get an even product from even × even, even × odd, and odd × even. The only time you get an odd product is when you multiply two odd numbers. So, hey, I'd rather have the even products. Forget the listing and counting of the 36 possibilities; I'm satisfied. Are you?

The Tangram Puzzle (page 83)

Extension 1: Area and Perimeter

This activity offers another way to look at the mathematical ideas in *Squaring Up, Double the Circumference*, and *The Area Stays the Same* from the measurement section. The Tangram pieces allow you to think about how area and perimeter relate by comparing shapes instead of resorting to standard units of measurement.

To compare the areas of the square, parallelogram, and middle-size triangle, rearrange the two small triangles to make each of the shapes. The areas of these three shapes are the same. Then match their edges to compare their perimeters. The parallelogram and middle-size triangle have the same-length perimeters, but the perimeter of the square is shorter. This is because the same amount of area is squashed together more compactly in a square, requiring less perimeter. If you rearranged the same area into a long skinny rectangle, you'd need a longer "fence" to surround it and the perimeter would therefore be longer. If you made a circle of the same area, however, the circle's circumference would be shorter than even the square's perimeter; the circle is the most economical shape for minimizing the distance around.

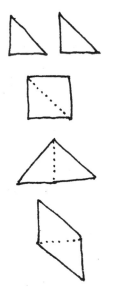

Extension 3: Using All Seven

This activity asks you to use all seven pieces of the Tangram to make different convex shapes. A convex shape is one with all of its interior angles measuring less than 180 degrees. Shapes with at least one interior angle greater than 180 degrees are called concave.

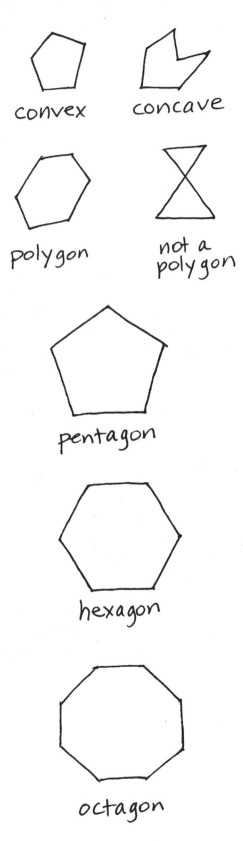

convex   concave

polygon   not a polygon

pentagon

hexagon

octagon

It's easy to spot them — children have told me, "They go in and out," or "They have dents."

The shapes you build with the Tangram pieces are all polygons. A polygon is a closed shape (which means it encloses an interior region the way a fence encloses a yard) made of connecting straight line segments. Sometimes a polygon is defined as a "simple closed curve." This seems contradictory, since the sides of a polygon are all straight line segments, but the definition has been in common use for quite some time. The "simple" part of the definition is important. It means that the line segments enclose one contiguous interior region; the inside of a polygon can't be divided into smaller regions. One way to think about this is to think of the corners where line segments meet — the vertices — as fence posts. Only two segments of the fence can touch each fence post.

The directions for this extension could have asked you to use the seven Tangram pieces to investigate convex polygons, instead of convex shapes. It's hard to decide when to use standard mathematical terminology or more common language. A good pedagogical approach is to use both — common language to provide access to an idea and correct terminology to help learners extend their mathematical vocabulary.

One more comment about the convex polygons you search for in this activity. Polygons are categorized by the number of sides they have — triangle, quadrilateral, pentagon, hexagon, heptagon, octagon, and so on. Any shape with four sides — squares, parallelograms, rectangles, and so on — is a quadrilateral. When a polygon has all identical sides and angles, it's called a regular polygon. A square is a regular polygon; so is an equilateral triangle. When we see pictures of pentagons, hexagons, and octagons, we typically see pictures of them as regular polygons.

The convex shapes you make in this activity, except for the square, are not regular. The rectangle shown below, for example, was made from the seven Tangram pieces, but it isn't a regular quadrilateral because its sides aren't all the same length:

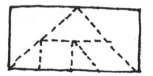

When doing this activity, be sure to name the different polygons you make.

Extension 4: Making Squares

I know it isn't possible to form a square from six Tangram pieces. I can't remember where I heard this, but my own experience experimenting with the Tangram pieces led me to believe that it is true. However, for a long time I wasn't able to explain why. (It's not enough to assert that I tried really hard to make a square from six pieces and couldn't — a proof calls for a convincing argument.) I was stymied. I don't mean to imply that I spent a lot of waking hours thinking about why I couldn't arrange six Tangram pieces into a square. But I remained intrigued by this fact and wondered about it whenever I taught a lesson using the Tangram puzzle.

In 1990, I raised this question at the annual retreat I hold with Math Solutions instructors. I formed a panel of four people who had a good deal of mathematical expertise, experience, and confidence but who hadn't yet thought about this particular problem and asked them to think about it together, out loud, while the rest of us observed. My idea was that it would be interesting not only to learn about why a square can't be formed from six Tangram pieces but also to have the chance to see mathematical thinkers in action.

So we observed four people rummage for ways to approach the problem. They cut Tangram pieces; they moved pieces about; they exchanged ideas; at times, one person would retreat into private thoughts and then reemerge to share discoveries; others would build on these ideas, as interested in how the others thought as they were in their own ideas. The group functioned in the way I want groups of students in the classroom to function.

Because of this experience I finally learned why making a six-piece square isn't possible. I offer my understanding knowing that it's hard to follow someone else's reasoning but hoping that my explanation will be useful to you and, perhaps, get you interested in this problem if you haven't been up to now.

Think about the small square Tangram piece as having an area of one square unit. As you may have learned from the first extension activity, the parallelogram and middle-sized triangle have the same area — also one square unit. The two small triangles that together form the square, parallelogram, and middle-size triangle each have an area of one-half square unit. Since the large triangles can be made from a square and two small triangles, they each have an area of two square units. Using these values, the square formed by all seven Tangram pieces has an area of eight square units. (Check to make sure you are with me this far; this information will be important a bit later.)

Now think about making a square with 2, 3, 4, 5, 6, and 7 Tangram pieces. First, you can make a square with two pieces by using the two small triangles. This square is the same size as the small square Tangram piece and therefore has an area of one square unit. And because you can find the area of a square by multiplying the length of a side by itself, it measures one unit on a side. If you use the two large triangles to make a square, however, each side measures two units (it's equal in length to two sides of a square), and its area is four square units. (Use your Tangram pieces to check that this is so.) This also makes sense because $2 \times 2 = 4$.

What about using three pieces to make a square? The chart on page 83 shows how to use two small triangles and the middle-size triangle to make a square. Its area is two square units. Each of its sides is equal in length to the long side of the small triangle — its hypotenuse. This is more than one unit but less than two units. How much is that, exactly? Although two is a small number that's generally easy for computations, in this situation it's easier to figure the length of a side for squares with larger but more cooperative areas. For a square with an area of 49 square units, for example, the sides are seven units (since $7 \times 7 = 49$). For a square with an area of 64 square units, the sides are eight units. In these examples, 49 and 64 are square numbers. (Take 49 or 64 pennies and you could arrange either number into a

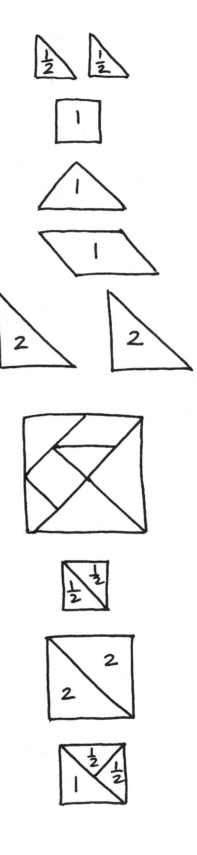

square array.) And 7 and 8 are the square roots of 49 and 64. We could say that the sides of those two squares are, respectively, $\sqrt{49}$ and the $\sqrt{64}$. Finding the square root of 2 isn't so friendly, so we could use a calculator, pressing 2 and then the square root key (my calculator displays 1.4142135, which makes sense because it's in between 1 and 2). Or we could just say that the side is $\sqrt{2}$ long.

Another way to figure the length of this side is to recall the Pythagorean theorem, which states that for a right triangle (and all of the Tangram triangles are right triangles because they all have a right angle), the hypotenuse (the long side) is equal to the square root of the sum of the squares of the other two sides. The theorem is often written as $a^2 + b^2 = c^2$. The illustration of a right triangle with sides that measure 3 and 4 and a hypotenuse that measures 5, and showing the sides squared, may help you see how the Pythagorean theorem makes sense. And the theorem can be a helpful clue for understanding this problem. To use the Pythagorean theorem to figure the length of the hypotenuse of the small Tangram triangle, I use the information that the shorter sides are each one unit, the same as the length of the side of the small square. The hypotenuse is the square root of $1^2 + 1^2$, which is $\sqrt{2}$. Then I use my calculator as above to get that messy number of 1.4142135.

Another clue is that if you examine the sides of all the Tangram pieces, they either are one unit, twice that (two units), $\sqrt{2}$ units, or twice that ($2\sqrt{2}$ units). (Again, use your Tangram pieces to make sense of this information.)

On to making a square with four pieces. Ah, that's possible. First I make a two-piece square using the two large triangles and then I replace one of the triangles with three pieces — the two small triangles and the square. The resulting four-piece square still has an area of four square units and measures two units on a side.

A five-piece square can be made from the five small pieces. It's the same size as the four-piece square — four square units — and its sides measure two units.

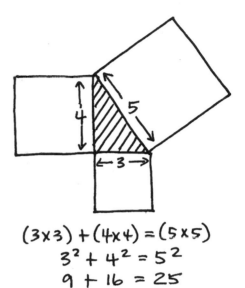

$$(3 \times 3) + (4 \times 4) = (5 \times 5)$$
$$3^2 + 4^2 = 5^2$$
$$9 + 16 = 25$$

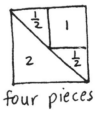

four pieces

five pieces

seven pieces

I already know about the seven-piece square. That's the square made from all seven Tangram pieces. Its area is eight square units and each of its sides is the length of the long side (the hypotenuse) of the large Tangram triangle piece. This is the same as twice the hypotenuse of the small triangle, which measures $\sqrt{2}$. So each side of the seven-piece square measures $\sqrt{2} + \sqrt{2}$, which can also be written as $2\sqrt{2}$.

For a square to be formed from six pieces, one piece of the Tangram puzzle has to be eliminated. The choices are to eliminate either one of the small triangles, one-half square unit; the square, parallelogram, or middle-sized triangle, one square unit; or a large triangle, two square units. So the area of a six-piece square would measure either seven-and-a-half square units, seven square units, or six square units. The side of a six-piece square, therefore, would have to measure either 17 1/2, 17, or 16. But there aren't any Tangram pieces with sides any of those lengths or combinations of those lengths. All we have are sides of lengths 1, 2, $\sqrt{2}$, or $2\sqrt{2}$, so it isn't possible to form a square with six Tangram pieces.

Convinced? If not, give it time. Remember that I thought about this problem for a long time — years — before finally making sense of it for myself. Try again when you're interested and rested. And don't forget the Tangram pieces; they contain many of the clues to thinking about this problem.

That's Just Half the Story (page 84)

This is the first of several activities that use the uppercase alphabet letters for geometric explorations. *That's Just Half the Story* investigates which of the letters have mirror symmetry, also called line symmetry. Some teachers make cutout block letters available, and children fold them to test for symmetry instead of using mirrors. This works well.

The letters that work only one way have exactly one line of symmetry — A, B, C, D, E, K, M, T, U, V, W, and Y.

Some letters have more than one line of symmetry — H, I, O, and X.

And some letters have zero lines of symmetry — F, G, J, L, N, P, Q, R, S, Z.

It's also possible for a shape to have an infinite number of lines of symmetry. If the O is formed as a perfect circle, for example, as long as a fold goes through the center of the circle, the two halves will match. Any line that goes through the center of a circle is a line of symmetry.

When children do this activity, they're often surprised and unsettled to find that N, S, and Z do not have lines of symmetry. I think this is because the letters appear to have a kind of balance that letters like F and G, for example, don't have. While N, S, and Z don't have mirror symmetry, they have rotational symmetry. This means that if you imagine each as a cutout letter attached to a surface with a pin through its center, you can rotate the letter 180 degrees so that it's upside down and it will look the same. Notice that the letters that have more than one line of symmetry also have rotational symmetry.

A note about rotational symmetry: Shapes can have rotational symmetry at other than 180 degrees. A square, for example, has rotational symmetry at 90 degrees, and an equilateral triangle has rotational symmetry at 120 degrees.

Interior Regions (page 84)

It's generally easy for children to sort the letters into those that do and don't have interior regions, so there's not much to discuss about this activity. But in the spirit of looking for connections among activities, revisiting this activity after writing the discussion for extension 3, Using All Seven, from *The Tangram Puzzle* made me wonder whether any uppercase letters were polygons. (If you aren't sure what a polygon is, read the explanation for Using All Seven.) The only letter formed only by straight line segments that enclose an interior region is A, but it has extra "tails," a feature that eliminates it from the polygon classification. Some of the letters that don't have interior regions would be polygons if their two dangling line segments were joined. For example, L and V would become triangles; M and W would become pentagons, actually concave pentagons. (Again, read the Using All Seven explanation if you're not sure what makes a shape concave.)

Straight or Curved (page 84)

Deciding which of the uppercase letters have only straight line segments, curves, or both is another easy sorting activity. Converting the chart to a Venn diagram, however, may be something new. A Venn diagram is a clever way to display sets of information when there is information that belongs in more than one set. (Venn diagrams are named for John Venn, a British mathematician, 1834–1923, who worked in statistics, probability, and logic.)

If this activity is your class's first experience with a Venn diagram, it may help to use cutout letters and two circles of different-color yarn. First form the two circles so that they don't overlap, then designate one for letters with straight line segments and one for letters with curves. The problem of where to put letters that have both straight line segments and curves comes up fairly quickly. Ask the children for suggestions. Some may suggest a third yarn enclosure, but that doesn't solve the problem of a letter such as B belonging in all three sets. Some students may suggest making three Bs; you can counter that you only have one of each letter and push them to think of an easier way than cutting out more.

If no one suggests overlapping the circles, then tell them about Venn's idea. Put the B in the intersection and have them verify that it's in both the yarn circle for letters with straight line segments and the yarn circle for letters with curves. While ideas like making three Bs might work, Venn diagrams have become accepted convention for displaying information like this, so children should become familiar with how they work.

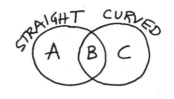

No-Lift Letters and More No-Lift Letters (page 85)

The house shape shown in *No-Lift Letters* is one that fascinated me as a young child. Once I realized that I could draw the house without lifting my pencil or retracing a line if I drew it in a certain way, I practiced and practiced until I could do it correctly every time. Then I experimented with other shapes.

Much later, from doing an activity like *More No-Lift Letters*, experimenting convinced me that the only shapes that could be drawn this way were those with zero or two odd vertices. Now I had a way to predict before I tried whether it was possible to draw a shape without lifting the pencil or retracing any line.

It was even later that I began to understand why it was possible to draw shapes with zero or two odd vertices without lifting the pencil or retracing any line. It seemed so strange that this was a rule that worked. Then I engaged in a different kind of experimenting, trying to understand why shapes with 1, 3, or more odd vertices didn't work. I came to see that an odd vertex was a dead end to be avoided, so zero odd vertices was best. Two odd vertices are okay because they provide places to begin and end. More than two odd vertices are trouble. And I haven't yet figured out how to draw a shape with just one odd vertex; maybe it's not possible.

My personal passage through this investigation shows how the same mathematical experiences can be appreciated in different ways at different ages. I returned to this problem over and over again for years. The discovery about odd and even vertices wouldn't have interested me as a young child trying to master how to draw a shape without lifting my pencil or retracing any line. Later, however, learning the rule was exciting to me, like uncovering a secret. But it wasn't until even later that I became interested in why the rule made sense. And perhaps there's still more to think about with this investigation — it wouldn't surprise me.

I sometimes hear teachers worry that students have done an activity in a previous year and therefore will no longer be interested. That hasn't been the case for me. I've found that children often enjoy returning to things they've previously learned. I've also found that revisits offer children the opportunity to see a situation in new ways and to bring to it their new maturity, experience, and learning.

Square Partitioning (page 89)

This activity demonstrates how rummaging around and getting immersed in a problem can reveal useful patterns that aren't obvious at first. At least that's what happened to me. For example, from fiddling with this activity I discovered a tried-and-true system for partitioning squares into any number of smaller squares in this sequence — 4, 7, 10, 13, 16, 19, and so on — with the numbers continuing to increase by 3. When you divide a square into four equal-size squares, the change from one square to four squares represents an increase of three squares, so the system is to divide any existing square into four equal-size squares. All of the numbers in the sequence are one more than a multiple of 3.

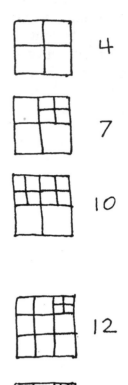

The next one that seemed easy to do was to partition a square into nine smaller squares, making a three-by-three array. Once I had nine squares, I could divide any square using the system I had discovered before and get three more squares. So this took care of 9, 12, 15, 18, 21, and so on. Or I could divide any of the nine squares into nine more squares, which added eight more squares, to solve the problem for 17, 25, 33, 41, 49, and so on.

But I was getting ahead of the problem with these large number solutions. What about partitioning a square into six, eight, or eleven squares? I stumbled into six from erasing some lines from the nine-square. And I found eight and eleven from dividing a square into a five-by-five array and then erasing some interior lines.

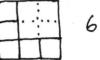

But enough. The fun in a problem like this is the discovering — if you like that sort of thing. I do. Once I have systems, I'm no longer interested, although at times I become delighted all over again when someone gives me a completely new way to look at a problem I thought I completely understood. The lesson is — be mathematically curious. It's a key to becoming mathematically competent.

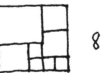

So what's the story with 5? It's not possible to partition a square into five smaller squares, a reminder that not every mathematical problem has a solution.

The Banquet Table Problem (page 89)

This problem uses the context of arranging tables for a banquet to explore the ideas of area and perimeter. Different arrangements of 12 square tables all have the same area but have different perimeters and, therefore, can seat different numbers of people. For example, putting all 12 tables in one row to make a long, thin table seats the most people — 12 on each side and one at each end for a total of 26. Arranging the tables into a 6-by-2 rectangle results in seating for 16 people — six on each side and two at each end. A 4-by-3 arrangement seats 14 people — four on each side and three on each end. These are the only rectangular arrangements that I had in mind when I wrote the problem. However, students have found ways to arrange the tables in other ways, leaving holes in the center.

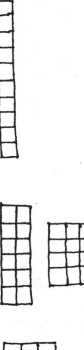

From time to time, students interpret a problem in a different way from the one intended. It's difficult to give precise directions all the time. My first impulse when a student built a table with a "hole" was to clarify that this wasn't what I meant, that I had meant only "filled-in" rectangles. I was locked into the goal I had for the lesson, for students to see the relationship between the number of small tables and the pairs of factors of that number. (For 12, the pairs of factors are 1×12, 2×6, and 3×4.) I wanted them to see that long, thin tables had longer perimeters than did more squarelike tables. When a student suggested a banquet table with a hole, and then others argued about whether or not people could sit inside the hole, I felt that I was losing mathematical control over the lesson.

I relaxed, however, and decided to see the diversion not as a potential disaster but as a way for students to follow their curiosity. The students continued to search for all possible tables and record their findings. Later, in a class discussion about the banquet tables made from 12, 24, and 100 small tables, I asked them to consider just those tables that were "filled-in" rectangles. This focused us on looking at the mathematics I felt was important.

For additional activities that also address area, perimeter, and relationships between them, see *Squaring Up*, on page 54, and *The Area Stays the Same*, on page 57. Also, *Spaghetti and Meatballs for All!*, a children's book I wrote, uses the context of a family reunion to show how rearranging tables can affect seating.

The Four-Triangle Problem (page 93)

This problem is an extremely versatile investigation that is valuable for and accessible to children at all grade levels. It helps students explore geometric concepts, learn geometric vocabulary in context, and develop spatial reasoning skills.

The triangles used for the investigation are right triangles; they all have one square corner. This is because the triangles come from cutting squares on the diagonal, leaving one of the square's right angles intact in each triangle. Also, all of the triangles are the same size, making them congruent right triangles. It's possible to arrange four congruent right triangles into a larger triangle and also into five different quadrilaterals, two different pentagons, and six different hexagons.

If you're interested in reading more about how to use this activity in the classroom, chapter 9 (pages 99–106) in *A Collection of Math Lessons From Grades 1 Through 3* describes the lesson in a first-grade class. And the *Math By All Means* unit *Geometry, Grades 3–4* (pages 16–25 and 77–82), offers a detailed explanation of the activity with older children.

Geoboard Line Segments (page 96)

There are 14 different-length line segments you can make on the geoboard by stretching rubber bands so that pegs of the geoboard are the endpoints of the segments. Four of them are parallel to the sides of the geoboard, measuring 1, 2, 3, and 4 units. Then there are four that are on the diagonal from one side or corner to the opposite side or corner. Children often think that the diagonal line segments are also 1, 2, 3, and 4 units, but that's not right. The line segment from a peg to the next diagonal peg is longer than the line segment from a peg to the peg directly above or below it. You can use a ruler or string to test that this is so. Or you can think about the Pythagorean theorem, since the diagonal is the hypotenuse of the right triangle. (You can read about the Pythagorean theorem in the explanation about extension 4, Making Squares, of *The Tangram Puzzle*.)

In addition to these eight line segments, there are six more, not parallel to any of the eight I described so far. The line segment that goes from one of the bottom corner pegs to the opposite top corner peg is the longest on the geoboard. The next to the longest goes from one bottom corner peg to the peg just under the opposite top corner peg. I think this is correct because the diagonal line segments are all hypotenuses of right triangles, and this particular one is the hypotenuse of a right triangle whose sides measure 4 units and 3 units. Use the Pythagorean theorem to calculate that this hypotenuse is 5 units, longer than the longest segment that is parallel to the sides of the geoboard. No other right triangle, except for one with both sides 4 units, has sides this large.

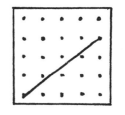

Area on the Geoboard (page 99)

If you can figure the area of the 26 shapes on page 99, you can probably figure the area of any shape on a geoboard. To do so, there are a few techniques that are useful.

One is to get good at spotting halves of squares. In shape A, for instance, there are two whole squares and half of another; its area is 2 1/2 square units. In shape B, there is one square intact topped by a parallelogram that is formed from two half squares. Keep an eye out for those halves and you'll do fine with shapes A through E. You can also confirm these areas by using small paper squares the size of square units, cutting them in half, and fitting them together to make all of the shapes from A to E.

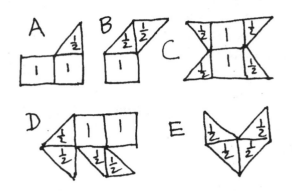

The next shapes get tricky. You can continue to use small paper squares, cutting them to fit the odd-looking shapes and adding up the bits and pieces. One problem with this approach is that measurement is never exact, and the lack of precision will be frustrating. Trust me, it's better to use your head than paper and scissors, at least for these problems.

Here's my advice. Think about rectangles. They're the easiest to figure because you only have to count whole squares. Look at shape F. It's not a rectangle, I realize, so I make it into one. The rectangle I drew has two square units; F is half of it; therefore, F is worth 1 square unit. (Okay, if you'd like, verify this by the paper-and-scissors method.)

Look at L. If I "rectangulate" it, the rectangle will have an area of 4 square units, so the area of L is 2 square units.

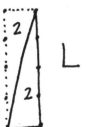

Nice work, you say, but you took the easy ones. What about M? Or N? Or O or P?

My advice is: Relax and rectangulate. My additional advice is that it's always easier to figure out what's outside the shape but inside your rectangle. Look at what happens when I draw a rectangle to enclose M. Its area is 8 square units. The triangle on the right side is the same as L and, therefore, has an area of 2 square units. The triangle on the left is half of the rectangle, so its area is 4 square units. Subtract these two areas from the whole rectangle, and you're left with 2 square units for M.

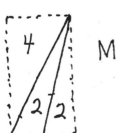

If you do N, O, and P the same way, you'll find that they each have an area of 2 square units. Does it seem peculiar that L, M, N, O, and P all have the same area? It made sense to me once I noticed that they all have the same-length base and the same height (which is the perpendicular distance from the base to the opposite vertex). Also, I know that you can figure the area of a triangle by multiplying the base times the height and dividing by 2 ($A = bh/2$). Looking at the illustration of "rectangulating" L helps show this; the area of the rectangle can be found by multiplying its base times its height ($A = bh$), and the triangle is half as big. Because L, M , N, O, and P all have the same base and height, their areas are also all the same.

With these techniques — rectangulate, figure out what's outside the shape but inside the rectangle, then subtract — I can figure the area of all the shapes on the page. Below are the answers (all in square units) so that you can check the answers you get.

A = 2 1/2
B = 2
C = 4
D = 4
E = 2
F = 1
G = 2
H = 1
I = 3 1/2
J = 3 1/2
K = 5 1/2
L, M, N, O, P = 2
Q = 3 1/2
R = 3
S = 2 1/2
T = 6
U = 6 1/2
V = 4 1/2
W = 8
X = 4
Y = 9
Z = 8 1/2

King Arthur's Problem (page 102)

The way I made sense of this problem was to investigate where the safe seat would be if there were only two knights, then three, then four, five, and so on. For example, for five knights, here's what I did:

I wrote the numerals 1 through 5 in a circle

I put my pencil on the 1 and said "You live."

I then moved my pencil to the 2, said "You die," and crossed it out.

I moved to the 3 and said "You live."

I then moved my pencil to the 4, said "You die," and crossed it out.

I next moved my pencil to the 5 and said "You live."

I then moved to the 1, said "You die," and crossed it out. Only the 3 and 5 were left.

I moved to the 3 and said "You live."

I moved to the 5, said "You die," and crossed it out.

The 3 was left, so it was the safe seat with five knights.

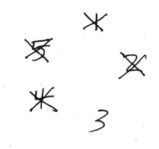

I recorded my findings on a table, hoping to find a pattern that would allow me to stop figuring and, instead, have a way to predict where the safe seat would be for any number of knights. Below is the table up through 20 knights:

Number of Knights	Safe Seat
1	1
2	1
3	3
4	1
5	3
6	5
7	7
8	1
9	3
10	5
11	7
12	9
13	11
14	13
15	15
16	1
17	3
18	5
19	7
20	9

A confession here: I didn't actually apply the method I described above to all 20 numbers. I started looking for patterns after 10 knights. I noticed that seat #1 was the safe seat when there were 1, 2, 4, and 8 knights. I recognized the pattern of these numbers, that each was the double of the previous one. (These numbers are the powers of 2.) That discovery led me to predict that with 16 knights, seat #1 would again be the safe one. I tried 16 and found that I was correct.

I also noticed that even-numbered seats were never safe. This makes sense because the live-die pattern alternates the same way even and odd numbers do. Knights in the even-numbered seats get killed in the first pass around the circle.

And I noticed that the odd-numbered safe seats followed a predictable pattern — 1, 3, 5, 7, and so on — until the next power of 2. After 16 knights, seat #1 would again be safe when there were 32 knights, and the safe seat numbers after 32 knights would go 3, 5, 7, 9, and so on up to when there are 31 knights. At that point, right before seat #1 again became the safe seat, seat #31 would be the safe seat.

Okay, this is all interesting, but the power of patterns is that they allow you to predict beyond the information you currently have. What if there are 50 knights at the table? How would I figure out the safe seat without writing the numerals in a circle and applying my crossing-out method? Here's how I thought about this. I know that seat #1 is safe for 32 knights, and the next time that seat #1 will be safe is for 64 knights. The safe seats for 33 to 63 knights will be consecutive odd numbers — 3, 5, 7, 9, . . . , 63. So, where will 50 hit? If you start with 32 (when the safe seat is #1) and count to 50, you count 19 numbers. (Check this out for yourself. I know that the difference between 32 and 50 is only 18, but I have to count both 32 and 50.) So the safe seat for 50 knights is the 19th consecutive odd number. The 10th consecutive odd number is 19; the 20th consecutive odd number is 39 (see a pattern?), so the 19th consecutive odd number is 37. It's my bet that 37 is the safe seat for 50 knights. I checked my prediction by making a partial table, from 50 up to 64, where I knew #1 would be the safe seat again. If seat #63 was safe for 63 knights, I'd be satisfied.

Number of Knights	Safe Seat
50	37
51	39
52	41
53	43
54	45
55	47
56	49
57	51
58	53
59	55
60	57
61	59
62	61
63	63
64	1

Hurray!

Okay, now what if there are 100 knights at the table? Again, I start with what I know, that after 64 knights, the next time that seat #1 is safe is for 128 knights. I also know that from 64 through 127 knights, the safe seat numbers will go in consecutive odd numbers — 3, 5, 7, 9, . . . , 127. All I need to figure out is how many consecutive odd numbers there will be to get from 64 to 100. The difference between 64 and 100 is 36, but I have to count both 64 and 100, so I need to find the 37th consecutive odd number. I remember that the 10th odd number is 19 (1 less than twice 10) and the 20th odd number is 39 (1 less than twice 20). I try a few smaller examples to check this pattern. The third odd number, 5, is one less than twice 3; the fourth odd number, 7, is one less than twice 4. So I'm comfortable figuring that the 37th odd number is one less than twice 37 — 73. So seat #73 is the safe seat for 100 knights.

More people have written to me about *King Arthur's Problem* than any other problem in *About Teaching Mathematics*. Some write short desperate pleas for help. Others write longer letters, often explaining in their own words what I offer above. Both the long-letter writers and the short-letter writers make the same request — WHAT'S THE FORMULA?

Sorry, but it isn't possible to reduce every math problem to a formula that you can use to get the answer you want. Well, I could concoct a formula for King Arthur. Let me see. Let n represent the number of knights. Let s be the safe seat. Let p be the power of 2 that is closest to but less than n. Then, the number of consecutive odd numbers to count would be $n - p + 1$, and to figure out what the safe seat number is would be $2(n - p + 1) - 1$. Mush the variables and you get $s = 2n - 2p + 2 - 1$, or $s = 2n - 2p + 1$. So, if you like formulas, there you go.

But here's what I know. I may not — and probably won't — remember that formula, but I know that I'll always be able to figure out how to solve the problem. And that's what counts in mathematical thinking.

The Prison Problem (page 105)

This problem has generated almost as much mail as *King Arthur's Problem*. When I first encountered it, I decided to solve a related but smaller problem. This technique often helps with math problems. Instead of thinking about a jail with 100 cells, suppose the jail only had 10 cells. What could I learn?

I wrote the numbers from 1 to 10 in a row to represent the cells. I followed the warden's first order, unlocked them all, and wrote U (for unlocked) under each number.

I then followed the warden's second order, left the first cell unlocked, locked the second, left the third unlocked, and so on. I wrote Us and Ls to indicate what I had done.

1	2	3	4	5	6	7	8	9	10
U	U	U	U	U	U	U	U	U	U
U	L	U	L	U	L	U	L	U	L

I continued following the warden's orders until I had to turn the key just in the 10th cell, keeping track as I went.

	1	2	3	4	5	6	7	8	9	10
Unlock	U	U	U	U	U	U	U	U	U	U
Leave 1	U	L	U	L	U	L	U	L	U	L
Leave 2	U	L	L	L	U	U	U	L	L	L
Leave 3	U	L	L	U	U	U	U	U	L	L
Leave 4	U	L	L	U	L	U	U	U	L	U
Leave 5	U	L	L	U	L	L	U	U	L	U
Leave 6	U	L	L	U	L	L	L	U	L	U
Leave 7	U	L	L	U	L	L	L	L	L	U
Leave 8	U	L	L	U	L	L	L	L	U	U
Leave 9	U	L	L	U	L	L	L	L	U	L

Boy, this was tedious. Clearly I had to do some fast thinking. I certainly didn't want to do this for 100 cells. What could I learn from what I had done so far?

For 10 cells, the ones that remained unlocked after all I did were cell #1, #4, and #9. But would they stay unlocked for the rest of the time if we did this for 100 cells? Well, I knew that cell #1 would for sure. It was unlocked the first time around, was skipped ever since, and would continue to be skipped no matter how many cells there were. And since we're now up to skipping the first 10 cells before turning the lock in any of them, all of the cells from #1 through #9 would now remain untouched.

Now I began to rummage in my mind. One clue: what we were doing by following the warden's orders was a kind of jailhouse version of skip counting. Skip counting is related to multiplication. The answer must have something to do with multiplication. Another clue: the numbers of the unlocked cells— 1, 4, and 9 — are square numbers. What do I know about square numbers and multiplication?

Okay, 1, 4, and 9 are square numbers because $1 = 1 \times 1$, $4 = 2 \times 2$, and $9 = 3 \times 3$. There's a tie to multiplication. I also know that square numbers are the only numbers that have an odd number of factors. All other numbers have pairs of factors. Think about 12, for example. Its factor pairs are 1×12, 2×6, and 3×4; 12 has six factors — 1, 2, 3, 4, 6, and 12. Each factor is paired with a different number to make 12. But with square numbers, you can multiply a number by itself, so one of its factors has itself as a partner, resulting in an odd number of factors. Think about 16, for example. Its factor pairs are 1×16, 2×8, and 4×5; 16 (a square number) has five factors — 1, 2, 4, 8, and 16.

So, what does this have to do with the locking/unlocking pattern? With the skip-counting method, each cell will have its lock turned once for each of its factors as it comes up in the warden's screwy system. For numbers that are not square, which all have an even number of factors, the lock will be turned an even number of times. It started locked, and after an even number of turns, it will again be locked. The only way it could be left unlocked would be if the lock were turned an odd number of times, which can happen for only the square numbers. For me, the problem was resolved.

The Three Sacks Problem (page 105)

When I start a problem like this, I first try to establish what I know for sure. In this situation, because each sack is mislabeled, I know the following:
- The sack labeled *Red* has either only blue cubes or a mixture of red and blue cubes.
- The sack labeled *Blue* has either only red cubes or a mixture of red and blue cubes.
- The sack labeled *Red and Blue* has only one color cube in it.
- I have to determine what really is in each sack by reaching into just one sack, removing one cube, and using only that information.

That's all I know.

To get started, I think about what might happen if I reach into the sack labeled *Red* and pull out a red cube. I'd then know that the sack must have both red and blue cubes in it, or else it wouldn't be mislabeled. This would solve the problem! The sack labeled *Blue* would then be the one with only red cubes, leaving the *Red and Blue* sack the one with only blue cubes. But . . . what if I reached into the sack labeled *Red* and pulled out a blue cube? I wouldn't be sure if the sack had all blue cubes or a mixture. I'd be stuck.

I'd be in the same situation if I decided to pull a cube out of the sack labeled *Blue*. If the cube I pulled was red, I wouldn't know if all of the cubes in the sack were red or if there were some blue in the sack as well. Again, I'd be stuck.

I guess I have to pull a cube from the sack labeled *Red and Blue*. But what would this tell? Since this sack is mislabeled, I know it has only one color in it — either only red or only blue cubes. Suppose the cube I pulled was red. Then the sack labeled *Red and Blue* should really be labeled *Red*. Of the two sacks left, one must have all blue cubes and one a mixture. The sack mislabeled *Blue* can't have all blue cubes, or else it wouldn't be mislabeled. So it must have a mixture and, therefore, should be labeled *Red and Blue*. And the sack mislabeled *Red and Blue* must have all blue cubes. And if I pulled a blue cube from the sack labeled *Red and Blue*, I could still identify what the other two contain following this same logic.

The best way to test my logic is to set up the three sacks, label them incorrectly, and try it.

The Orange Juice and Water Problem and the Two-Color Problem (page 108)

The problem about orange juice and water causes fiercely passionate discussion in classes, with staunch believers on three sides — some convinced that there's more orange juice in the water glass than water in the orange juice glass, some believing the reverse, and some sure that there's the same amount of each in each. My position is that after taking spoonfuls back and forth three times — or any number of times — there will always be the same amount of orange juice in the water glass as there is water in the orange juice glass.

The way I reason is that after moving spoonfuls, there's still the same amount of liquid in each glass, allowing some small difference for imprecise measuring technique. We started with the same amount of orange juice as water, but just mixed the two. Now, the quantity of water in the orange juice glass has replaced the same amount of orange juice, which in now in the water glass.

It may help, if my reasoning doesn't hold water (oops, sorry), to think about the next problem in the book, *The Two-Color Problem*. In this you have two sacks, one with 10 objects of one color and one with 10 objects of another color. You move the same number of objects back and forth, mixing the sacks each time. When you're done, you still have 10 objects in each sack, most likely a mixture of colors. If there are now three blues in the red sack (or whatever colors you used), for example, there have to be three red objects replacing those blues in the blue sack. As long as you wind up with the same number of total objects in each sack, the number of red in the blue sack and vice versa will be the same. I'm thoroughly convinced that this is the same as the orange juice and water situation.

Riddles with Color Tiles (page 109)

I've done this activity successfully with students as young as second graders as well as with middle school classes, adjusting the number and the complexity of clues to fit the situation. (If you're interested, vignettes of this lesson appear in two Math Solutions Publications books in the *A Collection of Math Lessons* series. See chapter 3 in the book for grades 1 through 3 and chapter 1 in the book for grades 6 through 8.)

Aside from the logical reasoning skills that these riddles promote, they also help develop or reinforce vocabulary — *more than*, *fewer than*, *half of*, and so on. With second graders, a clue such as "I have twice as many blue tiles as yellow tiles" often reveals that you need to teach children what twice means.

For the riddles on page 109, the color tiles in Riddle 1 included four tiles of each color; for Riddle 2 there are two yellow tiles and four blue tiles.

The Handshake Problem (page 124)

This is another problem that generates a fair amount of mail from readers. I include this long-winded explanation as an example of how to approach, in general, the problems in the Patterns, Functions, and Algebra section.

Typically, letters about *The Handshake Problem* don't request help with figuring out the number of handshakes for successive numbers of people; that seems to be something that readers are able to do from either acting it out, making a drawing, or in some other way. Here's the table completed for up to 10 people:

PEOPLE	HAND-SHAKES
1	0
2	1
3	3
4	6
5	10
6	15
7	21
8	28
9	36
10	45

People usually include in their letter their discoveries about how to continue the table by following the pattern in the handshakes column. The number of handshakes increases each time by one more than the previous increase — from 0 to 1 is 1 more, from 1 to 3 is 2 more, from 3 to 6 is 3 more, from 6 to 10 is 4 more, and so on. Continuing the pattern, there are 9 more handshakes for 10 people than there were for 9 people (45 (36 = 9), so the number of handshakes for 11 people would be 10 more than for 10 people. Since 45 + 10 = 55, if 11 people were each to shake hands with everyone else, there would be 55 handshakes in all.

Three questions are asked most frequently in the letters I receive: Why do handshakes generate this pattern? How can you figure out how many handshakes there will be for a large number of people, say 100 or more, without making a long table? What's the formula for this pattern?

In a way, all three questions are the same. The answer to question 1 is the rationale for the pattern of handshakes. This rationale can be applied to any number of people to answer question 2. And a rationale can often be expressed as an algebraic formula to answer question 3.

A rationale first. Suppose you are one of the people in the room. With how many other people will you shake hands? This depends, of course, on the number of people in the room and therefore changes for different numbers of people. What stays the same, however, is that you'll shake hands with everyone in the room except yourself. That means that the number of handshakes for you will be one less than the number of people in the room. The same is true for everyone else in the room: each person in the room shakes hands with one less than the total number of people.

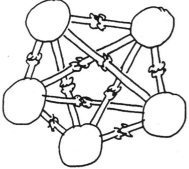

If there were five people in the room, for example, each of the five people will do four handshakes. You can try this by drawing five people is a circle and drawing hands connecting each person to every other person.

Every person shakes hands with four others. And if five people each do four handshakes, I reasoned, that makes 20 handshakes all together. Right?

Wrong! Look at the table above. According to the table, for five people, there are 10 handshakes, not 20.

When I first encountered this problem, it took me a while to figure out where the glitch was in my thinking. Then I had a lucky realization — a mathematical "Aha!" Counting all 20 handshakes is twice as many as there should be because I counted each handshake twice. For example, if you were in the room, then I counted shaking hands with you as one handshake. But I also counted your shaking hands with me as one handshake. This is double trouble.

So I refined my rationale. First I reasoned that each person shakes hands with one less than the total number of people. Then I figured out how many handshakes that makes all together (by multiplying the number of handshakes each person makes by the number of people). Finally, I cut the number in half.

I tried my refined rationale for another number. For six people, for example, each person shakes hands with five others. That makes 30 handshakes, which is twice as many as there really are, since each handshake has been counted twice. Half of 30 is 15. Check the chart! Also, try my rationale for other numbers to be sure it holds true.

Now I can answer question 2. Suppose there are 100 people in the room. Each person shakes hands with 99 others. If 100 people do this, it seems that there would be 9,900 handshakes, but that's double the correct answer of 4,950 handshakes.

To answer question 3, I need to translate my rationale to an algebraic equation. The number of people varies from room to room, and therefore we need to use a variable to represent it. Also, the number of handshakes depends on the number of people, so we need to use a variable to represent it as well. How about p for people and h for handshakes? Each person in the room shakes hands with one less than the total number of people, so each person makes $p - 1$ handshakes. With p people altogether, that makes p times $p - 1$ handshakes, which we can write in algebraic shorthand as $p(p - 1)$. But that's twice as many handshakes as we need, so I have take half of $p(p - 1)$, or divide $p(p - 1)$ by 2 to get the number of handshakes. Here are two ways to write a formula that works:

$$h = \tfrac{1}{2}p(p-1) \qquad\qquad h = \tfrac{1}{2}p(p-1)$$

$$h = \frac{p(p-1)}{2} \qquad\qquad h = \frac{p(p-1)}{2}$$

If you followed this, great. If you didn't, maybe you'd like another way to think about the problem. Here's another rationale. (Remember, there's usually more than one way to think about any math problem.) Well, it's not a totally different rationale. Go back to the way I began thinking about the problem, supposing that you're one of the people in the room, and figuring out that you'll shake hands with one less than the number of people in the room. So you do $p - 1$ handshakes.

Now suppose that I'm also in the room and I have to shake hands with everyone else. But I already shook hands with you. To avoid that double trouble later, I won't shake hands with you again and will, instead, shake hands with everyone else *except* you. This means I do $p - 2$ handshakes.

Now the third person shakes with everyone else except for you and me — $p - 3$ handshakes.

Continue thinking in this way and then add up the handshakes. For five people in a room, for example, you shake hands with the four others. Then I go around the room, skipping you and shaking hands with the three others. Then the third person skips both you and me and shakes hands with the two others. The fourth skips you, me, and the third person and shakes hands with the only other person in the room — the fifth person. The fifth person then doesn't have to do any more handshaking since he (or she) already shook hands with you, me, and the other two people. Total the handshakes — four for you, three for me, two for the third person, and one for the fourth person — $4 + 3 + 2 + 1 = 10$. Yup, it works.

Try it for six people. The first does five handshakes; the second does four; the third, three handshakes; the fourth, two handshakes; the fifth, one handshake; the sixth is finished. Add $5 + 4 + 3 + 2 + 1$ and you get 15.

This method will also work for 100 people — $99 + 98 + 97 + 96 + 95 + 94 + 93 + \ldots + 1$. Bleh. If I had to do this much adding, I might as well just finish the table and have the answers for all of the numbers up to 100.

A friend told me another way to think about the problem, however, that also led to a viable formula. Suppose everyone shook hands with everyone else, including shaking hands with themselves. For five people, that would be five handshakes per person, which is 5 times 5, or 25 handshakes. For six people, this reasoning means six handshakes per person, which is 6 times 6, or 36 handshakes. For any number of people (p), it's p times p or p^2 handshakes.

Ridiculous, I protested. That's way too many handshakes, and people don't shake hands with themselves.

Okay, my friend said, let's subtract the extras. Take out one handshake per person to eliminate the self handshakes. For five people, that means subtracting five handshakes; for six people, that means subtracting six handshakes; for p people, that means subtracting p handshakes. So now we're down to $p^2 - p$.

No way, I protested again. For five people, that's 25 minus 5, or 20 handshakes; for six people, it's 36 minus 6, or 30 handshakes. These numbers are twice as big as they should be.

Ah, my friend said, I counted each handshake twice, as you did before. So I'll just take half of $p^2 - p$ and I'll have the right answer. I used this logic to write two versions of the formula:

$$h = \tfrac{1}{2}(p^2 - p) \qquad h = \tfrac{1}{2}(p^2 - p)$$

$$h = \frac{p^2 - p}{2} \qquad h = \frac{p^2 - p}{2}$$

I tried the formulas for several other numbers. Bingo!

Now I had four options for formulas:

$$h = \tfrac{1}{2}\,p(p-1)$$

$$h = \frac{p(p-1)}{2}$$

$$h = \tfrac{1}{2}(p^2 - p)$$

$$h = \frac{p^2 - p}{2}$$

These four options are really all the same — if you recall how to work with algebraic expressions.

Two last thoughts. The first one is a mathematical connection: *Dot Connecting* (page 117) is mathematically identical to *The Handshake Problem*. Take a look. The sketches I made for *Dot Connecting* are just like the sketches I made for figuring out handshakes of people in a room, except they have just lines, not little hands. Ten lines connect five dots on a circle, for example, just as there are ten handshakes for five people in the room.

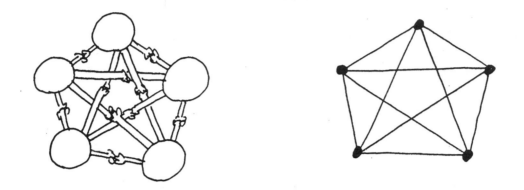

My last suggestion is to use the pairs of numbers on the table — (1,0), (2,1), (3,3), (4,6), and so on — and mark points on a coordinate graph. Look at the example about tricycles and wheels on page 113 if you need a reminder about how to do this. The points on page 113 go in a straight line, but the points for *The Handshake Problem* go in a curve. When you have $p \times p$, or p^2, in a formula, it's called a quadratic equation and makes a curve that's called a *parabola*. If this is a new idea for you, remember that learning something invariably leads to learning something new. Keep your mind open to learning about parabolas and other curves that come from graphing formulas. It may open a whole new aspect of math for you.

Number Sums (page 126)

This problem asks primary-age children to find all the possible ways to represent small numbers as the sum of addends. When I listed on page 126 the seven ways to write 4 as the sum of addends, I used an orderly approach to be sure to account for all the possible ways. I started by using all 1s as addends, then I listed the different combinations with 2s, and then I used 3s. My system isn't the only useful approach, but it works for me. I used the same system to find the 15 possible combinations for the number 5:

$$1+1+1+1$$
$$1+1+1+2$$
$$1+1+2+1$$
$$1+2+1+1$$
$$2+1+1+1$$
$$1+2+2$$
$$2+1+2$$
$$2+2+1$$
$$1+1+3$$
$$1+3+1$$
$$3+1+1$$
$$1+4$$
$$4+1$$
$$2+3$$
$$3+2$$

When I do this problem with young children, however, I typically find that the children don't use a logical approach but merely rummage to find different combinations. I sometimes show a class how I think about making a list to account for all the possibilities, but I do so with a light touch and don't push them to solve the problem my way. I've learned that as children get older, they're more inclined to think in a logical fashion. Besides, children's rummaging is valuable. It engages them in thinking about combinations of different numbers, which is useful addition practice. The activity also gives children informal experience thinking about commutativity and associativity.

While the addition is simple enough for older children, the problem can still be interesting for them, especially if the focus is on predicting how many ways there are to write sums for larger numbers. The summarizing section of the problem asks for predictions about the number of ways to write sums for 6, 7, and 8. The information in the table on page 127 helps in making these predictions. The numbers of ways to write sums for 3, 4, and 5 are 3, 7, and 15. The numbers of ways are odd. They're also each one less than a power of 2. (The powers of 2 are 1, 2, 4, 8, 16, and so on, the numbers that are so useful for *King Arthur's Problem*.) Using this information, my prediction is that for the number 6 there are 31 possible sums (because 31 is one less than 32, the power of 2 that follows 16); for the number 7 there are 63 possible sums; for 8 there are 127.

My predictions also make sense if I evaluate the existing data another way. Look at the differences between the 3, 7, and 15, the numbers of sums for 3, 4, and 5. The difference between 3 and 7 is 4; the difference between 7 and 15 is 8. These differences — 4 and 8 — are powers of 2. In a logical progression, the difference between 15 and the next number should be 16, the next power of 2. That would make the number 31, which is consistent with the prediction I made. The difference between 31 and 63 is 32, the next power of 2; and the difference between 127 and 63 is 64.

I didn't include in the problem thinking of all the ways to write sums for the number 2. Maybe I should have, but it didn't seem interesting, since there's only one way to write 2 as a sum — 1 + 1. But if I add that information to the table, I can see that it preserves the patterns I used for predicting, since 1 is one less than a power of 2.

Number	How Many Sums?
2	1
3	3
4	7
5	15
6	31
7	63
8	127
⋮	⋮

A teacher suggested to me that an easier problem for children would be to consider the different combinations of addends for each number without worrying about the reversals, so that 2 + 1 and 1 + 2 would be considered the same since they use the same addends. For the number 3, then, there would be only two possibilities:

$$1 + 1 + 1$$
$$1 + 2$$

In this version of the problem, the number 4 has four possibilities:

$$1+1+1+1$$
$$1+1+2$$
$$1+3$$
$$2+2$$

The number 5 has six possibilities:

$$1+1+1+1+1$$
$$1+1+1+2$$
$$1+2+2$$
$$1+1+3$$
$$1+4$$
$$2+3$$

Make a table of this information and predict the number of sums for 6, 7, and 8.

Either version of the problem is fine, and you may think of another. What's important is that the problem engages children in practicing addition and also looking for patterns.

Making Change (page 130)

Using the context of money, this problem calls for making a list of all possible ways and, in that way, it's similar to *Number Sums*, on page 126. The problems are also similar in that both involve thinking about different addition combinations. I approached solving the problem the same way I did for *Number Sums*, making a list in an orderly fashion that would exhaust all the possibilities for making change for $.25, $.50, and $1.00.

Instead of making a list, actually, I made a chart, writing the coins at the top and using each line for a different combination, indicating how many of each coin I would use. For $.25, for example, I made the following chart that produced 12 ways to make change:

10¢	5¢	1¢
2	1	0
2	0	5
1	3	0
1	2	5
1	1	10
1	0	15
0	5	0
0	4	5
0	3	10
0	2	15
0	1	20
0	0	25

I've learned to watch for patterns when I tackle a problem. In examining the chart above, I noticed a 2-4-6 pattern in the dimes column. There are two ways to use a dime twice, four ways to use a dime once, and six ways not to use a dime at all. This isn't a great discovery, but one that gave me some comfort that there was some order to what I was doing.

For $.50, here is part of the chart I made (this chart has an additional column to account for quarters as well as dimes, nickels, and pennies):

25¢	10¢	5¢	1¢
2	0	0	0
1	2	1	0
1	2	0	5
1	1	3	0
1	1	2	5
1	1	1	10
1	1	0	15
1	0	5	0
1	0	4	5
1	0	3	10
⋮	⋮	⋮	⋮

I found 49 ways to make change for $.50. The 2-4-6 pattern emerged again in the dimes column when one quarter was used, and also a 1-3-5-7-9-11 pattern in the dimes column when no quarters were used. Hmmm.

On to making change for $1.00. I knew that there would be many more ways to make change for $1.00, and I wondered if there was a way to find them other than starting another chart. Making such an elaborate list was going to be pretty exhausting.

I decided to use what I knew about making change for $.50. I added a first column to the chart for using a 50¢ coin, using a different-color pen to keep my previous work intact. Then I thought: if I added a 50¢ coin to each of the 49 ways for $.50, each would then be worth $1.00, and that makes 49 ways. Also, I could make $1.00 using only two 50¢ coins, so now I have 50 ways and, I think, have taken care of all possibilities using one or two 50¢ coins. Now I have to figure out the ways to make change for $1.00 without using any 50¢ coins.

I thought that if I used the chart I'd made for making change for $.50 and doubled the quantities for each coin, the amount on each line would double from $.50 to $1.00. That would give another 49 ways, bringing my total up to 99 ways. I wondered if doubling would take care of every other possibility, however. I realized that the ways I had considered so far used four quarters once and two quarters 24 times, but I hadn't considered any possibilities using one or three quarters. Oops. I went back to construct those.

It wasn't hard to figure that there were 12 ways with three quarters: I reasoned that because three quarters makes 75¢, I need 25¢ more, and I learned earlier that there are 12 ways to make change for 25¢. So if I added three quarters to each of those 12 ways, I'd have 12 new ways to make change for $1.00. That changed my total from 99 to 111 ways.

Now I thought that all I had to do was figure the ways using one quarter. With one quarter, I need 75¢ more. Maybe I can use the chart for $.25 again, this time tripling the quantities for each coin so that the amount on each line would triple from $.25 to $.75. That would produce 12 more ways to make change for $1.00 using one quarter, bringing the total to 123.

Was this saving time? Should I just have made the list to begin with? How did I know whether I had accounted for all the possible ways? I didn't feel right about this number 123. I don't know why, but I felt there were other possibilities. I took a break. I fixed a cup of tea and a snack. I phoned a friend (about something completely unrelated). I went to the store to do an errand.

Then it came to me. I was thinking that there were only 12 ways to make change for $1.00 using one quarter, but that couldn't be right. That would be the same as saying that there were 12 ways to make change for $.75 if I used only dimes, nickels, and pennies. But there were 12 ways to make change for $.25 with dimes, nickels, and pennies, so there should be lots more ways to make change for $.75 with these·same coins. I went back to work, this time making a chart for the ways to make change for $.75 with dimes, nickels, and pennies. I found 72 ways! (And 72 is the sum of 2 + 4 + 6 + 8 + 10 + 12 + 14 + 16, an extension of the 2-4-6 pattern I had noticed earlier.)

My chart included those 12 ways from tripling the quantities in my old chart for $.25, so I eliminated that step, went back to the previous total of 111 and added on the new 72 ways, to get a total of 183.

At this point I was sorry that I had ever put this problem in *About Teaching Mathematics* and even sorrier that I had committed to offering solutions. Now I had heaps of paper on my desk and an answer of 183 in which I had little confidence. I decided that I needed to give the problem a fresh look, but this was not the time. I took another break and didn't return to the problem for several days.

When I returned to the problem, rested, I took a new approach. To make change for $1.00, I thought, I can use two 50¢ coins; that's one way. Or if I used one 50¢ coin, then my former logic makes sense that there are 49 ways to make $.50 with quarters, dimes, nickels, and pennies, adding the 50¢ coin to the ways I already have brings each total to $1.00. So now I have 50 ways so far, as I had before. So far, so good.

Okay, I eliminated the 50¢ coins and thought about what happens with quarters. I can make $1.00 with four quarters, three quarters, two quarters, one quarter, or no quarters.

Four quarters is easy; there's only one way.

For three quarters you need $.25 more to make $1.00, and there are twelve ways to make that.

For two quarters, you need $.50 more, and there are 49 ways to make that. But I can't count the ways on my list of 49 that already use one or two quarters, because those ways use three and four quarters total, which I've already counted above. This eliminates 13 possibilities and leaves me with 36 more ways.

For one quarter, I need $.75 more. Let's see, the answer to that is somewhere in this heap of papers. (I hadn't thrown out anything.) Here it is — using only dimes, nickels, and pennies, there are 72 ways to make $.75.

There's only zero quarters left. How many ways can I make change for $1.00 with only dimes, nickels, and pennies? I started a chart. A 1-3-5-7-and-so-on pattern emerged for using ten dimes, then nine dimes, then eight, and so on. I didn't write all of the possibilities,

I merely added the odd numbers from 1 through 21 and got 121. Boy, I love patterns. So I'm going with 121 ways to make $1.00 using only dimes, nickels, and pennies.

What's my total this time? I have to add 50, 1, 12, 36, 72, and 121, which gives a total of 292. I hope this is right. But please write if you have a quarrel with my answer or my reasoning. I'd like to hear from you. Really. (I'll save my papers.)

How Many Sums? (page 131)

Egads, I thought, another problem of finding all the different possible sums. But this time there are only five possible addends, so it should be easier.

I began by making a list of the possible combinations using two addends. I found ten:

$$19 + 21$$
$$19 + 15$$
$$19 + 17$$
$$19 + 13$$
$$21 + 15$$
$$21 + 17$$
$$21 + 13$$
$$15 + 17$$
$$15 + 13$$
$$17 + 13$$

I knew that I didn't need to reverse these combinations, because I'm interested in different sums, and reversals would produce the same set of sums. Hey, I then thought, this is like *The Handshake Problem*, on page 124 — if five people shake hands with each other, there will be ten handshakes altogether. It's also like *Dot Connecting*, on page 117 — with five dots, I can draw ten lines connecting each one to every other one. (Keep an eye out for connections like these. They help build your mathematical intuition.)

I was feeling pleased with myself, but only for a moment. What if I was allowed to use the numbers more than once? Then I'd have to include 19 + 19, for example, and the other sums with both addends the same. But what does the problem call for?

I read it again. It wasn't clear. I could go either way. Well, it's my book, I thought. Which way was I thinking? I couldn't remember. (After all, I wrote the first edition of this book quite a while ago.) But I could remember why I included the problem. It gave practice with addition in a way that also called for logical reasoning. Either version does that. So there really are two problems here, one in which you use each number only once and one in which you can use each number as many times as you'd like.

I opted to continue the way I started and went on to make a list of the possible combinations of three addends, using each number only once in each combination. Again, I found ten.

$$19 + 21 + 15$$
$$19 + 21 + 17$$
$$19 + 21 + 13$$
$$19 + 15 + 17$$
$$19 + 15 + 13$$
$$19 + 17 + 13$$
$$21 + 15 + 17$$
$$21 + 15 + 13$$
$$21 + 17 + 13$$
$$15 + 17 + 13$$

For possible combinations of four addends, I found five ways.

$$19 + 21 + 15 + 17$$
$$19 + 21 + 15 + 13$$
$$19 + 21 + 17 + 13$$
$$19 + 15 + 17 + 13$$
$$21 + 15 + 17 + 13$$

For five addends, there's just one way:

$$19 + 21 + 5 + 17 + 13$$

All in all, there were 26 combinations of addends. But I wasn't done, because the problem asked for different possible sums, not different possible combinations of addends.

I returned to the ten combinations with two addends and figured the sums:

$$19 + 21 = 40$$
$$19 + 15 = 34$$
$$19 + 17 = 36$$
$$19 + 13 = 32$$
$$21 + 15 = 36$$
$$21 + 17 = 38$$
$$21 + 13 = 34$$
$$15 + 17 = 32$$
$$15 + 13 = 28$$
$$17 + 13 = 30$$

The sums were all even, which makes sense, because whenever you add two odd numbers, the sum is even. And there were duplicate sums. I looked again at the numbers and realized that they were consecutive odd numbers — 13, 15, 17, 19, 21. If I added the first and the last, the sum would have to be the same as if I added the second and the fourth because I would be increasing one addend by two and decreasing the other addend by two. So there's more to discuss with students than merely calculating sums, but seeing relationships among pairs of addends. For two addends, there were ten possible combinations, but only seven different sums. That's because 19 + 13 = 15 + 17; 19 + 15 = 21 + 13; and 19 + 17 = 21 + 15.

To think about the sums with three addends, I tried using this information to see which would be eliminated. First of all, I knew that all the sums would be odd, since adding three odd numbers always produces an odd number. That guaranteed that there wouldn't be any matches with the first set of sums, which were all even. But again there were duplicates in this set, which left me with seven different sums, making 14 altogether so far.

The combinations with four and five addends produced unique sums, which added five more. The grand total: 20 possible sums.

I'm done — unless I want to do the other version of the problem and use the numbers more than once. Well, not right now. Maybe later.

Change from a $10.00 Bill (page 131)

I found eleven solutions for the amount I could spend: $0.95, $1.85, $2.75, $3.65, $4.55, $5.00, $5.45, $6.35, $7.25, $8.15, and $9.05. The first one in the list has given people trouble because of the zero in the dollar place.

Multiplication Possibilities (page 133)

I used to view this as a ho-hum problem, just a twist on providing students with multiplication practice. Using trial and error to test different numbers certainly does support practice, but this problem can also help develop students' number sense and logical reasoning skills.

The first thing I wondered about was how to get a 6 in the ones place of the answer. In order for that to happen, the product of the one-digit multiplier and the ones digit in the three-digit top number had to end in a 6. I wondered about which pairs of numbers made this possible. I started a list with 1×6. Then I thought about 2 as a factor, and came up with 2×3. For 3, 3×2 was obvious. For 4, I came up with 4×4, which made me realize that I was being fairly narrow with 1, 2, and 3, thinking only about how to get to a product of 6. I had skipped over 2×8. And if 6 and 16 are possible products that ended in 6, so are 26, 36, 46, 56, 66, 76, 86, or 96. Now I began to think of ways to reach those products with two single-digit factors. My list evolved:

$$1 \times 6$$
$$2 \times 3$$
$$2 \times 8$$
$$3 \times 2$$
$$4 \times 4$$
$$4 \times 9$$

I skipped over 5. I knew that 5 times any number ends in either 5 or zero, so it wouldn't be a possibility. I continued.

$$6 \times 1$$
$$6 \times 6$$
$$7 \times 8$$
$$8 \times 2$$
$$8 \times 7$$
$$9 \times 4$$

I couldn't think of any others, but a dozen was a good start. Okay, I thought, now what do I do?

I'm a just-get-started kind of problem solver, happy to try something and think about it afterward. I put a 1 in the box to use as the multiplier. Aha, that works if I use 966 as the top number. I put a check next to 1×6 on my list.

I then tried 2 as the multiplier. Ah, I thought, this works if I use half of 966 as the top number. (Do you see why that makes sense?) Since 966 is even, that's possible. Now I had two possibilities. I put a check next to 2×3.

Next on the list was 2×8. Well, if I use 2 as the one-digit multiplier, I already know the answer — it's 483 — so 2×8 won't work. I crossed it off my list. But what if I used 8 for the one-digit multiplier and the 2 in the ones place on top? What times 8 equals 966? Here's where knowing how multiplication and division relates helps. Dividing 966 by 8 gives 120.75, and that won't fit in the three boxes for the top number, so 8 can't possibly be a multiplier. I crossed off 8×2 and 8×7. My list now looked like this:

$$1 \times 6 \quad \checkmark$$
$$2 \times 3 \quad \checkmark$$
$$\cancel{2 \times 8}$$
$$3 \times 2$$
$$4 \times 4$$
$$4 \times 9$$
$$6 \times 1$$
$$6 \times 6$$
$$7 \times 8$$
$$\cancel{8 \times 2}$$
$$\cancel{8 \times 7}$$
$$9 \times 4$$

Now I started to wise up. I knew that 1 and 2 were possible single-digit multipliers; I knew that 8 was impossible; the only other numbers I needed to test were 3, 4, 5, 6, 7, and 9. I didn't really have to make that list after all. I could have merely tried those numbers, using what I know about the relationship between multiplication and division.

Also, I could use what I knew about divisibility. A number is divisible by 3 if its digits add to a multiple of 3. I added 9 plus 6 plus 6 and got 21; since 21 is a multiple of 3, I knew that 3 would work. And I knew that 6 would also work, because even numbers that are divisible by 3 are also divisible by 6.

I did the divisions and found what I think are the only possibilities — 966×1, 483×2, 322×3, 161×6, 138×7. (Where's the answer book to check my work?)

I began to wonder what other problems like this one would be good for students to try. That got me thinking more about the 966 problem. Judging by all the thinking it sparked for me, it seems that 966 was a good choice of number. What other factors would produce a product of 966? How could I think about that? I identified the prime factors of 966 — 2, 3, 7, and 23.

Then I rearranged and combined the factors in different ways, applying the commutative and associative properties. I came up with other problems — $(2 \times 3 \times 7) \times 23$, or 42×23; $(2 \times 7) \times (3 \times 23)$, which is the same as 14×69; and 21×46. None fit the three-digit times one-digit format, but all produced the answer of 966. Who ever thought that I'd get so involved with 966?

So, what other numbers would be good to use in a problem like this to replace 966 and spark thinking? Here are three I tried that you might be interested in tinkering with. Or make up some of your own.

$$\begin{array}{r} \square\,\square\,\square \\ \times\ \ \square \\ \hline 510 \end{array} \qquad \begin{array}{r} \square\,\square\,\square \\ \times\ \ \square \\ \hline 870 \end{array} \qquad \begin{array}{r} \square\,\square\,\square \\ \times\ \ \square \\ \hline 594 \end{array}$$

The Postage Stamp Problem (page 134)

The arithmetic calculations required in this problem aren't particularly challenging, which makes it accessible to some primary students as well as to upper elementary students. And the patterns that emerge are interesting to students of all ages. I offer here how I thought about the problem of the possible postage to make with 3¢ and 5¢ stamps, and then with 5¢ and 8¢ stamps. I leave it to you to think about what happens with stamps of other denominations.

If I use only 3¢ stamps on an envelope, then the possible postage amounts are multiples of 3 — 3¢, 6¢, 9¢, 12¢, 15¢, and so on. Using only 5¢ stamps produces postage amounts that are multiples of 5 — 5¢, 10¢, 15¢, 20¢, 25¢, and so on. Combining both denominations produces other possible amounts. For example, one 3¢ stamp and one 5¢ stamp makes 8¢; two 3¢ stamps and one 5¢ stamp makes 11¢; three 3¢ stamps and one 5¢ stamp makes 14¢. These begin a pattern that increases by 3¢ each time and results in all new totals — 8¢,

11¢, 14¢, 17¢, 20¢. Oops, there's a repeat, caused because it uses five 3¢ stamps, which is the same as three 5¢ stamps. So there will be some new amounts and some repeats from using one 5¢ stamp with different numbers of 3¢ stamps.

It seems way too complicated to figure out all of the possible amounts. Maybe it would be easier to think about the amounts that aren't possible. Maybe there's a pattern there that would give a tidy solution.

Okay, I know from a bit of testing that it's not possible to use the stamps to make the amounts of 1¢, 2¢, 4¢, or 7¢. What is the next impossible number?

I listed the amounts from 1¢ to 25¢ and decided to try which I could make. After 7¢, all the amounts were possible, so I concluded that 1¢, 2¢, 4¢, and 7¢ were the only impossible amounts. The way I did my figuring was first to use trial and error to find solutions for all of the sums from 8¢ to 17¢. The next number, 18¢, was 10¢ more than 8¢, an amount I had already solved, which meant I could do 18¢ with two more 5¢ stamps. And 19¢ was 10¢ more than 9¢, another amount for which I had solution. Every subsequent number would be 10¢ more than something I had already done, which meant adding on two more 5¢ stamps to a previous solution. Actually, I could have done even less arithmetic and stopped once I found three consecutive numbers in a row with solutions — 8¢, 9¢, and 10¢. Then all I had to do was add a 3¢ stamp on to 8¢ to make 11¢, then 3¢ to 9¢, and so on, to make every subsequent amount. But adding 10 seems so friendly.

There are four impossible amounts using 3¢ and 5¢ stamps, and the largest is 7¢. Done.

Well, not really done. Next the problem asks me to use only 5¢ and 8¢ stamps. Hoo-hah, this was harder. I was looking for a consecutive string of five numbers with solutions so I could apply the same logic, this time adding a 5¢ stamp to make all subsequent amounts. I finally found a string — 28¢, 29¢, 30¢, 31¢, and 32¢. There were 14 impossible amounts, all smaller — 1¢, 2¢, 3¢, 4¢, 6¢, 7¢, 9¢, 11¢, 12¢, 14¢, 17¢, 19¢, 22¢, and 27¢, with 27¢ being the largest impossible amount.

The problem suggests also investigating what happens with other combinations of stamps. I fiddled with some and was intrigued by the differences when both stamps were even or odd, or when there was one of each. The problem can get complex. But the beauty of it is that the only skill you need to get started is addition, and adding gets you pretty far. In a classroom, some students won't progress beyond adding to find solutions while others will search for patterns to reveal what's happening. There's something here for everyone.

	3¢	5¢
1	—	—
2	—	—
3	1	0
4	—	—
5	0	1
6	2	0
7	—	—
8	1	1
9	3	0
10	0	2
11	2	1
12	4	0
13	1	2
14	3	1
15	)$\frac{5}{8}$	$\frac{8}{3}$
16	2	2
17	4	1
18	1	3
19	3	2
20	0	4
21	2	3
22	4	2
23	1	4
24	3	5
25	)$\frac{5}{8}$	$\frac{2}{5}$

Arrow Arithmetic (page 135)

In this activity, each arrow tells you to move one square on a 0–99 chart in the direction that the arrow is pointing. I like this activity and have had success with it in primary classes as well as in middle school classes; students generally delight in figuring out what the arrows mean. Doing this activity with students has taught me not to take for granted that the patterns that seem so obvious to me on the 0–99 chart are also obvious to students. Some students, even older ones, need to refer to the chart to check predictions if not actually to arrive at answers. But when they are given time to explore the activity, I've found that students make numerical discoveries that serve them beyond the arrow problems.

Young students typically continue to use the 0–99 chart as a reference for finding answers. Older students, however, either visualize the chart or translate the arrows to arithmetic calculations — an arrow pointing right results in adding one to the starting number; an arrow pointing down results in adding 10; an arrow pointing diagonally down to the right results in adding 11; and so on. Thinking arithmetically helps students develop strategies for adding and subtracting 11 and 9, which is good practice for developing their mental arithmetic ability.

Teachers sometimes ask me why I use the 0–99 chart instead of the 1–100 chart. The activity works equally well with either version, but on the 0–99 chart all of the numbers in the same decade, the 20s or 30s, for example, are on the same line. But this is a small preference, not a biggie. Take your pick of charts.

We're used to having one right answer to most math problems, and the extension problems offer the refreshing possibility for different interpretations. For 9 →, for example, I've heard of three different answers from students, all of which made sense according to how they reasoned.

1. The answer is 10, because → means *add 1*, and 9 + 1 = 10.

2. The answer is 0, because I think how the chart would look pasted on a cylinder, like a can of vegetables or soup. If you go one space to the right, you'll be back at the beginning of the same row.

3. There is no answer. Not all math problems can be solved, and this is an example of one of them.

All of these answers show reasonable mathematical thinking. The system of arrows suggested in this problem isn't one that has been established as a conventional part of mathematics. Different answers to potentially ambiguous situations can exist as long as they are justified.

BIBLIOGRAPHY

Bibliography

TEACHER RESOURCE BOOKS FROM MATH SOLUTIONS PUBLICATIONS

Bresser, Rusty, and Caren Holtzman. *Developing Number Sense, Grades 3–6.* 1999.

Burns, Marilyn. *Writing in Math Class: A Resource for Grades 2–8.* 1995.

Burns, Marilyn. *50 Problem-Solving Lessons.* 1996.

Burns, Marilyn. *Math: Facing an American Phobia.* 1998.

Burns, Marilyn, ed. *Leading the Way: Principals and Superintendents Look at Math Instruction.* 1999.

Burns, Marilyn, and Robyn Silbey. *So You Have to Teach Math? Sound Advice for K–6 Teachers.* 2000.

Chapin, Suzanne, and Arthur Johnson. *Math Matters: Understanding the Math You Teach, Grades K–6.* 2000.

Dacey, Linda Schulman, and Rebeka Eston. *Growing Mathematical Ideas in Kindergarten.* 1999.

Litton, Nancy. *Getting Your Math Message Out to Parents: A K–6 Resource.* 1998.

Ohanian, Susan. *Day-by-Day Math: Activities for Grades 3–6.* 2000.

Raphel, Annette. *Math Homework That Counts, Grades 4–6.* 2000.

Skinner, Penny. *It All Adds Up! Engaging 8-to-12-Year-Olds in Math Investigations.* 1999.

A Collection of Math Lessons Series
Burns, Marilyn, and Bonnie Tank. *Grades 1–3.* 1988.
Burns, Marilyn. *Grades 3–6.* 1987.
Burns, Marilyn, and Cathy Humphreys. *Grades 6–8.* 1990

Math and Literature Series
Burns, Marilyn. *Grades K–3.* Book 1. 1992.
Sheffield, Stephanie. *Grades K–3.* Book 2. 1995.
Bresser, Rusty. *Grades 4–6.* 1995.

Math By All Means Replacement Unit Series

Burns, Marilyn. *Place Value, Grades 1–2.* 1994.

Confer, Chris. *Geometry, Grades 1–2.* 1994.

Crawford, Jane. *Money, Grades 1–2.* 1996.

Tank, Bonnie. *Probability, Grades 1–2.* 1996.

Burns, Marilyn. *Multiplication, Grade 3.* 1991.

Burns, Marilyn. *Probability. Grades 3–4.* 1995.

Ohanian, Susan, and Marilyn Burns. *Division, Grades 3–4.* 1995.

Rectanus, Cheryl. *Geometry, Grades 3–4.* 1994.

Rectanus, Cheryl. *Area and Perimeter, Grades 5–6.* 1997.

TEACHER RESOURCE BOOKS
FROM OTHER SOURCES

Baratta-Lorton, Mary. *Mathematics Their Way.* Rev. ed. Addison-Wesley, 1995.

Barnett, Carne, Donna Goldenstein, and Babette Jackson, eds. *Mathematics Teaching Cases: Fractions, Decimals, Ratios, and Percents.* Heinemann, 1994.

Branca, Nicholas. *RecTiles.* Cuisenaire Company of America, 1991.

Countryman, Joan. *Writing to Learn Mathematics.* Heinemann, 1992.

Cuisenaire Company of America. The Super Source Series. *Grades K–2. Grades 3–4. Grades 5–6.* Cuisenaire Company of America. Various dates.

Driscoll, Mark. *Fostering Algebraic Thinking: A Guide for Teachers, Grades 6–10.* Heinemann, 1999.

Duckworth, Eleanor. *"The Having of Wonderful Ideas" and Other Essays on Teaching and Learning.* 2d ed. Teachers College Press, 1996.

EQUALS and the California Mathematics Council. *Assessment Alternatives in Mathematics: An Overview of Assessment Techniques That Promote Learning.* EQUALS, Lawrence Hall of Science, University of California, 1989.

Hiebert, James, et al. *Making Sense: Teaching and Learning Mathematics with Understanding.* Heinemann, 1997.

Kamii, Constance, with Leslie Baker Housman. *Young Children Reinvent Arithmetic: Implications of Piaget's Theory.* 2d ed. Teachers College Press, 2000.

Kaye, Peggy. *Games for Math.* Random House, 1998.

Labinowicz, Ed. *The Piaget Primer.* Addison-Wesley, 1980.

Lane County Mathematics Project. *Problem Solving in Mathematics (Grades 5–7).* Dale Seymour, 1997.

Ma, Liping. *Knowing and Teaching Elementary Mathematics.* Lawrence Erlbaum, 1999.

Mason, John, Leone Burton, and Kaye Stacey. *Thinking Mathematically.* Addison-Wesley, 1982.

Mokros, Jan. *Beyond Facts and Flashcards: Exploring Math with Your Kids.* Heinemann, 1996.

Mokros, Jan, Susan Jo Russell, and Karen Economopoulos. *Beyond Arithmetic: Changing Mathematics in the Elementary Classroom.* Dale Seymour, 1995.

Moon, Jean, and Linda Schulman. *Finding the Connections: Linking Assessment, Instruction, and Curriculum in Elementary Mathematics.* Heinemann, 1995.

National Council of Teachers of Mathematics. *Assessment Standards for School Mathematics*, 1995. *Curriculum and Evaluation Standards*, 1989. *Principles and Standards for School Mathematics*, 2000. *Professional Standards for Teaching Mathematics*, 1991. National Council of Teachers of Mathematics.

National Research Council. *Everybody Counts, 1989. Measuring Up: Prototypes for Mathematics Assessment*, 1989. *Reshaping School Mathematics*, 1989. National Academy Press.

Richardson, Kathy. *Developing Number Concepts.* Book 1, *Counting, Comparing, and Pattern.* Book 2, *Addition and Subtraction.* Book 3, *Place Value, Multiplication, and Division.* Dale Seymour, 1998.

Russell, Susan Jo, Rebecca Corwin, and Susan Friel. *Used Numbers: Real Data in the Classroom.* Dale Seymour, 1990.

Schifter, Deborah, ed. *What's Happening in Math Class? Vol. 1, Envisioning New Practices Through Teacher Narratives.* Vol. 2, *Reconstructing Professional Identities.* Teachers College Press, 1966.

Steen, Lynn Arthur, ed. *On the Shoulders of Giants: New Approaches to Numeracy.* National Academy Press, 1990.

Stenmark, Jean Kerr, ed. *Mathematics Assessment: Myths, Models, Good Questions, and Practical Suggestions.* National Council of Teachers of Mathematics, 1991.

Stenmark, Jean Kerr, Grace D. Coates, and Brian Gothberg, eds. *Family Math for Young Children.* EQUALS, Lawrence Hall of Science, University of California, 1997.

Stenmark, Jean Kerr, Virginia Thompson, and Ruth Cossey. *Family Math.* EQUALS, Lawrence Hall of Science, University of California, 1986.

Thompson, Virginia, and Ann Humphrey Williams. *Family Math, The Middle School Years: Algebraic Reasoning and Number Sense.* EQUALS, Lawrence Hall of Science, University of California, 1998.

CHILDREN'S BOOKS FROM MARILYN BURNS

Brainy Day Books

Burns, Marilyn. *Spaghetti and Meatball for All!* Scholastic, 1997.

Burns, Marilyn. *The Greedy Triangle.* Scholastic, 1994.

Friedman, Aileen. *A Cloak for the Dreamer.* Scholastic, 1994.

Friedman, Aileen. *The King's Commissioners.* Scholastic, 1994.

Neuschwander, Cindy. *Amanda Bean's Amazing Dream.* Scholastic, 1998.

Brown Paper School Books

Burns, Marilyn. *Math for Smarty Pants*. Little, Brown, 1982.

Burns, Marilyn. *This Book Is About Time*. Little, Brown, 1978.

Burns, Marilyn. *The Book of Think*. Little, Brown, 1976.

Burns, Marilyn. *The I Hate Mathematics! Book*. Little, Brown, 1975.

Hello Math Readers

This series from Scholastic includes such titles as *A Quarter from the Tooth Fairy, Monster Money, Stay in Line, One Hungry Cat*, and more than thirty others. The books are organized into four levels: Level 1: PreK–1; Level 2: K–2; Level 3: Grades 1–2; and Level 4: Grades 2–3.

Other

Burns, Marilyn. *The Good Time Math Event Book*. Creative Publications, 1977.

Burns, Marilyn. *The $1.00 Word Riddle Book*. Math Solutions Publications, 1990.

ARTICLES BY MARILYN BURNS

"Making Sense of the Math Standards." *Creative Classroom*, March/April 2000.

"Tough to Teach: Tackling the Third R." *Creative Classroom*, March/April 1999.

"Can I Balance Arithmetic Instruction with Real-Life Math?" *Instructor*, April 1998.

"Nine Questions That Make Math Happen." *Early Childhood Today*, January 1998.

"How I Boost My Students' Number Sense." *Instructor*, April 1997.

"What I Learned from Teaching Second Grade." *Teaching Children Mathematics*, November 1996.

"How to Make the Most of Math Manipulatives." *Instructor*, April 1996.

"The 8 Most Important Lessons I've Learned About Organizing My Teaching Year." *Instructor*, September 1995.

"Writing in Math Class? Absolutely!" *Instructor*, April 1995.

"Math Questions? Ask Marilyn Burns." *Instructor*, April 1994.

"Arithmetic: The Last Holdout." *Kappan*, February 1994.

"The 12 Most Important Things You Can Do to Be a Better Math Teacher." *Instructor*, April 1993.

"Introducing Division Through Problem-Solving Experiences." *Arithmetic Teacher*, April 1991.

"Organizing the Classroom for Problem Solving." *Arithmetic Teacher*, May 1988.

"Helping Your Students Make Sense Out of Math." *Learning Magazine*, January 1988.

"Dice Advice." *Instructor*, January 1988.

"Teaching the Basics Through Problem Solving." *Arithmetic Teacher*, September 1987.

"Alphabet Math." *Instructor*, September 1987.

"Give the Kids the Scoop on School." *Instructor*, August 1987.

"Those Pesky Word Problems." *Instructor*, November 1986.

"Does Math Make Good Homework?" *Instructor*, September 1986.

"Teaching 'What to Do' in Arithmetic vs. Teaching 'What to Do and Why.' " *Educational Leadership*, April 1986.

"Graph Tactics." *Instructor*, March 1986.

"The Role of Questioning." *Arithmetic Teacher*, February 1985.

"Good Math Practice—Is It Worth $1.58?" *Learning Magazine,* November 1983.

"Put Some Probability in Your Classroom." *Arithmetic Teacher*, March 1983.

"Statistics and Probability: A Sure Thing for Elementary Classrooms." *Learning Magazine*, January 1983.

"The $1.00 Word Search." *The Oregon Mathematics Teacher*, September 1982.

"How to Teach Problem Solving." *Arithmetic Teacher*, February 1982.

"Groups of Four: Solving the Management Problem." *Learning Magazine*, September 1981.

"Making Sense Out of Word Problems." *Learning Magazine*, January 1981.

"Getting Kids Ready for Computer Thinking." *The Computing Teacher*, April 1980.

"The Math Connection Is Yours to Make." *Learning Magazine*, January 1979.

VIDEOTAPES BY MARILYN BURNS

Mathematics: What Are You Teaching My Child? Math Solutions Publications, 1994.

Mathematics: Assessing Understanding (Grades K–6). Cuisenaire Company of America, 1993.

Mathematics: Teaching for Understanding (Grades K–6). Cuisenaire Company of America, 1992.

Mathematics for Middle School (Grades 6–8). Cuisenaire Company of America, 1989.

Mathematics with Manipulatives (Grades 6–8). Cuisenaire Company of America, 1987.

AUDIOCASSETTES BY MARILYN BURNS

Marilyn Burns Talks About Math Teaching Today. Math Solutions Publications, 1999.

Topic 1: "What's Reform All About?" (Grades K–8)

Topic 2: "Teaching the Basics" (Grades K–8)

Topic 3: "Linking Assessment and Instruction" (Grades K–8)

BLACKLINE MASTERS

Area and Perimeter

From *About Teaching Mathematics* © 2000 Math Solutions Publications

Geoboard Dot Paper

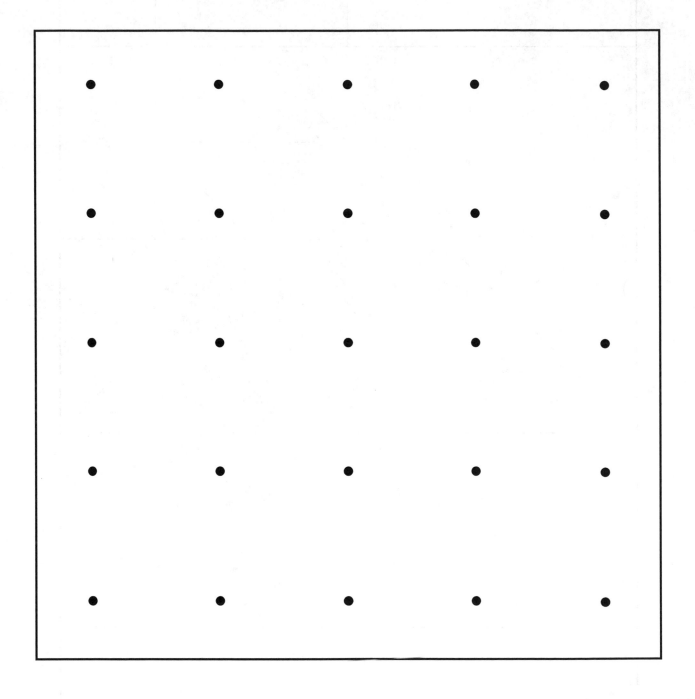

Geoboard Dot Paper

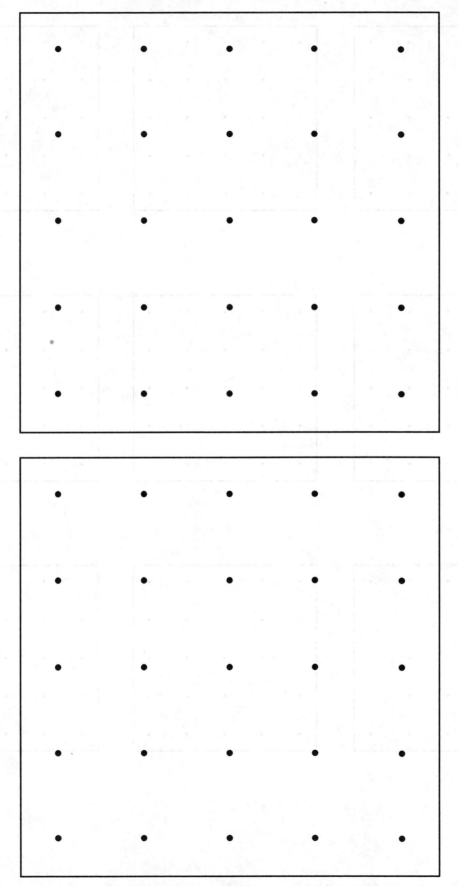

From *About Teaching Mathematics* © 2000 Math Solutions Publications

321

Geoboard Dot Paper

Pattern Block Triangle Paper

0–99 Chart

0	1	2	3	4	5	6	7	8	9
10	11	12	13	14	15	16	17	18	19
20	21	22	23	24	25	26	27	28	29
30	31	32	33	34	35	36	37	38	39
40	41	42	43	44	45	46	47	48	49
50	51	52	53	54	55	56	57	58	59
60	61	62	63	64	65	66	67	68	69
70	71	72	73	74	75	76	77	78	79
80	81	82	83	84	85	86	87	88	89
90	91	92	93	94	95	96	97	98	99

0–99 Charts

0	1	2	3	4	5	6	7	8	9
10	11	12	13	14	15	16	17	18	19
20	21	22	23	24	25	26	27	28	29
30	31	32	33	34	35	36	37	38	39
40	41	42	43	44	45	46	47	48	49
50	51	52	53	54	55	56	57	58	59
60	61	62	63	64	65	66	67	68	69
70	71	72	73	74	75	76	77	78	79
80	81	82	83	84	85	86	87	88	89
90	91	92	93	94	95	96	97	98	99

0	1	2	3	4	5	6	7	8	9
10	11	12	13	14	15	16	17	18	19
20	21	22	23	24	25	26	27	28	29
30	31	32	33	34	35	36	37	38	39
40	41	42	43	44	45	46	47	48	49
50	51	52	53	54	55	56	57	58	59
60	61	62	63	64	65	66	67	68	69
70	71	72	73	74	75	76	77	78	79
80	81	82	83	84	85	86	87	88	89
90	91	92	93	94	95	96	97	98	99

0	1	2	3	4	5	6	7	8	9
10	11	12	13	14	15	16	17	18	19
20	21	22	23	24	25	26	27	28	29
30	31	32	33	34	35	36	37	38	39
40	41	42	43	44	45	46	47	48	49
50	51	52	53	54	55	56	57	58	59
60	61	62	63	64	65	66	67	68	69
70	71	72	73	74	75	76	77	78	79
80	81	82	83	84	85	86	87	88	89
90	91	92	93	94	95	96	97	98	99

0	1	2	3	4	5	6	7	8	9
10	11	12	13	14	15	16	17	18	19
20	21	22	23	24	25	26	27	28	29
30	31	32	33	34	35	36	37	38	39
40	41	42	43	44	45	46	47	48	49
50	51	52	53	54	55	56	57	58	59
60	61	62	63	64	65	66	67	68	69
70	71	72	73	74	75	76	77	78	79
80	81	82	83	84	85	86	87	88	89
90	91	92	93	94	95	96	97	98	99

0	1	2	3	4	5	6	7	8	9
10	11	12	13	14	15	16	17	18	19
20	21	22	23	24	25	26	27	28	29
30	31	32	33	34	35	36	37	38	39
40	41	42	43	44	45	46	47	48	49
50	51	52	53	54	55	56	57	58	59
60	61	62	63	64	65	66	67	68	69
70	71	72	73	74	75	76	77	78	79
80	81	82	83	84	85	86	87	88	89
90	91	92	93	94	95	96	97	98	99

0	1	2	3	4	5	6	7	8	9
10	11	12	13	14	15	16	17	18	19
20	21	22	23	24	25	26	27	28	29
30	31	32	33	34	35	36	37	38	39
40	41	42	43	44	45	46	47	48	49
50	51	52	53	54	55	56	57	58	59
60	61	62	63	64	65	66	67	68	69
70	71	72	73	74	75	76	77	78	79
80	81	82	83	84	85	86	87	88	89
90	91	92	93	94	95	96	97	98	99

From *About Teaching Mathematics* © 2000 Math Solutions Publications

Multiplication Table

1	2	3	4	5	6	7	8	9	10	11	12
2	4	6	8	10	12	14	16	18	20	22	24
3	6	9	12	15	18	21	24	27	30	33	36
4	8	12	16	20	24	28	32	36	40	44	48
5	10	15	20	25	30	35	40	45	50	55	60
6	12	18	24	30	36	42	48	54	60	66	72
7	14	21	28	35	42	49	56	63	70	77	84
8	16	24	32	40	48	56	64	72	80	88	96
9	18	27	36	45	54	63	72	81	90	99	108
10	20	30	40	50	60	70	80	90	100	110	120
11	22	33	44	55	66	77	88	99	110	121	132
12	24	36	48	60	72	84	96	108	120	132	144

From *About Teaching Mathematics* © 2000 Math Solutions Publications

10-by-10 Grids

Toothpick Dot Paper

Hexagon Fill-in Puzzle

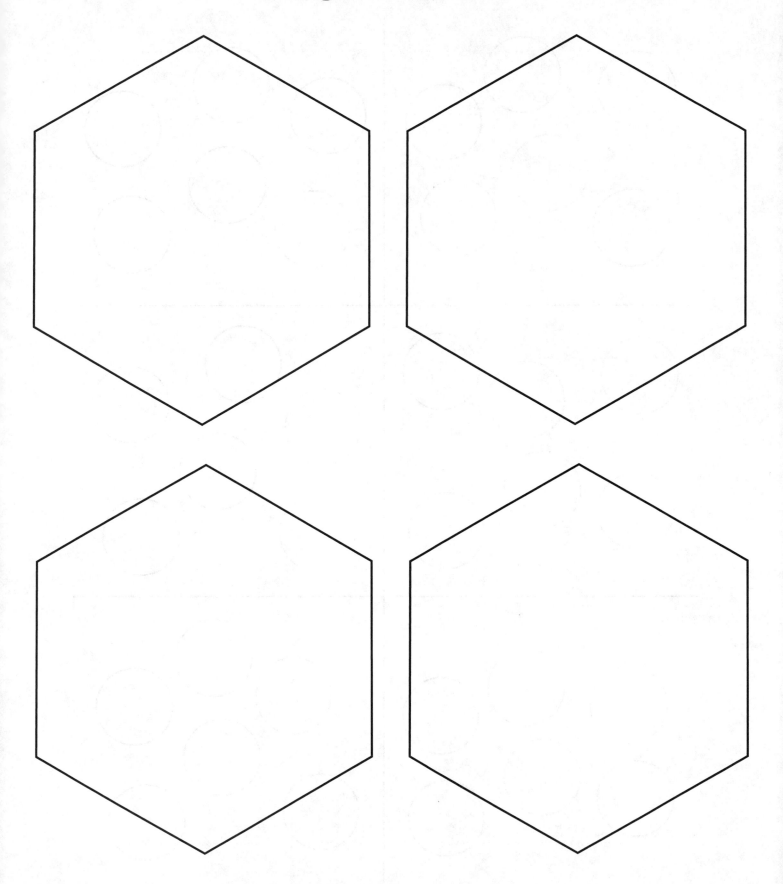

Shake and Spill

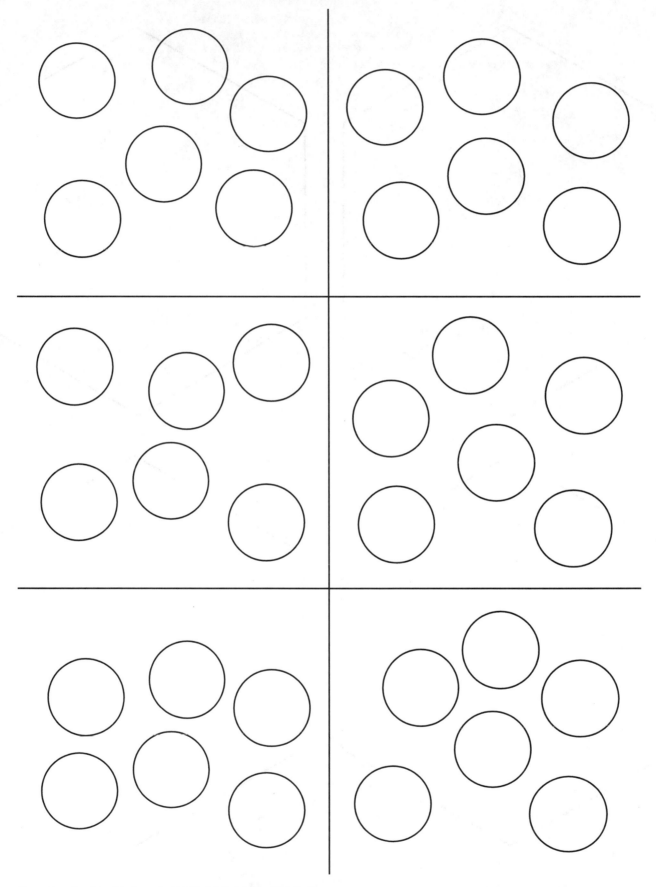

Isometric Dot Paper

From *About Teaching Mathematics* © 2000 Math Solutions Publications

Palindrome Recording Chart

No.	Steps	Palindromes	No.	Steps	Palindromes	No.	Steps	Palindromes
10			40			70		
11			41			71		
12			42			72		
13			43			73		
14			44			74		
15			45			75		
16			46			76		
17			47			77		
18			48			78		
19			49			79		
20			50			80		
21			51			81		
22			52			82		
23			53			83		
24			54			84		
25			55			85		
26			56			86		
27			57			87		
28			58			88		
29			59			89		
30			60			90		
31			61			91		
32			62			92		
33			63			93		
34			64			94		
35			65			95		
36			66			96		
37			67			97		
38			68			98		
39			69			99		

Fractions on Grids (4-by-4 squares)

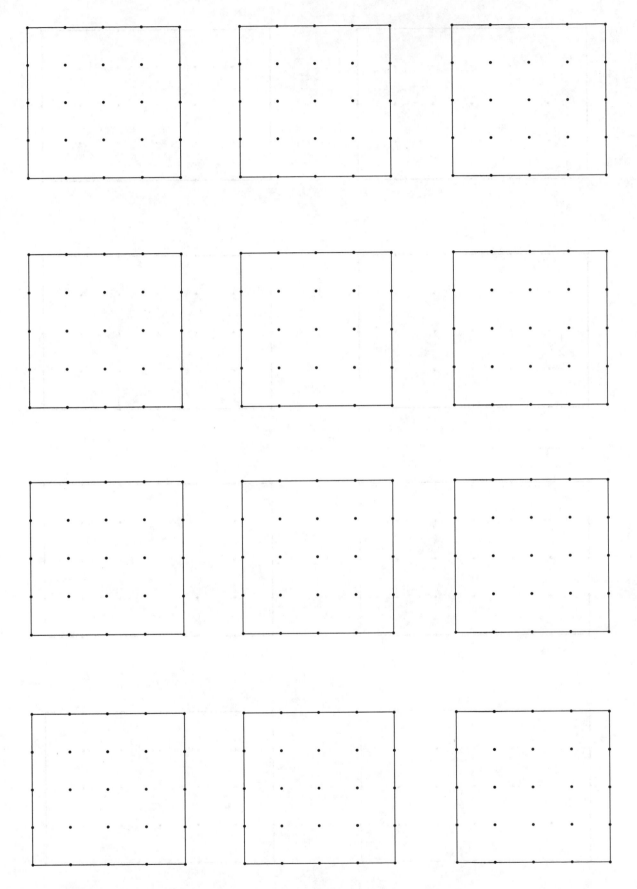

Fractions on Grids (6-by-4 squares)

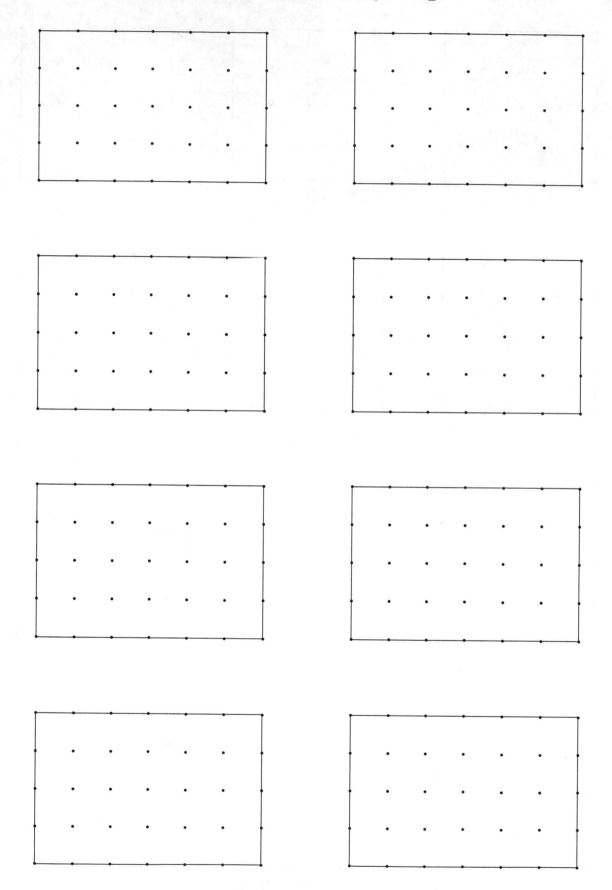

Fractions with Cookies

1-Inch Squares

1/2-Inch Squares

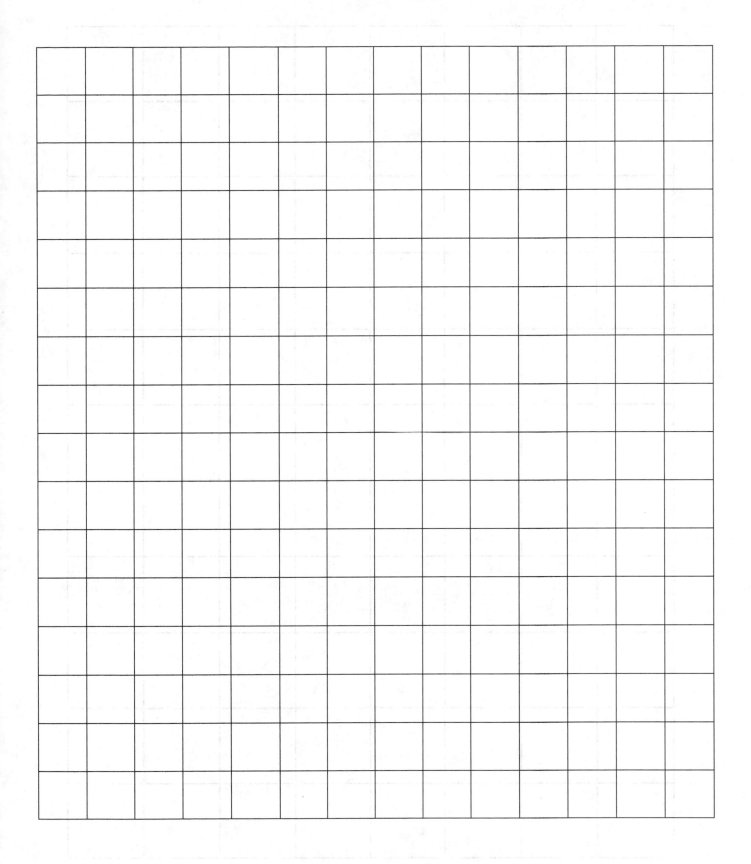

From *About Teaching Mathematics* © 2000 Math Solutions Publications

2-Centimeter Squares

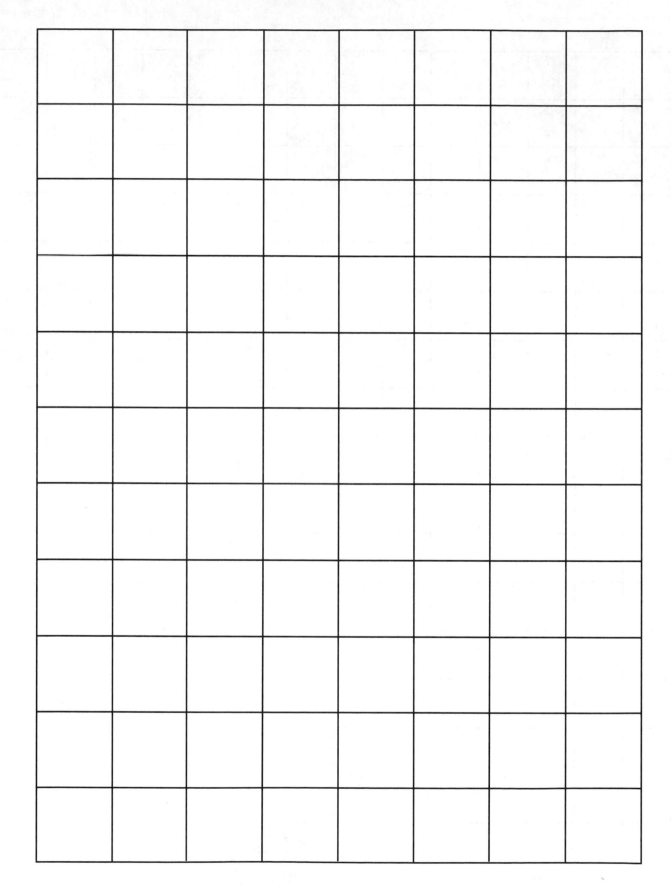

From *About Teaching Mathematics* © 2000 Math Solutions Publications

1-Centimeter Squares

List of Activities

The activities marked with an asterisk are discussed in Section IV.

Index